WHO BUT GOD!
RIDING THE WHIRLWIND

Copyright © 2020 by James T. Draper and Carol Ann Draper

Published by HeartSpring Media, Sunset, Texas USA

All rights reserved. This book or parts thereof may not be reproduced in any form, stored in a retrieval system, or transmitted in any form by any means—electronic, mechanical, photocopy, recording, or otherwise—without prior written permission of the publisher, except as provided by United States of America copyright law.

Paperback ISBN 978-1-58695-014-9
Hard Cover ISBN 978-1-58695-016-3

Library of Congress Control Number: 2020941314

Cover photo: Fred Mahusay
Cover design and layout: Russell Lake

Printed in the USA

First Edition

Additional copies may be available at JimmyDraper.com.

WHO BUT GOD!
RIDING THE WHIRLWIND

JIMMY & CAROL ANN DRAPER

Published by HeartSpring Media
a division of Seed Studios, Inc.

DEDICATION

To our three remarkable children, Randy, Bailey & Terri, who traveled much of this road with us. They not only survived, they thrived and have provided us with nine grandchildren (three are married and we claim their wives as our own), two great-grandchildren and more on the way! Each of them is living out their own legacy of Faith and Devotion to the Lord Jesus Christ. We wanted them to know our journey in ways they would not ever know otherwise.

TABLE OF CONTENTS

INTRODUCTION i

1: THE WHIRLWIND BEGINS 1

2: THE DRAPERS & FLOYDS 13

3: JIMMY'S STORY –
   WHERE SOUTHERN GOSPEL MUSIC BEGAN 19

4: CAROL ANN'S STORY – SAN ANTONIO ROSE 57

5: ROMANCE, MARRIAGE & BAYLOR 75

6: LIVING IN AGGIELAND 83

7: SEMINARY, INTERIM PASTOR & PART-TIME JOBS 101

8: SNUFF CITY & IREDELL BAPTIST CHURCH 107

9: DEEP IN THE HEART OF TEXAS 121

10: REMEMBER THE ALAMO 131

11: HOME IN MID-AMERICA 159

12: WHERE THE WIND COMES SWEEPING
    DOWN THE PLAINS 207

13: NEW ROLE IN BIG "D" 239

14: IN THE HEART OF DFW 263

15: A HILL TO DIE ON 331

16: MUSIC CITY, USA 359

17: STILL RIDING THE WHIRLWIND 417

WHO BUT GOD! RIDING THE WHIRLWIND

JIMMY AND CAROL ANN DRAPER

INTRODUCTION

This is our story, Jimmy and Carol Ann Draper. It is not a typical memoir or autobiography; just things that we remember and how we felt as we experienced them. Our walk down Memory Lane may not always be precise or accurate, but it is what we remember and how we remember it. We have not made any attempt to footnote or document our memories, but to simply share some of the more memorable moments of our journey together that now spans over 64 years.

This book is simply a reflection of our life in ministry together. Although I have done the preaching, Carol Ann has always been an essential part of our ministry. I have never done anything in ministry that she was not deeply involved in through and through. I may be a bit biased, but many believe just as I do – she is a premier leader in her own right. Across these 64 years she has spoken, counselled and encouraged women and their families not only in America but on five continents. As we have put this book together, we've both contributed greatly, one of us starting a story and the other adding bits of details along the way. For your sake, just assume it is Jimmy speaking unless otherwise noted with a (CA) beside it, but rest assured this is a labor of love on both our parts. We lived it together and are telling it together, just as it has always been between us.

It will also help to understand that am a long-time history buff. I've always believed that understanding where you come from plays into how you see things, what you value, and what you believe. This has certainly been true for both of us and we believe it to be true for our country as well. That said, in recalling the more significant events in our lives, I thought it would be helpful to understand the context of times—the social and cultural mores of the times, the political climate, America's involvement in world affairs and wars, and our economy.

And so, here's your first history lesson…

The United States and the world were transformed by two Industrial Revolutions that took place between 1790 and 1920. The first began in 1790 and ended somewhere around 1870, nearly 80 years. During that time industry moved from home businesses producing products that were largely hand-made with manual labor-based. Also during this time, 95% of people lived in rural areas and only 5% lived in cities. Today, these numbers are more closely reversed as 80% of our population today live in cities and urban areas while only 20% live in rural areas.

Samuel Slate, who was known as the "Father of American Industry," established the first water-powered cotton mill in 1790 in Pawtucket, Rhode Island. From there, he helped begin the development of textile factories in Lowell, Massachusetts in 1823, which later became known as the "Cradle of the Industrial Revolution." During that time industrial production saw the development of not only textiles, but also coal, iron, and the railroads.

INTRODUCTION

Importantly, Robert Fulton introduced the use of steamboats during these years and opened the door to the use of the nation's waterways to transport goods and facilitate travel by boat.

The Second Industrial Revolution began in 1870 and saw the production of steel, intended to replace iron, plus electricity and petroleum. Many, many significant inventions came about during the next fifty years that helped to further establish the United States as an industrial powerhouse including:

- The Transcontinental Railroad opened in 1869.
- Alexander Graham Bell patented the telephone in 1876.
- Thomas Edison and Joseph Swan perfected the design for the electric light bulb in 1879.
- The internal combustion engine was invented in 1878 but was impractical for public use. It only became available to the general public as liquid fuels were developed.
- Elias Howe invented the sewing machine during this time, allowing for a faster and more efficient way to produce garments.

The introduction of all these innovations and conveniences was not without its problems. With the increasing development of factories, disgruntled workers called for the first railroad strike in 1877. As a result, violence erupted in many areas. Vigilantes, the National Guard, and Federal Forces were all involved in settling the strike and protecting citizens from the rising hostilities.

During this time, John D. Rockefeller founded Standard Oil Company in 1870. At its peak Standard Oil controlled 90% of the petroleum production in the United States. Rockefeller stepped aside from control of the company in 1897 and was known as the wealthiest man in the world at the time.

WHO BUT GOD! RIDING THE WHIRLWIND
JIMMY AND CAROL ANN DRAPER

This Second Industrial Revolution ended around 1920 and transformed life across the United States. Major changes in transportation, manufacturing, and communications swept across the nation. The last few years of this period resulted in the first global war as World War I began in 1914, though rumblings in the Balkans began as early as 1908.

The second quarter of the twentieth century was a mixture of war and violence as well as rapid advancement in almost every area of human progress. Still, few countries in the world escaped the turmoil of those years.

In many ways, our life together through these years was like trying to ride a whirlwind. Things were not only changing quickly but changing in such a way that they would never be the same again. We were both born in the midst of the Great Depression that impacted every country in the world, especially the United States. Although we were poor, we didn't know it! Our parents struggled to endure and to survive, but they never passed on any anxiety to us about our lives or about the future.

Both of us were raised by godly parents who had a deep faith and lived as proof that what they believed was the truth. Neither of us ever heard our parents shout at or quarrel with each other. Divorce was rare in our communities. I was 12 years old before I knew of a divorce in our town. Families ate meals together and discussed the activities of the day and things relating to our lives. We attended church on Sunday as regularly as we attended school on Monday. It was never questioned, and we loved every moment of it.

Most homes did not have dryers for wet clothes, so it was common to hang clothes on the backyard clothesline to let the sun dry them. Since there were no televisions as we grew up, we played

INTRODUCTION

till dark and came home in time for dinner. Games like hide & seek and kick-the-can were always our favorites. We also enjoyed team sports like baseball, basketball and football whenever we could play. And unless we got permission to go somewhere else, we were always within the sound of our parents' voices.

Churches did not run off their pastors or staff very often, and if a dismissal had to be made because of inappropriate actions, it was handled quietly with no public discourse throughout the community. Just in my lifetime things have changed tremendously! In our Southern Baptist Convention today, we see upwards of 1,500 pastors fired or forced resignation every year and probably more staff members than pastors are asked to leave— a tragedy that impacts so many lives.

Neither of us ever saw a television until our high school years. Color television was still years away, so we enjoyed our shows in black and white with only 2 or 3 stations operating. Few cars had air conditioning, and many did not have radios. It was not unusual for us to leave the keys in our unlocked cars at night as we had no fear of anyone stealing them. Doors were unlocked all night and windows left open with only a screen between the outside and inside of the house.

Blue laws were enforced during our growing up years in Texas which prohibited retail stores from opening and doing business on Sundays. Services for lodging, grocery stores, and what were considered necessary services were allowed to operate, but not general retail stores. Schools never planned activities on Wednesday nights and Sundays as those were for church activities. The pastor was one of the leading influencers in the town or city and the church was the center of community life.

WHO BUT GOD! RIDING THE WHIRLWIND
JIMMY AND CAROL ANN DRAPER

School children would get in trouble at school for shooting paper wads with rubber bands or talking too much. Teachers were free to discipline children in school as it was needed. As a young boy, I knew that if I got a spanking at school, I would get another one at home. Imagine that!

We were taught to respect all adults, regardless of their ethnicity or position. "Yes, sir," "Yes, ma'am," and "No, sir," and "No, ma'am" were always our answers when asked anything by adults. We never called adults by their first name. Even our relatives were called "Aunt Ruth" or "Uncle L.M." We also grew up with great respect for the older people in our communities.

Laws were made to be obeyed, not ignored or violated. Drug use was not unknown, but never easy to find. The hardest drug we saw in high school was marijuana. It took several decades for the emergence and widespread use of strong and illegal drugs to become normal in our society.

Things like sex, abortion, promiscuity or illegal behavior were not even mentioned in most places. It was not that bad things did not happen or that the age itself was some kind of "golden age," but respect, politeness, hard work, honesty, and integrity were the dominant attitudes in our communities. Many contracts were sealed with a handshake rather than a signature.

Even in a city as large as Houston, where I went to high school, violence wasn't commonplace. Public transportation was the norm, not the exception, and was how we got to school and other places. It was considered a safe and desirable means of getting around. I did not have a car until my junior year in Baylor.

The generation of our parents is known as the "Greatest Generation." It impacted how they raised us in every way and how

INTRODUCTION

we sought to raise our children. We are grateful for this life of faith and the peaceful, happy homes we were each raised in. We also realize this gave us tremendous advantage that was not available to everyone during these years.

But, the world we grew up in was not a good world. Two global wars occurred within 15 years of each other in the first 35 years of the twentieth century. The devastation and barbarism of those wars is still hard to grasp and the violence those wars perpetrated on enemy soldiers and innocent citizens is almost beyond belief. It is no wonder that veterans of those wars seldom talk about their experiences. It was a time of violent greed among nations as empires crumbled and many nations were overcome by enemy invaders.

Our early years were spent living in a world torn apart by dual personalities. Simplicity and respect were seen in much of the United States among its citizens, but at the same time brutality and hostilities that caused civil, territorial, and global wars dominated the world. It was a Jekyll and Hyde kind of world, a description made famous by Robert Louis Stevenson in his book, "The Strange World of Dr. Jekyll and Mr. Hyde" about a man with dual personalities.

While not a perfect world, we were taught that evil was to be rejected and good was to be embraced. Seldom did we ever see the two mingle. Each kept their distance from the other. For us, it was a great time to live. We were, and continue to be, blessed beyond measure as we have lived through our eight-plus decades of life.

We ask you to join us on this journey and experience a little of what we faced along the way.

Jimmy & Carol Ann Draper
Spring 2020

WHO BUT GOD! RIDING THE WHIRLWIND
JIMMY AND CAROL ANN DRAPER

1

THE WHIRLWIND BEGINS!

It was known as the Tunguska Event, or more commonly called the 'Russian Explosion,' and it occurred early the morning of June 30, 1908, in a remote area of Siberia. It is the event that best symbolizes the first half of the 20th century. It was an explosion that impacted 830 square miles of a remote area in Siberia, Russia, near the Tunguska River that flattened over 80 million trees and is believed to be the largest impact on Earth in recorded history.

The best scientists can explain it, the explosion was an airburst from a large meteoroid or possibly a fragment of a comet that exploded five to six miles above the earth's surface. Fortunately, since it occurred in such a remote area, only three were known to have died, although its impact was felt for many miles from the center of the explosion.

It is estimated that the explosion was the equivalent of a 20-30 megaton bomb, more powerful than the 15-megaton atomic bombs dropped on Nagasaki and Hiroshima, Japan, in 1945. If such an explosion were to happen in the Dallas/Fort Worth metroplex today, it would destroy the entire area.

WHO BUT GOD! RIDING THE WHIRLWIND
JIMMY AND CAROL ANN DRAPER

As an example of the force of the explosion, one man in Vanavara, Siberia, was sitting on his front porch when the blast occurred. He was hurled from his chair and described the heat as being so intense it felt as if his shirt was on fire—and he was 40 miles from the center of the explosion! This Russian Explosion continues to hold the fascination of scientists today because, despite its verification by many, no crater of impact has ever been found. Over 1,000 scholarly papers have been written about this devastating and destructive, unknown, and unexpected phenomenon.

I believe the mystery, devastation, turbulence, turmoil, and violence of the world during those first decades of the 20th century is symbolized by the Tunguska Event. The western world was torn and swept away in the throes of discontent and rumblings of war from the first decade. At least nine wars ranging from territorial conflicts to civil wars created unrest and chaos across much of the world, climaxing with the beginning of the first global war in the history of the world as World War I began in August 1914. The tipping point that triggered the beginning of WWI was the assassination of Archduke Ferdinand, the Austrian/Hungarian heir in Sarajevo, Bosnia, on June 28, 1914.

Battle lines were drawn between France, Russia, and Britain on one side and Germany, Austria/Hungary, and Italy on the other. Several years into the war, President Woodrow Wilson declared war on Germany on April 6, 1917, although the United States was never the primary combatant in the war. This declaration of war came after Germany resumed unrestricted submarine warfare in January 1917. Already the British ocean liner, the Lusitania, had been sunk in May 1915, killing 123 Americans. When seven U.S. merchant ships were

THE WHIRLWIND BEGINS!

sunk by German subs in early 1917, it was the last straw and war was declared.

The nations involved in this war had been in an arms race since the early 1900s. Conflicts appeared everywhere across Europe and beyond. In Morocco, one Sultan was deposed and succeeded by his brother. The Bosnian crisis erupted in 1908 when the Austria-Hungarian Empire annexed Bosnia and Herzegovina. In October 1908, Bulgaria declared its independence from the Ottoman Empire and a struggle known as the Young Turk Revolution erupted against the Ottoman Empire. Few European nations escaped involvement in these conflicts.

The results of World War I were tragic—resulting in 8.5 million deaths of military personnel and 13 million civilian deaths. The influenza epidemic of 1918, known as the Spanish flu, killed an additional 50-100 million people worldwide.

World War I was the turning point for our modern world in virtually every way: politically, culturally, economically, socially, and even theologically. No spiritual or philosophical area was not impacted by this first global war. It was called 'The War to End Wars', because it was begun in the midst of so many revolutions and disputes. It also provided the kindling for the fires of Nazi Fascism to be born and to become aggressive and powerful within 14 years of the official ending of World War I.

In the aftermath of this first global conflict, four empires disappeared: the Russian, German, Austria-Hungarian, and Ottoman empires. Numerous nations won independence, and new nations were begun even as civil wars and other revolutions continued to break out across the world.

WHO BUT GOD! RIDING THE WHIRLWIND
JIMMY AND CAROL ANN DRAPER

The Treaty of Versailles eventually ended World War I on June 28, 1919, although the effective date of the end of the war was January 20, 1920. Since Germany was the first country to declare war on another country, this treaty placed the blame for the war on Germany. Germany was also the primary reason for Austria-Hungary entering the war. This left the majority of Germans feeling humiliated and resentful. There was an active denial of war guilt and deep resentment most Germans felt towards the reparations demanded of them as well as the continued Allied occupation. This widespread revision of the meaning and memory of the war by Germany was widespread.

As for the Nazis, they waved the banners of domestic treason and international conspiracy in an attempt to galvanize the German nation into a spirit of revenge. Nazi Germany sought to redirect the memory of the war to the benefit of its own policies. The Fascism of Adolph Hitler and Nazism rebounded quickly. Less than 14 years after the end of the war, **Hitler became Chancellor on January 30, 1933.**

The whirlwind of events globally continued to feed the hysteria, and rising turmoil in the U.S. The Stock Market crashed on October 29, 1929, and led the United States into the Great Depression. From the day of the crash until Franklin Roosevelt was elected president in 1933, manufacturing decreased by one-third. As a result, prices for manufactured goods fell 20%, which caused tremendous deflation of the dollar and made repaying most debts almost impossible. Unemployment increased from 4% to 25%, and of those who remained employed, a full 33 % were downgraded to part-time work and smaller paychecks. Almost 50% of the nation's work-power

THE WHIRLWIND BEGINS!

was left idle by the Depression. Social and economic turmoil was rampant across the globe in the aftermath of the war.

When thousands of banks closed and depositors lost their savings, there was no national safety net, no public unemployment insurance, and no social security. Conditions worsened each year, and demand for relief skyrocketed as resources soon became insufficient to meet the need. This devastating whirlwind of change tore away at the heart of the United States.

The decade of the 1930s brought unprecedented challenges. The number of unemployed in late 1929 was 1.5 million but rose to 4 million by spring and 7 million by December of 1930. The Bank of the U.S. became the largest bank failure in history when it shut down and erased the life savings of 400,000 depositors. Throughout 1930, approximately 1,300 banks failed, and almost 2,300 closed in 1931. Despite $500 million available for emergency funds for banks and large companies, little help was available for the unemployed or the nation's economy.

> *This devastating whirlwind of change tore away at the heart of the United States.*

The move from rural to urban centers accelerated, and by the end of 1931, nine million Americans were unemployed. U.S. steel cut wages for over 220,000 employees, and other companies quickly followed suit. The downward spiral and deterioration of dismal circumstances continued at a rapid pace.

1932 proved to be a pivotal year for the country. Democratic candidate Franklin D. Roosevelt was elected President while other Democratic candidates took control of more than 70% of the House of Representatives and Senate. Roosevelt served as president for four terms from 1933 – 1944. By the time he was first sworn in, farm income had fallen by over 50% since the Stock Market crash, an estimated 840,000 non-farm mortgages were foreclosed upon, and 5 million home mortgages were foreclosed upon.

Malnutrition was a fact of life in every part of the country. Starvation set in quickly and gave power to the developing whirlwind of efforts to solve the economic problem. During Roosevelt's first 100 days, there were 15 major pieces of legislation passed to deal with the Depression. In passing these bills so quickly, Roosevelt was able to start the process of restoring the nation's morale.

On February 15, 1933, Giuseppe Zangara, an unemployed brick mason, fired five shots at then President-elect Roosevelt while in Miami. He missed Roosevelt, but hit five bystanders, including Chicago Mayor Anton Cermak, who was killed in the shooting. Instances such as these were typical examples of the turmoil, discontent, and desperation that characterized America in the first half of the 20th century.

> *an estimated 840,000 non-farm mortgages were foreclosed upon, and 5 million home mortgages were foreclosed upon.*

THE WHIRLWIND BEGINS!

In March 1933, Roosevelt broadcast what was to become a series of 30 Fireside Chats on the radio. In each episode, Roosevelt urged Americans to face the difficult days ahead with patience, understanding, and faith. He always appealed to God or Providence at the end of almost every broadcast and followed it with the Star-Spangled Banner. Through those broadcasts, he was able to begin to restore confidence and lift the nation's morale. He introduced the New Deal in 1933 and the Second New Deal in 1935. More than 100 government agencies and commissions were begun under Roosevelt.

As 1934 began, the whirlwind continued to pummel our nation. Although more than 2.5 million people began to find work and wages began to rise, some 11 million people were still unemployed, and even more were still receiving relief support. Crops across the heartland were hit by the worst drought the U.S. had ever seen started, and natural disasters took center stage as earthquakes struck a number of western states over a period of three continuous hours during the month of March. Fortunately, the stock market began turning upward as industrial production began to rise slowly.

As 1935 began, the collapse of the United States economy was identified as a full-scale depression. The financial crises produced more profound efforts to solve long-term problems. Many legislative decisions were made by Congress. The Social Security Act, designed to safeguard Americans against financial difficulties of old age & unemployment, was established and became law in August. The Banking Act of 1935, which restructured the Federal Reserve System to allow increased control of banking and credit, passed the same month.

WHO BUT GOD! RIDING THE WHIRLWIND
JIMMY AND CAROL ANN DRAPER

In 1936 President Roosevelt won re-election by 60.8% majority, the largest margin since James Monroe in the early 1800s. Democrats won 79% of House and 77% of Senate. Unemployment insurance began in January. That same month, the Union Strike at the General Motors plant in Flint, Michigan, occurred.

March saw the drought broken as heavy rains & melting snow caused severe flooding in the Northeast. Water rose to 14 feet in the streets of Johnstown, PA. When waters receded several weeks later, 171 deaths were confirmed in the flood.

Floods on the Ohio, Mississippi, and Allegheny Rivers caused severe damage in the early weeks of 1937, with over 900 dead and 500,000 homes flooded. A 44-day sit down strike ended at the General Motor plant in Detroit on February 11. Soon thereafter, in March two of the United States' largest steel companies, U.S. Steel & Carnegie Illinois Steel, were faced with a threat of sit-down strikes. Both companies agreed to recognize another CIO Union, the United Steel Workers, and adopt the 40-hour work week. Union turmoil continued when a violent taxi strike erupted in the Chicago Loop area. Drivers wrecked cars and fought with police.

A dock strike on the West Coast brought all shipping to a halt as 39,000 workers walked off the job for 98 days. May ended with Police firing on steelworkers and their families demonstrating near the South Chicago plant of Republic Steel with ten killed. The Labor movement called it the "Memorial Day Massacre." The whirlwind of chaos and violence continued.

As 1938 began the recession worsened. The Stock Market reached its lowest point in four years, and by May, the Federal Reserve index of industrial production fell drastically.

THE WHIRLWIND BEGINS!

President Roosevelt told Congress that the United States needed a stronger military urgently. He asked Congress for funds to build a navy capable of protecting both the Atlantic and Pacific coasts, and the funds were quickly approved.

Hurricanes hit New England in September, killing 600. H.G. Wells' "War of the Worlds" was a fictional account of an invasion from Mars that was broadcast on the radio on October 30. The broadcast was so compelling, thousands of listeners thought it to be real and flooded the radio stations, police headquarters, and newspapers in hysteria.

Fascism spread across Europe rapidly in 1939. Germany invaded Czechoslovakia, claiming that the chaos there was a threat to the safety of German Nationals. Hitler claimed annexation of Memel, Lithuania, and a Baltic port near Danzig and demanded access across Poland to Danzig. Germany attacked and overwhelmed Poland on September 1. Two days later, England & France declared war on Germany.

The war economy began to improve domestic conditions even as scientists begin to develop a new kind of bomb. The Advisory Commission on Uranium held a meeting to consider making an atomic bomb. The time would soon come for the United States to enter another global conflict. The involvement of the United States became increasingly apparent as the cyclonic turmoil of the 1930s ended.

It was in this whirlwind of systemic change, chaos, poverty, governmental and cultural turmoil that two families were moving toward a merger that would mark the beginning of a new family from the two. An energetic and passionate young minister and remarkable, beautiful, and devoted Christian young lady were on a collision course under the Sovereignty of God that would link them together for the rest of their lives.

Those two, Jimmy Draper and Carol Ann Floyd, grew up in the homes of wonderful parents who loved each other and the Lord, and taught their children to do the same. Although Jimmy & Carol Ann actually met casually at ages 8 and 6, and again in their middle teenage years, their stories and how God brought them together is one that cannot be told properly without the guiding hand of God.

Who but God could have orchestrated such a whirlwind to accomplish His perfect will in the lives of these two willing individuals?

THE WHIRLWIND BEGINS!

Jimmy age 3   Carol Ann age 1

WHO BUT GOD! RIDING THE WHIRLWIND
JIMMY AND CAROL ANN DRAPER

Jimmy with his mother, grandmother Keeling and great Grandmother Compton 1935

THE DRAPERS & FLOYDS

The earliest Drapers migrated from England in 1647 and settled in Boston, Massachusetts. The Draper ancestry traces all the way back to the Lord Mayor of London, Sir Christopher Draper, in 1566. His coat of arms is the official one for the Draper family today and still hangs in Ironmongers Hall in London.

The Draper family has deep roots in New England. There were seven Drapers listed as having fought at Lexington and Concord during the Revolutionary War. In the 19th century, the family gradually moved to Arkansas. Jimmy's great-grandad was Benjamin Franklin Draper. Benjamin, his wife Sarah, and family settled atop a bluff on the edge of Malvern, Arkansas. Fittingly, it was named Draper Ridge. Benjamin was a deeply committed Christian and a strong layman in the First Baptist Church of Malvern. He was well versed in the Bible and carefully followed the teachings of the Bible.

Benjamin worked to stay well informed about national, state, and local issues and was frequently referred to in news articles as "one of Malvern's pioneer citizens." When he died, the local newspaper said of him, "He was a man among men and, at his going, Hot Springs County loses one of her best citizens." His funeral was conducted by

WHO BUT GOD! RIDING THE WHIRLWIND
JIMMY AND CAROL ANN DRAPER

Leonard Marcellus Keeling

L.M. Keeling, Jimmy's maternal grandfather, and pastor of First Baptist Church in Malvern. There were eleven honorary pallbearers for the service, including one congressman, one judge, two doctors, and other prominent citizens.

Jimmy's dad was born in 1913 in southeast Arkansas. A few months later, his mother died, and he was left to be raised by his father. Around his tenth birthday his dad could no longer provide for the children, so they were placed in foster homes at that time. Jimmy's dad was raised by a wonderful family named Macomber. Two girls were in that home and became known to us as Aunt Flossie and Aunt Sugar. He was raised into his teenage years in that home in Warren, Arkansas.

Jimmy's dad, Jimmie, was saved in his early teens. Although he had been raised in the Methodist Church, he wanted to be baptized by immersion. When he told his Methodist pastor of his conversion and how he wanted to be baptized, his pastor told him that if he really felt that way, he should go to the Baptist church. Jimmie took him at his word and was baptized at the Immanuel Baptist Church in Little Rock, and that is how he became a Baptist!

Jimmie felt the call of God on his life to the ministry soon after his conversion.

Jimmie Draper

THE DRAPERS & FLOYDS

Knowing the deep devotion of his grandfather to the Lord and his commitment to honor the Lord in all his ways, he and a close friend, Loyal Pryor, decided to ride their bicycles 46 miles to Malvern to tell his grandfather about his decision. The distance proved too great for them to make it, and they turned around and came back home. Sadly, before they could get to Malvern at a later date, Benjamin was killed in a fire on Draper Ridge at age 82.

Later Jimmy's dad would marry Lois, the daughter of L.M. and Pearl Keeling, and the providential moving of God continued as the Draper legacy grew. Lois was struck with polio when she was 10 months old and was cripple all of her life. By the time she was 15 years old, she had had more than a dozen surgeries. Many of the surgeries required her to travel by train to St. Louis by herself. Her early years were filled with physical challenges that impacted

Lois Keeling Draper

her all of her life. In spite of those challenges, she was a strong and creative woman whose spirit was contagious. She was characterized by gratitude, determination, and courage throughout her life. Typical of her attitude was her reply to one of her niece's question about the possibility of going to an assisted living facility. Mom said, "Well, I probably won't want to go, but if I go I'll be the happiest person there!"

****

WHO BUT GOD! RIDING THE WHIRLWIND
JIMMY AND CAROL ANN DRAPER

Carol Ann comes from both the Floyd and Huffhines families. The Floyds came to Texas from near Murfreesboro, Tennessee. John Huffhines was a pioneer in Dallas County and the father of this branch of the family. John married Elizabeth Wright on March 8, 1821, and they had 14 children who lived to be adults. John came to Texas with 11 of his children in 1853. The trip took several weeks as they traveled by carriage, covered wagons, and on horseback. He raised registered stock and entered a stallion in the Dallas County Fair. After the stallion won the top prize for four straight years, they refused to let him enter a fifth time.

John was a firm believer in the Bible and education. He often brought educational books home for the benefit of the children as they grew up. Although he was too old to serve during the Civil War, his family had eight sons and four sons-in-law serve, three of whom died in the war.

Carol Ann's parents, Finis Floyd and Lucille Huffhines, were both graduates of Richardson High School in Texas. They had dated for seven years before deciding on December 13, 1929, to have a church wedding. Ten days later, in a whirlwind of planning, they were married on December 23, 1929, and were married for 57 years. Lucille died at the age of 80 in 1988, and Finis died at the age of 94 in May of 1998.

Carol Ann's mom was the last born of five girls. Her dad was named George Washington Huffhines. He was married twice and was widowed twice. He raised

George Washington Huffhines

his daughters to adulthood by himself, but Carol Ann never got to know him as he died shortly after she was born. When he heard that Lucille had a girl, he wrote her a letter suggesting that she be named Minnie Lucille. Carol Ann is grateful the mail took several days to arrive back then because by the time the letter arrived, she had already been named and she much prefers being known as Carol Ann! In fact, her name has a bit of a story behind it. Lucille had previously held a good job in Dallas at a bank, and because of her admiration for her then-boss, Mr. Carroll, she named Carol Ann after him.

Carol Ann's dad was born in Forney, Texas, to a farming family. He was one of 13 original children in the family, of which only ten lived to adulthood. Life was hard on the farm, but they had a loving family. Carol Ann never had the opportunity to know her Floyd grandparents nor the opportunity to visit her grandparents on holidays or vacations and still misses the opportunity to have had those memories.

This account of the lives of Jimmy Draper and Carol Ann Floyd must begin with a look at their early lives. Jimmy was born in the middle of the Great Depression in an obscure town in West Central Arkansas named Hartford. Carol Ann was born in San Antonio, Texas, with its Hispanic heritage and Spanish speaking population. Though born in different states and in different size cities, both would end up moving before long as God continued to direct their paths toward one another.

WHO BUT GOD! RIDING THE WHIRLWIND
JIMMY AND CAROL ANN DRAPER

Jimmy 22 months

WHERE SOUTHERN GOSPEL MUSIC BEGAN

JIMMY'S STORY - HARTFORD, ARKANSAS

I was born in Hartford, Arkansas, on Oct. 10, 1935. Hartford is located in the Poteau Mountains in Sebastian County and is contiguous to the Oklahoma state line. Hartford was a significant rural town and was incorporated as Hartford in 1900 when the Rock Island Railroad came through. Before this, it was known as Gwynn from the time of its original settlement. It was a mining town at the turn of the 20th century and home to the last working coal mine in the state of Arkansas.

It is significant that one of the earliest music companies to produce both shaped note music and early Southern gospel music was the Hartford Music Company established by E. M. Bartlett in 1918. He wrote scores of popular hymns, including the most famous of all, 'Victory in Jesus.' He came to Hartford to teach people how to read music and how to sing—with or without instruments.

WHO BUT GOD! RIDING THE WHIRLWIND
JIMMY AND CAROL ANN DRAPER

In 1931 E.M. Bartlett merged his new company with his former employer, the Central Music Company, the company that had originally hired him when he first arrived in Hartford. Once the companies merged, they quickly grew their distribution to over 100,000 music books a year across 35 states. Today Hartford Music Company is still recognized as one of the most successful music publishing companies in the first half of the 20th century.

Bartlett was a prolific composer and went on to establish the Hartford Music Institute in 1921 to teach individuals how to sing the music that was being produced. He introduced a monthly magazine called 'The Herald of a Song,' which featured the ongoing story of the great quartets that developed during the first half of the 20th century. In addition to 'Victory in Jesus,' Bartlett wrote 'Everybody Will Be Happy Over There,' 'Just a Little While,' 'He Will Remember Me,' and 'Camping in Canaan's Land.' He also had a great sense of humor and wrote secular favorites like 'Take an Old Cold Tater and Wait,' made famous by Little Jimmy Dickens, and 'You Can't Keep a Good Man Down.'

Bartlett's contribution to the development of Southern gospel music was only exceeded by his protégé, Albert Brumley. Brumley was a native of the Choctaw Nation area in Spiro, Oklahoma. He attended the Hartford Music Institute and graduated in 1926. There he met well- known gospel singers who became lifelong friends. Brumley became a traveling singer, a schoolteacher, and a composer. His most famous song was 'I'll Fly Away,' which has remained a favorite at gospel music events ever since. He also wrote 'Turn Your Radio On,' 'Jesus, Hold My Hand,' 'I'll Meet You In The Morning,'

WHERE SOUTHERN GOSPEL MUSIC BEGAN

'If We Never Meet Again,' and many more gospel songs that have remained popular with Southern Gospel fans.

Hartford High School also has the distinction of having been the first high school football team in the state to play under electric lights. The athletic teams at Hartford High School were known as the Hartford Hustlers and were active for over 100 years until the high school closed at the end of the school year in 2018.

My life began in that special little rural town with such a great tie to Southern gospel music, which probably explains why Southern gospel music has always been my favorite. Even though I was supposed to be born in Fort Smith, I arrived so quickly that I was actually born in the parsonage of the First Baptist Church in Hartford, where my dad was pastor. It seems like I have been riding the whirlwind ever since!

There was a fine mist and gentle breeze blowing in Hartford, Arkansas, when Oct. 10, 1935, greeted the dawn of a new day. Jimmie and Lois Draper were not yet ready for the arrival of their firstborn child but had planned to make the 24-mile trip to the hospital in Ft. Smith when the time was ready. Only a trace of rain could be found in Hartford, and though my arrival was nearing, no one realized just how anxious I was to arrive!

And then it happened. The water broke, contractions began, and before they could even think about making the trip to Ft. Smith, there I was—James Thomas Draper, Jr.—born right there in the parsonage of the church. From the beginning, I was called Jimmy, but my parents spelled my name Jimmy, rather than like my father, Jimmie.

WHO BUT GOD! RIDING THE WHIRLWIND
JIMMY AND CAROL ANN DRAPER

Some of the earliest memories I can recall are of Southwestern Baptist Theological Seminary in Ft. Worth where my dad had begun his seminary training in 1937, before my second birthday. We lived on the ground level of a two-story quadruplex on campus as the whirlwind of my life accelerated. The Naylor Student Center sits on the location of those quadruplex apartments.

Another memory stayed with me for many years afterward because of the scar I received from it. While playing with my friend Doreen Margrett, I was carrying a small bucket with a shovel sticking out of it when I tripped and fell. The end of the shovel caused a small cut on my forehead that left a slight scar as a reminder for many years afterward.

Doreen's mother, Anne Margrett, was the granddaughter of the Bagby missionary family, who were the pioneer Southern Baptist missionaries in Brazil. She was the widow of an English businessman who had lived in Argentina and was studying to return to Argentina as a missionary after graduating from seminary. When Doreen and her mother moved to Argentina, we stayed in touch and became pen pals throughout our teenage years. During one of her teenage years Doreen had emergency surgery to remove her appendix. She stayed with us for several weeks to recuperate while her mother traveled telling the story of their mission work in Argentina. Doreen later studied at Mary Hardin Baylor in Temple while I attended Baylor.

Two other notable events occurred while we were at Southwestern that were unforgettable for me. I tasted my first green apple…and suffered the consequences of a stomachache and its accompanying conditions. I also vividly remember having my tonsils out in the doctor's office and then being brought home for recuperation. The bright spot of my operation was that ice cream was one of the few things my sore throat could tolerate!

My dad preached at a half-time church in Forester, Arkansas, a sawmill town in the Ozark Mountains. By half-time, I mean that the same building was used on alternate Sundays by the Methodists and Baptists; each denomination used it half-time. Because our family had no car, my dad would ride a train as far as he could before catching a bus as close as he could get to Forester. Once there, one of the members of the church would meet him and take him on to Forester.

Forester was founded in 1930, so it was a new company town for the Caddo River Lumber Company. It became the largest and most productive sawmill in the state, with a huge lumber shed 80 ft. by 1,000 ft. that stored millions of board-feet of kiln-dried planed lumber. The town finally closed in 1952 and had only two town Marshalls during that time with little crime. Being a company town it had free healthcare for the residents provided by the company doctor.

Since the church had no budget to pay a pastor, each week an offering would be taken. At the end of the service, a paper bag was passed around and then given to my dad. When he got home, we would gather around to empty the sack on the bed and count the coins and the occasional dollar bills. It was always a big family event to see how much he received. Some weeks the offering was better than others, but it was always an exciting time for our family. It made such an impression on me that when someone would ask me, "Why does your dad preach?" I would eagerly exclaim, "For the money!" Life was never dull for our family during those years at Southwestern Seminary in the late 1930s.

Vacations were few and far between for our fledgling Draper family. On the years when it was possible, we would go to Albuquerque, New Mexico, where all of my mother's siblings had moved by the mid-1930s. One year on our way to Albuquerque, I was in the beginning stages of whooping cough. The trip was filled with stops to 'whoop' and to take a sip of the honey and lemon mix my mother had made for the trip. Being the generous child that I was, I actually managed to give the whooping cough to the majority of the family in Albuquerque!

CLARKSVILLE, ARKANSAS

When I was five years old, we moved to Clarksville, Arkansas, the county seat of Johnson County. It was 1941, and I was set to enter first grade six weeks shy of my sixth birthday. Starting to school was a significant event for me as I was the youngest in my class. But the most important event occurred a few months before that—when I was saved. Mother had taken me one weekend to a revival my dad was preaching in another town in Arkansas. It was a Saturday evening service when God began to move in my heart. I was on the front row with another young boy, and during the invitation I turned to that boy and said, 'I'll go if you will.'

Neither one of us moved, but later on, back at the parsonage where we were staying, I talked with my parents about trusting Jesus as my Savior. It was right there—beside a cot on a screened-in porch—that I invited Jesus into my heart. It was such a definitive point in my life that whenever people ask me how I know for sure I was saved, I've always responded, "Because I was there when it happened!"

World War II was entering its third brutal year in Europe, and the economy was still mired in a slow, painful depression. I still have some very vivid memories from our time in Clarksville. One of my favorites was the gathering of some of the mothers of the church as they brought their children to the river to enjoy playing in the shallow parts. Catching tadpoles and keeping them till they grew into frogs was one of the highlights of those gatherings.

I also remember during our years in Clarksville, our family had a huge garden where we harvested all the vegetables for our food. It was also the place I had the measles and had to stay quarantined for two weeks under a tent made from a sheet over my bed. The sheet was meant to prevent any outside light from reaching me and to contain my germs.

I also got a brother while we were in Clarksville. My brother, George Leonard, was born six years after I arrived and was named after our grandfather, Leonard Marcellus Keeling, and the doctor who delivered him named George.

BAY CITY, TEXAS

In 1943 our family moved to Bay City, Texas. It was quite a change from the lush Ozark foothills in Clarksville with the beautiful Arkansas River flowing through it. So much so, the flat prairie of South Texas seemed like an alien world to us in the beginning. I especially remember the heat and humidity there because we were only about 20 miles inland from the Gulf of Mexico. It was also the county seat of Matagorda County. The city was formerly named 'Bay

WHO BUT GOD! RIDING THE WHIRLWIND
JIMMY AND CAROL ANN DRAPER

Prairie' as the natural ecosystem that surrounded the city was mostly prairies crisscrossed by creeks that led into Matagorda Bay.

The First Baptist Church of Bay City dated back to 1850. When we were there, it was a growing and active church with a fruitful ministry. One year during my dad's service there, the church baptized 83 people. That was a significant number—especially when the average attendance was close to 250. A hurricane had previously destroyed the sanctuary in 1909, but a beautiful sanctuary had been rebuilt on the same site.

During our Bay City years, my dad had the privilege of officiating the wedding of Dwight Eisenhower's grandson. This was especially meaningful as General Eisenhower later became the country's 34th president. Some years later, when the grandson died, and his widow tried to have the will probated, she was surprised to find the courthouse where they had been married had burned to the ground, and there was no record that their marriage ever existed!

My dad told me about that when I was licensed to preach. A minister's personal record of weddings is admissible in court as confirmation of a wedding. The woman was able to finalize all the issues of her husband's death because of my dad's personal record of the wedding. That is also why my dad presented me with a 'Pastor's Record' book to keep detailed records when I became a pastor.

The church parsonage was one block away from the church and, as always, was regularly filled with guests—especially during revivals. The evangelistic team would always stay with our family, and we were introduced to so many well-known preachers and singers of the time. Our visitors included one of Southern Baptists' most prolific and famous hymn-writers B.B. McKinney, Herman Westmoreland, pastor at the South Main Baptist Church in Houston, and J. Howard Williams, who later became president of Southwestern Seminary when I began my seminary training.

Although our family was there only for two years, several things stand out vividly. With World War II in its final stages, I took a special interest in keeping track of our country's armed forces as they made their way towards victory. I had a map of the world on my bedroom wall with stick pens in it. Each day as news of the progress of our Allied troops was announced on the news, I moved the pins to reflect their progress. Without the benefit of television, we only had radio broadcasts to keep us aware of what was happening, but my map was a great way to track their advancement.

Another thing I remember about Bay City was that my dad would regularly play tennis with some of his friends. Mother would bring George and me to the tennis court to watch them play. That was the only sport I ever saw my dad personally play until he began playing golf a few years later. While we were in Bay City, we also began to raise ducks, and when we moved to Jacksonville, we had to take two of them with us. We were especially fond of them and had named them "Dr. Westmoreland" and "Dr. Williams" after two of the evangelists who had stayed with us.

The thing that really makes those years memorable is that I made my public profession of faith and was baptized at First Baptist Church of Bay City. I was such a shy youngster at that time in my life that when I went forward, I simply sat on the front pew rather than go to my dad, who stood in the altar. I remember C.E. Matthews, who later taught at Southwestern Seminary, was the preacher for the week. There were many people saved that week, including some of my friends who were also baptized then.

Probably the most outlandish event that happened to our family in Bay City was when my three-year-old brother George managed to ride his tricycle more than a mile to the city's hospital. When George heard mother say dad had gone to visit the hospital, he wanted to go too! He rode that tricycle across railroad tracks and one of the city's busiest thoroughfares to get there, but he made it!

There's one other special memory I have about Bay City—it was there I first met Carol Ann even though I don't remember it. It was 1943, and I rode with my dad to Lake Jackson, some forty miles away. Dad went to preach the constitutional sermon for First Baptist Church Lake Jackson when the church formally constituted that afternoon. I was only eight-years-old, and she was six, and we were among the children who played together at the school while the service was being held. Even though we both clearly remember being there that day, neither one of us remembers meeting the other. But memory of it or not, every day I'm grateful the good Lord allowed our paths to continue crossing in years to come.

JACKSONVILLE, TEXAS

In 1945 our family packed up and moved again—this time to Jacksonville in far East Texas. That part of the state was home to the Piney Woods and Jacksonville was known for its tomatoes. The town was called 'The Tomato Capital of the World.' The high school football stadium was called the Tomato Bowl and was built out of red

WHERE SOUTHERN GOSPEL MUSIC BEGAN

iron ore rock in one of the Works Progress Administration's projects during the Great Depression.

Jacksonville's population was around 5,000 and was becoming known for something beyond tomatoes – basketball. The city was home to Lon Morris College, the oldest junior college in Texas at the time. It had become a national powerhouse in junior college basketball. Players from Lon Morris regularly moved on to major colleges after their junior college years. It was a mainstay of entertainment for me watching those excellent players.

One significant thing for our family was that, when we arrived there, we did not have a car. Now imagine a pastor in a town the size of Jacksonville with no car. This made it very difficult for us as my mother had suffered from polio when she was ten months old and remained cripple all her life. When we came to Jacksonville, I was nine years old, and my younger brother, George, was only three. It was quite some time before we actually owned a car.

While we did not have a car, we did have ducks! The ducks we brought with us from Bay City took over our backyard in Jacksonville. We had a drake, we called 'Hawkie,' who ruled the backyard. If a stranger came into our yard by himself, he would be greeted with Hawkie flying three feet off the ground right at him. He did not like intruders! We also had hens, and at one point, we had 41 baby ducks waddling around our back yard!

When we came to Jacksonville, I was in the fifth grade. At my new elementary school, my principal was a wonderful leader for all of us and a very committed Christian. One day, as he was filling in for our teacher, he talked with us about eternal life and gave us

WHO BUT GOD! RIDING THE WHIRLWIND
JIMMY AND CAROL ANN DRAPER

an example about how long eternity really is. He told us to imagine a great boulder of granite that was one-mile wide and high. Then imagine that a bird came by once a year and rubbed its wing against that boulder one time. He concluded that, when the birds who came had worn the granite down completely, eternity would have just begun! It was a vivid description of eternity.

There were three elementary schools, creatively named East Side, West Side and North Side Elementary Schools. Each of us had a football team. We didn't wear cleats, and some even played barefooted. We did have uniforms and enjoyed the competition. Most Sunday afternoons, after our naps, about eight or ten of us would play touch football. We got pretty good for elementary age boys.

Jimmy - Bottom Row 2nd from the left

I never liked to go barefooted when I was a boy. It probably was because of the grass burrs we had all over town! I was one of the few who wore shoes for the games. Charlie Brazil, who was a year older than I, was one of the boys who regularly played quarterback. Charlie and I were a good combination. We often played football in our neighborhood. He would throw the ball, and I would be his receiver. In one of our games against West Side, I was playing left end, and Charlie told me to just run for the goal line, and he'd get the ball to me. I made a run for the goal, Charlie threw me a great pass, and I was in the clear heading to the end zone except for one problem—my shoes. They slowed me down just enough for the other team to catch me just shy of the goal line on the two-yard line!

Charlie never let me forget about how my shoes cost our team a touchdown. He razzed me about it every chance he got for years and years. Apparently, Charlie started feeling a little convicted about this because I recently received an email from him that said, "I never did ask you to forgive me for giving you such a hard time about wearing shoes in the football game at East Side, and I need to do that now." Hard to believe we're both in our eighties now, and that game is still so vivid in our memories to both of us!

Charlie went on to become a great high school football coach and ended his career at Jones High School in the Houston area. His son is also a football coach at Hebron High School in the Dallas area and won a state championship several years ago.

My dad was called to serve as pastor of Central Baptist Church in Jacksonville, Texas, from 1945-1951. The church was founded in 1906 and held its first revival five days after organizing. Dr. George W. Truett led the revival as 32 new members joined that week. He was pastor of First Baptist Church Dallas. Central Baptist Church was destroyed in 1919 in a devastating fire, but the church rebounded stronger than ever the next year, adding 92 new members at the next revival.

Not only did the church grow during our time there, so did our family. My second brother, Charles William Draper, was born six years after George was born. Being 12 years older than the youngest child in the family, I did a lot of babysitting in my time.

WHO BUT GOD! RIDING THE WHIRLWIND
JIMMY AND CAROL ANN DRAPER

My first job came while we were in Jacksonville. I was a stock boy for Brookshire Brothers Grocery when I was 12 years old. Don't guess anyone worried about child labor back then! I worked all day Saturday each week and was paid in change from the cash register at the conclusion of each workday. I don't recall how much it was, but it could not have been over $3 or $4.

When I got my first "sack" of coins for my first day at work, I brought it with me to church the next morning and when the offering plate was passed I put the sack and all its coins in the offering plate. God has gifted me as a preacher but giving may be my strongest gift. Throughout much of our marriage we have given from 25% to 35% of our salaries to the Lord and his church. We have learned that we cannot out-give God!

Each summer, the youth at our church attended camp at Piney Woods Baptist Encampment near Groveton, Texas. It was always a highlight of the year for my friends and me. While there in 1948, God moved in my heart to commit my life to special service. I did not know what God was calling me to do, but knew He was calling me to a special ministry. Dr. Boyd Hunt, pastor of First Baptist Church in Houston, was the preacher for the week, and he later became one of my professors at Southwestern Seminary.

One night as the invitation was given, I went forward and shared with one of the counselors that I felt God was calling me to a special ministry. I thought that I had to know what God wanted me to do right then, so I stayed up late and even snuck out of the dorm that night to go for a walk as I was seeking a word from God about the specific direction His call would take.

WHERE SOUTHERN GOSPEL MUSIC BEGAN

At that time, the only options I knew about were to serve as pastor, minister of music, or as a missionary. That evening I could never envision all the many types of ministry that would develop during my lifetime. Even though I could not confirm exactly what my call from God meant that night, I had no doubt God had a special task for me.

Our summers in Jacksonville were terrific. We had Vacation Bible School, Youth Camp, and the annual summer Youth Revival which was planned and led by the youth under the guidance of the adults who worked with us. During the summer of 1950, Baylor students, Bailey Stone and Buckner Fannin, came to preach that week in our Youth Revival, and on Saturday of that week, I formally surrendered my life to the gospel ministry.

That week was saturated with a great move by God. Normally there would be a time of fun-filled fellowship and refreshments for the youth and their workers after each of the services. But one night, the fellowship turned into a prayer meeting that lasted throughout the night. The overwhelming presence of God Himself filled that fellowship hall during those remarkable hours.

Bailey Stone and I witnessed to many students that week. One was a close friend of mine who lived just a block away from our house. My friend Darrell was in the service on Saturday evening, and Bailey was preaching. Standing on the back row of the choir for that service, I was praying for Darrell when God spoke to me with alarming clarity. He asked me a startling question, "How do you expect Darrell to be saved when you are not willing to do what I want you to do?" Though not audible, that question dominated my heart at that moment. I knew without any doubt that God had called me to preach the Gospel of the Lord Jesus Christ, and so I walked to the altar to announce my call to preach.

That was August 26, 1950 and was also my dad's 37th birthday. And even better—the next morning, Darrell made his profession of faith! Little did I know then that I would preach my first sermon just eight days later. The same night I surrendered to God's call to preach, Medford Hutson, a returning military veteran, also surrendered to preach. He became a fast friend for the Draper family. When Medford and his fiancée, Dorothy, were married, the ceremony was conducted by my dad in the Draper parsonage. Medford and Dorothy served more than thirty years as Home Mission Board missionaries in Utah.

Early the next week, Medford called me to tell me that the First Baptist Church in Mixon, Texas, had asked him to preach on the next Sunday—Labor Day weekend. He couldn't do it but asked if I could, and I quickly agreed! It was to be my first sermon, and I worked hard on it all week. Drawing from every source I could find—my dad, granddad, George W. Truett, and others, I had that sermon down and could deliver it in 30 minutes. It was from Matthew 22:42—'What Think Ye of Christ?' When the time came for me to preach, I delivered that message in 12 minutes! Since then, some of my deacons have jokingly asked what happened to my 12-minute sermons.

Many of the church people from Central Baptist Church came to hear me preach that night. First Baptist Church Mixon even set the service to begin early so my dad could attend and get back to Central Baptist to preach. It all happened so fast, I even got back in time to hear my dad preach! That service was a turning point for me because it cemented my heart and mind in the confidence that God had called me to preach the gospel.

One of my closest friends was Grady Nutt. He became a nationally known comedian using his incredible sense of humor in his presentations. He always made sure to include a biblical message in his comedy routines. He became so well known as a comedian that he was one of the early cast members on the TV series, "Hee Haw." He appeared in 37 shows from 1979 – 1982. We spent a lot of time together and even had our first double date with the Wheatley sisters during these years.

Grady and his wife, Eleanor, remained friends until Grady was killed in a plane crash returning from an engagement in 1982. It happened during my tenure as president of the Southern Baptist Convention. The night of the crash, I had led a group of Jewish leaders and Southern Baptist leaders to Israel at the special invitation of the Israeli government. Our group was in Safed, Israel, and had just finished dinner when Carol Ann called to tell us of Grady's death. Bailey Stone, who had been preaching when I had surrendered to preach, was with me on the trip and had also introduced Grady and Eleanor. Together, we sat on the steps of the hotel and wept when we heard the news.

In all the years we lived in Jacksonville, I participated in football, basketball, and baseball. The word about my newfound commitment to ministry quickly circulated around Jacksonville. One day during football practice, one of the players lit up the air with profanity. Everything turned quiet, and everyone looked at me. Coach Osburn

Amburg seized the moment and asked me, "That wasn't nice was it, Draper?" Without further comment, I simply said, "No, coach, it wasn't." As a young man now called to ministry, I saw the world differently. It was obvious that those around me saw me differently as well.

The wonderful thing about Central Baptist Church was their strong heart for leading the youth of the church in their spiritual development. I will forever be grateful for men like W.H. Brown, Frank Huttash, Herbert Coleman, Frank Wagoner, W.W. and Luman Holman, Carter and Obie Childs, A.J. Brazil, George Williamson, C.P. Mosley, James Craddock, the Tidwell family, and too many others to name.

HOUSTON, TEXAS

In the early spring of 1951, our family moved to Houston, Texas—the largest city in Texas and fourth-largest in the United States. I stayed in Jacksonville to finish my sophomore year in high school and joined the family at the end of school. Houston was the second most populous metropolitan area in Texas at the time, second only to the Dallas/Fort Worth area

Houston was founded by land speculators on Aug. 30, 1836, at a point known as Allen's Landing. The city was named after Gen. Sam Houston, who was president of the Republic of Texas after having won the battle for Texas' independence from Mexico at the Battle of San Jacinto, just 25 miles east of Allen's Landing. Houston also served briefly as the capital of the Republic of Texas in the 1830s.

The devastating effects of a hurricane in 1900 destroyed Galveston as the primary seaport in Texas, but the construction of the Houston ship channel, along with the Texas oil boom, allowed the Port of Houston to become the primary port in Texas. It now ranks first in international waterborne tonnage handled in the United States.

Houston's economy rapidly emerged in the 20th century. It became the home for the Texas Medical District, the world's largest concentration of healthcare and research institutions. It also became the home of the NASA Johnson Space Center and the mission control center for the country's space launches. It also is famous for building the first totally enclosed athletic baseball field in the nation, the Astrodome, known as the 8th Wonder of the World. The first baseball game played in the Astrodome was April 9, 1965, an exhibition game with the New York Yankees. The first "official" game was on April 12 against the Philadelphia Phillies.

My dad became pastor of the Park Memorial Baptist Church in Houston. It was the third-largest church in the city at that time and had a great youth group. Once I moved to Houston, I plunged into speaking every chance I could get at Sunday School fellowships, social events, the Star of Hope Mission, and even at school!

Park Memorial Baptist Church
Houston, TX

In the summers, the youth would attend church camp at Palacios, Texas. It was a thriving conference center located on the shores of Matagorda Bay. It had a long history of hosting great camps for youth and families. One of my earliest memories of the Bay City years was of a family camp at Palacios where families would fill the pavilion, and when it overflowed, they would sit on quilts surrounding the pavilion.

While my family was living in Houston, Carol Ann and I had our second 'casual' meeting at Palacios Baptist Encampment that summer. Again, we were both there at the same time, even though we don't remember specifically meeting each other that week.

I entered Milby High School as a junior in 1951. Several students joined with me in my senior year in discussing the formation of a Christian Student Union at Milby. We had never heard of such an organization in any other high school, but it seemed like a great idea to us. Even back then, it was not an easy thing to get approved. Several of us approached our principal about forming the group to have before-school devotions twice a week. We had plans to be responsible for all the organizing and leading.

He agreed with the stipulation that we had to get 1,000 signatures in support of it. That seemed like an insurmountable task as the total enrollment for Milby High School that year was 1,850 students. We got busy and got all 1,000 signatures, and the Christian Student Union was born. He also told us we had to have a teacher sponsor. Mrs. Anna Stracener, one of our English teachers, gladly agreed to be our sponsor. I was elected as the first president, and we regularly drew a crowd of over 300 students at our devotions.

Mrs. Stracener came to hear me preach in revivals several times. I always remember she really emphasized to me that I needed to get the object of prepositions correctly. So many of us would say 'to my friend and I' or 'for you and I,' and she taught me that it is never 'I' after a preposition, but always 'me.' She reminded me of this lesson very regularly. To this day, I often hear speakers on radio or television, even PhD's, make this mistake, and I think of Mrs. Stracener.

Near the end of the year, we had our first Christian Student Union banquet. I had asked Bill Tanner, pastor of Broadway Baptist Church not far from Milby High School, to be our banquet speaker. Later on, this would be special to me for two different reasons. First, he was the son-in-law of Kyle Yates, one of my professors I graded papers for at Baylor. Secondly, during the fall of my freshman year at Baylor, Bill Tanner came to speak at Chapel. Even though I had only met him once before on the night of the banquet in high school, he immediately remembered my name. I couldn't believe it! I felt so blessed that he remembered my name that I made it my resolve to try my best to remember the names of everyone I met from that day forward. This commitment has turned out to be a great strength in the ministry the Lord has allowed me to have.

Not long after we got our Christian Student Union up and running at my high school, my friend Ronnie Boswell, who attended Austin High School, asked me to help him begin one at his school. We worked together, and I helped him know what appeals to make, and what details were necessary. Later that year, Austin High School began its own Christian Student Union.

During my junior year in Milby High School we had a highly successful revival at our church, Park Memorial Baptist. It was led by the man who was preaching when I made my profession of faith, C.E. Matthews. He was a compelling evangelist and amazingly his invitations sometimes lasted longer than his sermons. At Park Memorial that week, a remarkable thing happened. Our Sunday morning service was broadcast on live radio each Sunday. One listener tuned in after the sermon during the invitation. Just listening to the invitation that Dr. Matthews extended, the man got dressed and made it to church before the invitation was over to make his profession of faith!

My best friend at the time was Charles Dan Oglesby. Even though he attended Austin High School, one of my school's biggest rivals, his family was very active at our church. Charles Dan and I had both surrendered to preach and often prayed together that God would use us to reach Houston for the Lord. Since I didn't have a car, we always had to use his Ford coupe. With both car doors open, we would kneel in our driveway by each door across the front seat to pray together. We were so enthusiastic in our beliefs at the time, we really believed we could actually win Houston to Christ

We made an agreement with one another that if one of us was asked to preach a revival, we wouldn't accept it unless both of us could come. As time went by, God answered our prayers to preach together. Charles Dan was asked to preach a youth revival at the Mason Drive Baptist Church in January 1953. The church was on 75th Street – the dividing line between Milby and Austin High Schools. He told the pastor that he couldn't come without me to share the preaching, and the pastor agreed. That was the beginning of a remarkable string of 22 revivals from January 1953, until September of that year when we both went off to Baylor.

From that first night we preached the church auditorium was completely filled with over 250 people. I remember the church did not have any air conditioning or a P.A. system, but none of that seemed to matter. Crowds overflowed that auditorium, and many stood on the outside to participate in the services outside the building. At the end of the first week there had been such a move of God that the principals of both Milby and Austin High Schools called us in to ask that we continue the revival due to the impact it was having on students at both schools.

We extended the revival one more week, and by the end of those two weeks, there were more than 400 professions of faith, mostly from students at the two schools. Most of the time, Charles Dan and I would trade off preaching one night and leading music the next. This went on for several months before we felt the need for another singer so we could focus on preaching every other night. We asked Chuck Swindoll to lead our music for the revivals. He was a year ahead of me in school and had already graduated but was still at home working for his dad in his sheet metal business.

It was a whirlwind of activity for us three young ministers at the time. We were soon swept up in its wake. During the week, Charles Dan and I would go to class, and Chuck would work for his dad; then, we would all meet at the church wherever the revival was being held. It was an amazing time for us as young preachers and the thousands who came to know the Lord during these revivals. We preached revivals all over Houston and many of the surrounding cities as well. We even made the front page of the newspaper with a headline, "East End Billy Grahams." Those days were truly a Spirit-led whirlwind!

The reception the pastors and churches gave our revival team was remarkable. It is hard to imagine today, but during these revival meetings, pastors of churches of all sizes would open their pulpits to us—three teenage kids excited about sharing Christ! During the summer after we graduated from high school, we occasionally led Vacation Bible Schools in the morning and revival services at night. Looking back, the encouragement and enthusiastic support of so many pastors in so many cities during this time was one of God's greatest blessings on our lives.

One evening while I was preaching, I looked up and saw Dr. Glen Commander—a very prominent pastor from another church in Houston listening to me preach! Needless to say, I got nervous and anxious, even though I continued to preach. Dr. Commander must have sensed my anxiety. He came up to me after the service, put his hand on my shoulder and simply said, "Jimmy, we are for you!" That was such a much-needed word of encouragement in those early days. It made such a strong impression on me as a young preacher that I have always tried to be an encourager in my own ministry.

At the same time, the three of us were preaching and singing in those revivals, another evangelist was beginning to make a name for himself, Freddie Gage. He was a former youth gang leader from the north side of Houston and had been dramatically saved, along with his wife Barbara, a few months before our revivals began. Freddie had been saved out of drugs and gang violence, and he wanted everyone to know of the saving grace of Christ. He went on to become one of the most powerful evangelists in the 20th century. At his prime, he truly had no equal!

Freddie's activity as an evangelist is staggering. He preached over 1,350 crusades and shared his testimony in over 3,000 school assemblies while talking about the dangers of drug use. He also preached in over 300 prisons and jails and to over 500 civic groups. More than 1,000,000 people made professions of faith as a result of his ministry.

WHERE SOUTHERN GOSPEL MUSIC BEGAN

Freddie was not a theologian and nor did he sound like one. He used the language of the street, much like Jesus did in His ministry. Jesus spoke in the *KOINE* Greek of his day, which was the language of the street in the first century. Freddie preached and ministered in this same pattern of ministry. Freddie and Barbara became close friends and, in the late 1970s, moved to Euless, Texas, where I was their pastor for over a dozen years. It was my privilege to preach the coronation services for both Freddie and Barbara.

During May, 1953, Billy Graham arrived in Houston for his first crusade. Both my dad and Charles Dan's dad were on the Executive Committee for that crusade. On the last day of the crusade, the service was moved to Rice Stadium to accommodate the crowd. Roy Rogers and Dale Evans, the most famous of the Cowboy singers and actors/actresses of their day, were scheduled to give their testimonies on the final day of the crusade. Charles Dan and I pulled a few strings with our dads, and we were given the coveted assignment to escort Roy and Dale to the platform.

Because the speaker's platform was at the far end of the stadium, Charles Dan and I escorted Roy and Dale the entire length of the field to the platform. Hundreds of youth would show us pictures during that summer that were taken as we walked to the platform. While we waited in the ramp to enter the stadium, we had the privilege of meeting Billy Graham, Cliff Barrows, Bev Shea, and Grady Wilson. These men treated us like we were really important, and it marked the beginning of a lifelong friendship with them and many others.

Just as he did with many other young ministers over the years, Billy Graham and his team had a significant impact on my ministry. Carol Ann and I have had the opportunity to visit Billy and Ruth over the years. While doing a conference at the Billy Graham Conference Center back in the 1990s, we had the privilege of spending an afternoon with Billy and Ruth Graham in their home and again with Billy after Ruth's death.

After this first meeting at the crusade, I became lifelong friends with Cliff Barrows. He even wrote the forward to my 1974 book, 'Say Neighbor, Your House is on Fire.' T. W. Wilson, Billy's daily companion for many years, and his wife Mary Helen, also became some of our closest friends.

Years later, while serving as president of LifeWay, we regularly traveled to LifeWay's Ridgecrest Conference Center in North Carolina, and we always made time for a visit with T.W. and Mary Helen in Black Mountain. Bev Shea lived on the same street as the Wilsons and was also a dear friend. One of my most cherished books is Bev's book, 'How Sweet the Sound' that Bev sent to me with a lengthy inscription and signature.

As a side note, I had taken this very special book with me on a trip and accidentally left it on the plane. I felt such a loss since Bev had gone to such lengths to personally inscribe the book and send it to me. I was wonderfully surprised about a week later when I received the book—my book—in the mail from a flight attendant on my flight who had found the book and took the trouble to look me up and return it to me. She had seen the personal inscription and knew it would be special to me.

The Billy Graham crusade was a tremendous success, and to this day, we still have many unforgettable memories of Billy Graham and his team, the celebrities who shared their testimonies, and the enthusiastic crowds during those exciting days.

WHERE SOUTHERN GOSPEL MUSIC BEGAN

Just before the crusade in early May, a devastating tornado swept through Waco, Texas, the home of Baylor University. It killed 114 people and remains as one of the deadliest tornados in Texas history. After the crusade, Charles Dan and I drove to Waco to see the damage caused by the storm. Even though the downtown area of Waco was still restricted to necessary personnel and the clean-up crews, the scene closely resembled a war zone. Fortunately, Baylor's campus was mostly spared from the destruction.

Racial violence had been prevalent in Waco, dating back to the Civil War. Tragically, an African American teenager, Jesse Washington, was tortured, mutilated, and burned to death in the town square of Waco in 1916. Even worse, 15,000 people watched it happen. It wasn't until 2016 that the then-mayor of Waco issued a formal apology to the Washington family.

In light of Waco's prominent history of racial hostility, it is interesting that Baylor had the first African American football player to ever play on a Southwest Conference team. It was 1965, and his name was John Westbrook. He was a gifted and very popular player. Westbrook's father, grandfather, and great-grandfather were all pastors. His father was an all-American football player at Paul Quinn College and the first in the family to graduate college. According to John, his dad had long-since predicted that one day his son would play football for Baylor.

Waco is known today for two delicious soft drinks that originated there. Dr. Pepper was first created in Waco in 1885 at Morrison's Old Corner Drug Store by Charles Alderton. Later in 1937, a special cream soda that eventually came to be known as "Big Red" was also created by Grover Thomsen and R.H. Roark. Waco was also the location of the White House Press Center during George W. Bush's years as president. Whenever Bush was at his ranch in Crawford, Waco was home to all the members of the press.

Above all, though, Waco is best known as the home of Baylor University, originally founded in Independence, Texas, in 1845 and moved to Waco in 1846. It is the oldest continually operating university in Texas with students from all 50 states and 80 countries outside the U.S. When Charles Dan and I came to Baylor in September 1953, and enrolled as freshmen, Baylor had about 5,000 students. Enrollment today tops 16,000.

My Baylor years were wonderful. I received a double major in History and Bible. One of the highlights I had was the privilege to grade papers for over two years for Dr. Kyle Yates. At the time, Dr. Yates was the premier Old Testament scholar in America. He was chosen by Cecil B. Demille to be the Old Testament scholar as a consultant during his making of 'The Ten Commandments' movie in the mid-1950s. I took every class he taught and grew to love him. He and my father had served as fellow pastors during the same years in Houston. He served as pastor of Second Baptist Church of Houston at the same time my dad was pastor of Park Memorial Baptist in Houston.

I was active on campus throughout my Baylor years and was an avid and enthusiastic fan of the Baylor Bears in whatever sports season it was at the time. When Baylor and Texas clashed in football in 1953 in Waco, some of us thought it would be a great idea to take an air horn to the game and blow it every time Baylor made a good play. The game was televised nationwide because both teams were nationally ranked. We found out later that every time we blasted the horn, television screens all over the country would flutter with interference!

'Singspiration' was a regular part of my Baylor years. It was a weekly get-together at the Student Center where up to 400 students would gather to sing and praise the Lord each week. It was my privilege to lead one of those services during my sophomore year. At the end of my junior year, I was elected president of the Ministerial Alliance at Baylor. More than six decades later, I still have many friendships from that group.

While at Baylor, I continued to preach on weekends and in the summers. Over the years, I preached revivals all over Texas including many times in Houston, as well as Huntsville, Sonora, Blanco, Lufkin, Trinity, Herty, Dallas, Fort Worth, Rusk, Carthage, Texas City, Brazoria, Kemah, Baycliff, LaPorte, Pearland, Rockport, Flat, Diana, Austin, Kilgore, Cedar Bayou, Willow Springs, Anahuac, Huffman, Kerrville, Franklin, Axtell, and Addicks. I also preached revivals in Little Rock, Albuquerque and Memphis.

Just before I began school for my sophomore year in Baylor in August of 1954, I went to Little Rock, Arkansas, to visit with my granddad, L.M. Keeling, who was in the last stages of liver cancer. He was bedridden at that time and rarely got out of bed except for his morning coffee. During that trip, two very significant things happened.

First, even though I had been preaching for five years by that time, my granddad had never heard me preach. One of his close friends had a daily fifteen-minute radio broadcast in Little Rock, and asked me to preach on his broadcast just so Granddad could hear me. I did the broadcast, and when I came back to the house, my granddad told me, "That is the same Gospel I have been preaching for 54 years!" That comment was so important to me.

The second thing happened one morning as we sat by his small table looking out to Battery Street from his living room window. With a twinkle in his eye, he asked me, "Little Jimmy, would you like to know where to find a good sermon?" Of course, I answered, "I sure would!" With that, he picked up his preaching Bible and hugged it like a mother might hold her newborn baby. With a smile, he said, "From Genesis to Revelation." He believed in the full authority and sufficiency of God's Word and is a strong reason for my own theological position today.

He passed away a few weeks later, but I will always cherish that time I got to spend with him during that August. He will always be one of the finest text-driven expository preachers Southern Baptists have ever produced!

It was in the fall of my sophomore year that I met Bill Anderson. He came as a freshman and was there on a football scholarship. We both attended Seventh and James Baptist Church and were in Training Union together on Sunday evenings. Our friendship has strengthened over the decades and still continues to this very day. Bill married before we got out of Baylor and He and Cookie served at First Baptist Church of McGregor just outside Waco for several years. Then he became pastor of First Baptist Church of Euless and would recommend me there when he moved to Calvary Baptist Church in Clearwater, Florida.

He was also the chairman of the Board of Trustees for the Sunday School Board in 1991 when I was elected to become the 8th president of that institution. He has been an important part of our lives over the years, and his daughter, Karen, was roommate with our Terri when they attended Baylor.

One of the more traumatic memories of my time at Baylor happened midway through my sophomore year. I was in an automobile accident returning to school from Houston right after New Year's with my dear friend, Clynton Pylate. Clynton lived nearby in Houston and had a brand-new Oldsmobile 88. On this particular trip, I was driving his car on Highway 6, just north of Hempstead. Even though it had been raining for quite some time, I was speeding and going much faster than I should have been. As we topped one hill, there was a car on our side of the road and a long line of cars that he was trying to pass.

I only had time to swerve hard to the right. As soon as the car got off the pavement, it began to roll and turned over several times before clearing a fence and landing upright in a pasture. Those who witnessed the accident said that I was thrown as high as the telephone poles along the highway between the fence and the highway itself. Thankfully the rain had softened the ground, so I had no broken bones. As it turned out, however, I was considerably more injured than I first thought.

My friend, Clynton, was thrown out of the car level with the ground and clipped a fencepost before landing in the pasture. Although he had severe injuries from hitting the fencepost, he recovered much quicker than I did. Even with no broken bones, I suffered severe injuries in my back, hip, and leg. Clynton recuperated from his injuries and returned to classes before I did.

The nearby hospital had been told by one witness that I was probably already dead, so they only sent one ambulance. When the attendants realized I was alive, I squeezed into the front seat of the ambulance because I refused to stay on that cold, wet ground and wait for another ambulance to arrive. Later on, when I admitted to the highway patrolman that I had been speeding, he promptly wrote me a speeding ticket! I ended up missing a fair amount of school, including my exams, but was eventually able to make everything up. And when I did return, I had to bring a pillow with me to classes just to be comfortable.

The following spring, in 1955, was also a significant time for me as I led a revival for high school students in Albuquerque, New Mexico. During that week, I preached at two different churches near two different high schools. Before school, students from Del Norte High School came for special services, and in the afternoon, students from Highland High School came to services. It was a remarkable time for those students and me, as many decisions were made for Christ.

Albuquerque has always held a special place in my heart for another reason too. My mother had five sisters and two brothers, all of whom moved to Albuquerque in the 1930s. I spent several summers there living with my aunt and uncle, Ruth and R. T. Baker, and their children, Richard and Betty Nell. Richard and I were born within six weeks of each other, and I had a special bond with his family for many, many years. His sister, Betty Nell, is like a sister to me and we still stay in touch after all these years.

It was during one of the summers I stayed with the Bakers that Richard and I got into a little (well, a lot!) of trouble with the family car. Richard had a paper route that he threw each morning from a bicycle. When his parents were gone for the week, he told me he

WHERE SOUTHERN GOSPEL MUSIC BEGAN

knew where the keys were to the new car that his dad had just bought. Even though he had been told not to drive the car, the temptation was just too great. The two of us threw his paper route one morning while he drove the car.

Everything was going fine until we hit a curb, and the tire went flat. So, not only were we driving a forbidden car, but we'd gotten a flat tire on it! And his parents were due home shortly. We tried our best to get it all completely repaired, but just couldn't get it back to its original condition by the time his folks arrived. To say the least, my uncle was not a happy camper with the two of us!

Several other significant things happened in Albuquerque in my life during my visits there. My mother's family were all members of First Baptist Church Albuquerque, so that's naturally where we always went when I was in town. One year my dad was scheduled to come to Albuquerque to preach the first revival for the new mission of First Baptist Church that later became known as Hoffmantown Baptist Church. I was already visiting from college, and when the pastor found out circumstances were going to keep my dad from arriving in time to preach on Sunday night, he asked me to preach the opening service of the revival. Today, Hoffmantown is one of the great churches in the country, and I'm grateful I got to share in that church's beginning days. I also was invited to preach the 50th anniversary service for the church a number of years ago.

I made many lifelong friends during my days in Albuquerque. Larry Walker became one of my great friends from there. Even though Larry was an All-State basketball player in New Mexico and played ball his freshman year at Baylor, he didn't continue his basketball career because he was already preaching around the country and had his own evangelistic team patterned after Billy Graham's. I became close friends with Larry's song leader, Dwayne Marrow, during our Baylor years as well. I stayed close friends with both of these men until their respective deaths. The team's piano player was Bobby Taylor and he was also a Baylor classmate. Later he would marry Dr. James Sullivan's daughter, Beth. Dr. Sullivan also served as president of the Sunday School Board from 1953-1976.

I couldn't match Larry's natural athletic abilities, but we both managed to play golf fairly well. One day, while I was in Albuquerque, we went to a local course to play 18 holes of golf. At the end of that round, we had tied on every hole. We decided to just keep playing until one of us won. After another 18 holes, we were still tied, so we played another round. By the end of the day, we had played 54 holes of golf and amazingly tied on every hole!

Another thing about Larry was his ability to play the violin. It was an unusual combination for an all-star basketball player to also be the first chair in the violin section of the Albuquerque Symphony Orchestra. In many of the mission trips we took over the years, Larry would show up just to play the violin. We also had lots of impromptu services. On some of these trips, whenever we got to a busy intersection in the city, Larry would start playing the violin. Before long, a crowd would gather, and I would share the Gospel. Many people came to know the Lord at these pop-up services.

I also became fast friends with Billy Wagner in Albuquerque. Years later, he and his wife, Sally, spent several decades in Europe as missionaries for our Foreign Mission Board. I will tell a special time of ministry with Billy later in our journey.

While my family was living in Houston, I often hitchhiked home.

WHERE SOUTHERN GOSPEL MUSIC BEGAN

I even hitchhiked to Albuquerque several times while I was at Baylor. On one of these trips at Thanksgiving, I was let off at Central Drive, the main street through Albuquerque, and about a mile from the Bakers' house. I walked the remaining distance to their house even though it was close to 2:00 a.m., and the temperatures were in the thirties. When I got to the house, I didn't want to wake anyone up, so I laid down on a couch on the front porch with plans to sleep until early morning. It got so cold that I finally rang the doorbell at 3:30 a.m., and my cousin, Betty Nell, immediately cried out, "He's here!" It turns out they had been waiting for me to arrive the whole time.

All four of my uncles who lived in Albuquerque were in insurance sales. Uncles Charlie Keeling, R.T. Baker, and L.M. Keeling traveled all over the state each week selling life insurance, and Uncle Ed Egli was a local insurance agent for car and house insurance. After that particular Thanksgiving holiday, my Uncle L.M. drove me to Hobbs, New Mexico, and I had plans to hitchhike back to Waco for classes. I made it as far as Lubbock and found myself in the midst of a West Texas snowstorm. I stood beside the road for several hours, but no one was stopping to help me get on to Waco. Fortunately, I had just enough money to buy a bus ticket to Waco and managed to get back in time for classes.

On another trip, I rode a bus from Albuquerque and the bus broke down about ten miles out of Rotan, Texas. We were told to leave our belongings on the bus, and they would be delivered to us when a new bus arrived. My mistake was in not taking my briefcase, which held my Bible, all my sermons from the last four years, and my record book dating back to my first revival in 1953. Sadly, it was all stolen, and I was left with no record of the early revivals I preached.

WHO BUT GOD! RIDING THE WHIRLWIND
JIMMY AND CAROL ANN DRAPER

Jimmy preaching in Possum Walk Baptist Church New Waverly, TX 1952

Charles Dan Oglesby & Jimmy

Jimmy Baylor Graduation

WHERE SOUTHERN GOSPEL MUSIC BEGAN

Youth Revival team reunited, Jimmy, Chuck Swindoll & Charles Dan Oglesby

Jimmie & Lois in college

WHO BUT GOD! RIDING THE WHIRLWIND
JIMMY AND CAROL ANN DRAPER

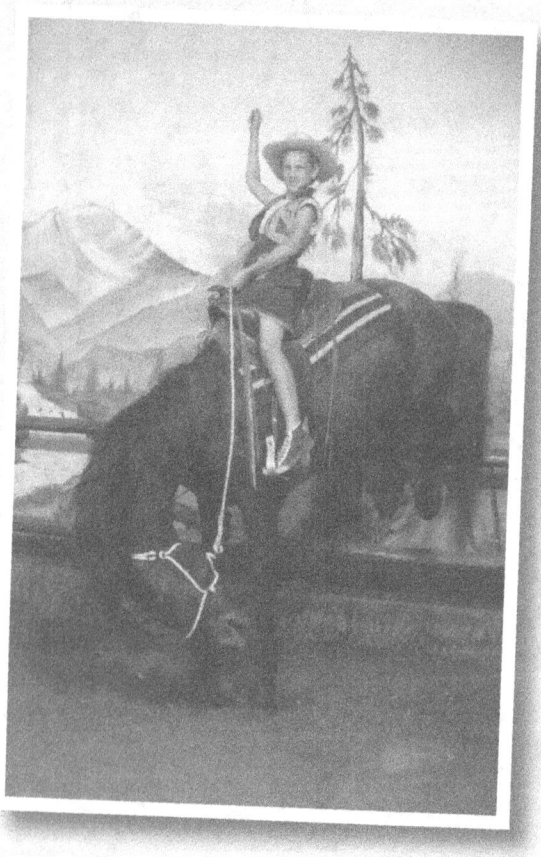

Carol Ann
nine years old

4

SAN ANTONIO ROSE

CAROL ANN'S STORY – SAN ANTONIO, TEXAS

Everyone has a story...and this is my story of God's amazing grace and divine guidance. I was born in San Antonio, Texas, the citadel of Hispanic heritage and culture in Texas. Spanish was the language of the streets when I was born on November 3, 1937 in one of the most unique hospitals in the United States. Not only was it just a few blocks from the historic Alamo (I am quick to point out that I was not born in the Alamo!), but the Nix Hospital occupied the top six floors of a 23-story high rise medical office building.

It was built and established in 1930 as the Nix Professional Building and was the first medical 'mall' in the United States. It contained not only the hospital, but doctors' offices, rehab facilities, and other medical services.

San Antonio was one of the oldest and largest Spanish settlements in Texas. It was founded on the west side of the San Antonio River near San Pedro Springs. The Presidio San Antonio de Bexar was the site of the first inhabitants of San Antonio. Mexico had won its independence from Spain in 1821, and Anglo settlers, alongside Hispanic settlers, were invited by the Mexican government to settle on the areas east and northeast of San Antonio. This was outlined in the Constitution of Mexico of 1824. Santa Anna was elected president of Mexico in 1833 and quickly rescinded the 1824 constitution.

Violence broke out almost immediately as the 'Tejanos,' as the Anglo and Hispanic settlers called themselves, demanded a return to the 1824 Constitution. In 1835 the Tejanos managed to defeat General Martin de Cos, Santa Anna's brother-in-law, and forced the Mexican military to retreat from Texas.

Santa Anna, seeking revenge on his brother-in-law's defeat marshaled the army for an assault on San Antonio, which became known as the Battle of the Alamo. It began on February 23, 1836, and concluded with the Mexican forces crushing the resistance in the Alamo on March 6, 1836. From the ruins of the Alamo, the cries of "Remember the Alamo" resounded across the forces of resistance, and on April 21, 1836, at the Battle of San Jacinto, Texas won its Independence.

Still proud of its Spanish heritage and culture, San Antonio is one of the great cities of America. Traditions such as the annual Fiesta parades attract millions of spectators. The two street parades are spectacular, but few events are as impressive as the nighttime floating parade on the San Antonio River each year. Called the Flambeau Parade, it attracts over 600,000 people each year by itself.

Several unique things stand out about the Fiestas in San Antonio. The governing board of the Fiestas is an all-volunteer board, and no

SAN ANTONIO ROSE

one receives any funds from the government to provide for the parades. The largest of the street parades has 75,000 volunteers and is the only parade in the U.S. that is staffed by all women volunteers. The Fiesta Commission is a non-profit organization, and all donations come from the businesses and interested individuals in San Antonio itself.

My mom and dad, Finis and Lucille Floyd, were wonderful examples to my brothers and me growing up. They were a loving couple, devoted parents, and deeply in love with Jesus. I still thank the Lord daily for the blessing to have been born into the hearts and arms of my parents and the wonderful childhood they provided for our family. Of all the many decisions God has allowed me to make throughout my life, I'm grateful He took care of this one for me.

Before I came along, my parents already had two boys—Richard and Don Ray. When I was conceived, my Dad had been mostly in bed and out of work for many months with a heart condition. Being in the midst of the Great Depression, I'm sure they wondered how they could take care of another child, but I'm so grateful they trusted the Lord and believed in His provision to make a way. When I arrived, Richard was 5-1/2, and Don Ray was just 18 months old. I am sure life was hard for my parents, but as children we never felt anything but God's grace and peace and our parents' love. We always had lots of friends, fun, and plenty of food.

We moved to Houston, Texas, when I was three years old because my dad was offered a good job there. We left San Antonio and moved into a new community and a new church home. My folks always took us to Sunday School and church. There was never any question—we went to church on Sunday just like we went to school on Monday. It was just a way of life for our family.

WHO BUT GOD! RIDING THE WHIRLWIND
JIMMY AND CAROL ANN DRAPER

In 1942, my dad was offered a new opportunity at the new Dow Chemical Company that was too good to turn down. This meant another move, this time closer to the Gulf coast near Freeport, Texas. The company was bringing in so many new employees, they actually built a company town called Lake Jackson. We were one of the first five hundred families to move in and begin a wonderful journey with new friends and a wonderful faith family.

Lake Jackson was a wonderful town to grow up in. We could walk to town where we had a movie theater, two grocery stores, a bank, clothing store, drug store, beauty shop, doctor's office, service station, and the Dairy Bar—where I had my first formal job. We also had a city library and Elementary School and Junior High School and several churches. If we needed anything not inside our little town, we drove just a few miles to Freeport.

One of the best parts of living in such a new community is that we knew almost everyone in town. Our lives centered around First Baptist Church, school, and the community. In elementary school, my girlfriends and I would make the outline of our make-believe houses on the sidewalk during recess and have hours of fun pretending each week.

Growing up in Lake Jackson gave me so many cherished memories and blessings. Life was not a whirlwind at that time. It was laid back, easy, and fun. Lucy Lester was a special friend who lived on the next street, and we always walked to school together. I would like to say it was three miles away, uphill both ways, but it was actually about a quarter of a mile. One day while in junior high, we decided to skate to school, but we never did that again because we ended up with blisters all over our feet!

SAN ANTONIO ROSE

My friends from growing up in Lake Jackson are some of my sweetest memories. One of my best friends was Carolyn Johnson, who was a very small girl due to a handicap from birth. Shirley Beth Pruitt and I got our last dolls on Christmas day when we were eleven years old. My doll was a boy doll, and I named him Jimmy Lee. Some of my other good friends I went all through elementary, junior, and senior high with were Deanna Smith and Cherrie Mae Jarrell.

I met many new friends in high school because it was a consolidated high school in Freeport named Brazosport. My three years there with new friends, teachers, and lots of ball games, band concerts, and parades were exciting. I was in the high school band and played the baritone saxophone when I was not marching as a majorette for the band.

My parents taught my brothers and me to love the Lord and His church. We loved, respected, and honored our parents and, with few exceptions, were obedient children. We had a lot of freedom but clear boundaries for our behavior. We learned that whenever faced with a dilemma to ask ourselves, "What would Jesus do?" Mom and dad always lived consistent, godly lives. They loved us and disciplined us as needed to teach us right from wrong. I always knew I was loved and protected.

My most cherished memory as I grew up was having a mom who did not work outside the home and was always there when we came in from school with cookies or a snack. My Dad was in a carpool and got home at 5:30 every day. We all sat at the table for dinner together and talked about what happened that day. Because we had no dishwasher, Richard, Don Ray, and I were responsible for washing and drying the dishes except for the rare occasions when we used the good china. This helped us learn to work together and to be thankful for food to eat and a stable family life. We did not have a lot of clothes, but we took care of what we had. We had school clothes, and we had play clothes. The school clothes were kept mended, cleaned, and ironed. We took our school clothes off when we got home and put on our play clothes.

My brothers and I grew up in a small frame, three-bedroom, one-bath house with no air conditioning, just a window fan. We played outside close to home and at nearby friends' houses. We could run in the streets and play sports in the yards because the yards weren't fenced. It also helped us get to know our neighbors well. We could walk to town a mile away with our friends. It was a wonderful way to grow up.

One of our town's most famous residents was King Hill, an All-American quarterback for Rice University and number one NFL draft pick. He was such a good athlete during his college years he lettered in football, basketball, and golf. Both my brothers were athletes as well, and close friends with King. My brother, Richard, was an outstanding baseball pitcher and was offered a Major League bonus and contract after pitching for the Navy baseball team while he was enlisted, but he declined the offer to pursue his career as an architect.

Our church, First Baptist Church of Lake Jackson, was a model for Baptist churches of the time. Our congregation was known to be unselfish and committed to missions, evangelism, and the community's youth. It sponsored virtually all of the other Baptist churches that began in the Lake Jackson area the 40+ years after it was constituted in 1943 and was often in the top 10 contributors to the Southern Baptist Convention's Cooperative Program in the last half of the 20th century. It was also very special to me because it was where I was saved and surrendered my life to the Lord.

My parents were consistent in their lifestyle, and their lives reflected Jesus and His Love. God worked through them to bring me to the place of receiving Christ into my heart when I was seven years old. I invited Jesus to save me, forgive me, and come into my Heart forever and He did.

After Jesus saved me, I wanted to become more like Him and less like me. I read my Bible daily and claimed His many promises and found Him to be faithful and true, just as He promised. When I was nine, I felt Jesus tug at my heart once again. This time I walked the aisle and committed my life to special service for the Lord. My tender, young heart told me that I was to be an old maid schoolteacher in Africa, teaching boys and girls about Jesus.

I was very active in school and played the soprano saxophone beginning in the sixth grade. In high school, I switched to the baritone saxophone and became a twirler in the band.

The summer before my sophomore year in high school, Richard, and his wife, Joan, and another friend were heading to the Brazos River to water ski. Because they knew how much I loved the water and wanted a chance to ride in a boat, they took me along. Joan was pregnant at that time, so she mostly sat on the bank and watched the guys ski. I thought it looked really hard and had no desire to learn that day.

As a background to my story, mom had given me a 'Bobbie home permanent' earlier in the day. She had rolled my hair on bobbie pens, and I was to leave it that way until it dried, so that's how I went.

WHO BUT GOD! RIDING THE WHIRLWIND
JIMMY AND CAROL ANN DRAPER

I was having a great time until Richard told me it was my time to ski. When I declined, he called me 'chicken,' and that's all it took. I quickly pulled two swim caps on over my pin curls and jumped in. I put on the skis, held the rope, and hoped for the best. The boat roared off, and I popped right up on top of the water. No one had given me any instructions on what to do, so I just hung on. I managed to make several good turns before I fell, but there was only one problem—I was so worried about keeping the skis on my feet that I forgot to let go of the rope.

The first few seconds, I felt like I was drowning or about to be stuck in the mud on the bottom of the river. Either way, by that time, both my swim caps were long since gone, and my swimsuit was down to my waist. When the rope finally came out of my hand, I had to quickly get my swimsuit in place before the guys got back to pick me up. In the meantime, my hair had gotten totally soaked—when it was supposed to dry completely before I could take the bobby pins out.

Two days later, my hair was mostly dry, and the bobby pins were beginning to rust, so we took them all out and washed and dried my hair. I had corkscrew curls all over my head and burst out into tears! Mom took me to the beauty shop, and the stylist cut all my curls off, but left me with very short hair. Mom reminded me my hair would eventually grow out, but that didn't stop my tears and knowing I would be the only sophomore girl in my high school with such short hair. It took longer than I had hoped, but mom was right—it finally did grow back.

What I want you to know about me is that I am an ordinary person who had the privilege of growing up with loving and godly parents and two normal brothers. My only claim to fame is that Jesus is my Lord and Savior. I desired from early in my life to be less like me and more like Jesus. I've always loved to read the Bible, claim God's promises, and live my life in such a way that He would receive the glory and honor.

NOW FAST FORWARD – Little did I know what God had planned for my life. Looking back, I now know that my young commitment to special service was not life as a missionary in Africa, but more of a, "Yes Lord, to your will and to your way." In Jeremiah 29:11-12, God says, "I know the plans I have for you, says the Lord, plans for your well-being, not for disaster, to give you a future and a hope." And that has been true throughout my entire life.

The Lord's lifelong plan for me began to take shape in August 1955. I was to be a senior at Brazosport High School, a consolidated school in Freeport. I rode a school bus like many of the kids because very few high school students had their own car.

I loved my high school years and the many new friends I met from other towns. It was in high school that I met my best friend, Wanda Jean Richardson. We bonded quickly and remained best friends until she died in 2018. Through the years, we often spoke on the phone, exchanged notes and letters, and even led retreats together. We called them 'Two Friends Retreats' because the only requirement to come was to bring a friend. Wanda Jean's husband, Jim, did the cooking for our retreats. These went on for over seven years and impacted hundreds of ladies.

Just before the start of my senior year, my church had planned a youth-led revival for the third week of August. Unfortunately, the person originally lined up to lead the music for the revival had to cancel about six weeks before the start of the meeting. My pastor,

WHO BUT GOD! RIDING THE WHIRLWIND
JIMMY AND CAROL ANN DRAPER

Bro. Johnny Beard, had just come to the church and was praying and seeking God for someone to come and lead the music.

As it turned out, Jimmy Draper, a young college minister from Houston, was the answer to that prayer. Even though he had been preaching every week all summer long, he had this week open, and he could sing.

AND NOW MY STORY TAKES A TURN – WHO BUT GOD? The week of the revival finally came. We were prayed up and ready to see what God would do in our midst. We came expecting lives to be changed and friends to be saved. It was an exciting time of anticipation.

I was wrapping up a great summer, heading into my senior year of high school, and planning to go to Baylor after that. I'd had a few boyfriends, but certainly wasn't looking for one then and certainly hadn't thought about marriage. I was happy and content, but I did get excited when I saw Jimmy was coming! He was single, a Baylor student, was so good looking, and had a heart for Jesus.

As Jimmy was leading music throughout the revival, I made sure to sing on the front row of the youth choir every night. After church on that first Sunday night, the youth had a fellowship. Jimmy led the fellowship, playing and singing a silly song about having supper in heaven and eating "cornbread and buttermilk and good old turnip greens." I was chosen to read a comedy about Cinderella, only in the story, she was known as 'Rendacella.' It was funny, but I was so embarrassed and glad when I finally got to the end.

We all introduced ourselves to Jimmy and shook his hand, and I remember I went with home with a smile on my face and thinking, "This college guy is a real person and has a heart for Jesus."

SAN ANTONIO ROSE

Jimmy and Harold Proctor, the preacher for the week, stayed in the parsonage of Bro. Johnny and Marti. Bro. Johnny told Jimmy that I was a popular but quiet girl and that he should get to know me and report back to him. That was also the week Jimmy bought his first car, a 1951 four-door Chevrolet with no A/C or radio! He asked me to help wash the car, and we had fun doing that.

Jimmy ate a meal in our home, and we made visits together to prospects for the church revival. We prayed together with other youth and were together almost daily. He was a good singer and very energetic about everything.

My mom realized we were spending time together and knew he would be gone by Sunday night. When she realized what was happening, she told me, "Single evangelists are like sailors; they have a girl in every port." I heard her but didn't want to believe that it was true about Jimmy. But then my suspicion grew…On Saturday night we had a great crowd, but from the choir, I saw three new young people come in. It was a boy and two girls, and I suspected one of the girls must have come to see Jimmy from another revival. Sure enough, they stayed and visited with Jimmy after the service, but he took me home that night.

Six months later, I would be in Sweeney for an Associational G.A. meeting and saw one of the girls. She recognized me and shared that she had come to the revival at Lake Jackson and was upset that Jimmy did not want to spend time with her. She asked if anything worked out for me, and I showed her my new engagement ring with a smile! That said it all.

On Sunday, the last night of the revival, Jimmy and Harold stood down front and let people come by and express their gratitude for their preaching and singing and to praise God for their ministry. When my mom came by Jimmy and expressed her thanks for him and his servant's heart, Jimmy said, "Mrs. Floyd, you have not seen the last of me yet!"

That was the true beginning for us. Jimmy was preaching two more revivals before returning to Baylor to begin his junior year, and both were in the Houston area. When we found out about those meetings, Mom and Dad took me to one of the services just to hear him preach and I got to know him a little better. **It was wonderful to hear him preach the Word!**

When Jimmy got to Baylor, I began to get a letter from him every day. I was a senior in high school, my busiest year ever, but I raced home every day from school to the letter I knew would be waiting for me. Mom always placed it on the table in the living room. I took each one to my room, shut the door, and read and reread his letter several times. Before long, he started driving to Lake Jackson on the weekends every time he was not preaching elsewhere.

My heart was falling for this guy I hardly knew, but his letters let me into his heart! I was falling in love! I earnestly prayed, "Help Lord! He is going to be a pastor someday, and I'm not qualified to be a pastor's wife." The Lord heard my prayer and answered graciously. With arms of love around me, He spoke to my heart and said, "I haven't called you because of who you are, but for Who I am and what I can do with a yielded vessel." My response was simple, "I want to be a yielded vessel. I want to be Your vessel."

Our love deepened, even though we only saw each other once or twice a month. We had daily letters and, once in a while, a phone call. Sometimes he would call collect, and my dad would accept the charges but remind us to, 'keep it short!' Back then, most people only had one phone, and you didn't use it just to chat with others; it was usually reserved for business or information.

The letters from Waco kept coming, and in the meantime, Jimmy had swept me off my feet and found a way into my heart. We were falling in love! It was obvious to everyone that we were building a serious relationship. On one weekend visit, Jimmy and my dad went outside in the back yard to visit because Jimmy had come to ask his permission to marry me. He would not ask me to marry him until my parents agreed. My dad gave his blessings for us to be married and we were thrilled!

Jimmy came for a visit in December with plans to propose. After dinner at our house, we were planning on going to my high school's basketball game. Knowing what was going on, mom pulled him aside and said, "If you are going to give her a ring tonight, do it before you go to the basketball game as she will want to show it off."

When we were finished with dinner, Jimmy made up an excuse to go to Bro. Johnny and Marti's house because he was staying there and mentioned he needed to change socks. It seemed like a strange thing for him to do, but I went along with it. When we got there, no one was there because Jimmy had asked Bro. Johnny and Marti to leave the house so we could be alone when he proposed.

I waited in the living room while Jimmy went to change. When he returned a few minutes later, I thought he was acting a little unusual, even sort of nervous, but I mostly just chalked it up to being tired from all he had going on.

After an awkward but brief silence, he asked me if I loved him. I quickly answered, "Yes," to which he then asked, "Do you love me enough to wear this?" as he pulled out an engagement ring. Needless to say, I was beyond thrilled and speechless. Later on, he admitted to having a romantic speech all prepared, but he forgot it when it came time to propose. I used to kid him that he never really asked me to marry him and that he hasn't been speechless since then! We went on to the basketball game and I got to show off my ring.

After the excitement of the proposal, I returned to finish my senior year in high school. With his mom and dad living in Houston, sometimes we would drive up to see them on Saturday. Whenever we pulled into the driveway, Charlie, Jimmy's 8-year-old brother, would run out of the house, shouting, "Carol Ann's here!" It was just one of the many ways the Draper family showed they loved and welcomed me.

Over the years, Jimmy has expressed and demonstrated his deep love for me time after time. I am so thankful for my 'one & only' that God brought into my life at a time when I was not looking or even thinking about marriage. Who but God knows every day of our lives before we were ever born? I praise Him for blessing me with Jimmy, a man of God, committed to Him and to me. How blessed I am today and forever!

We both have a rich heritage of love and faithfulness in our parents and family. Our families never argued, fussed, or said unkind words to each other. The love we shared in our homes was evident all the time. Not only did God give me a godly boyfriend who became my husband, but godly in-laws who would call me their 'daughter-in-love!'

It is a constant blessing in my life to know all of our family is saved and heaven-bound and that one day we will all be there together! I am forever grateful God has brought me into this family.

SAN ANTONIO ROSE

My family update –

Richard was very smart and athletic. He played quarterback in football, center in basketball, and pitcher in baseball. He went to Rice University and played baseball in college. He joined the Navy and was a pitcher for the Navy baseball team while he was in the Navy. After his service in the Navy, he completed his studies at Rice and became an architect.

He married Joan Bean, and they had four children, raising them all to love and serve the Lord Jesus. Carol Denise, their oldest child, married Randy Johnson. Randy was a minister and spent nearly three decades as Youth Minister at First Baptist Church Richardson. Ricky was born next, married Tammy, and made his home in Garland. He has spent his career in construction management for a commercial building company. Next came Leigh Ann, married to Greg, and living in San Antonio. Their youngest is Gary, an excellent singer/songwriter living in California.

Richard and Joan are both in heaven and have seven grandchildren. Carol and Randy had two children, both daughters. Ricky and Tammy had three sons. Leigh Ann and Greg had two children, a son and daughter. Gary has never married.

Don Ray was only 18 months older than me, and we have always been very close. He is a wonderful man who serves the Lord faithfully. In fact, both my brothers were ordained deacons. Don Ray waited until he was 36 years old to marry. We wondered if he would ever find Miss Right, and when he did marry, it was to a wonderful lady, Barbara Boyd.

Don Ray graduated from North Texas University and taught school and coached high school before moving into the banking

WHO BUT GOD! RIDING THE WHIRLWIND
JIMMY AND CAROL ANN DRAPER

business for several years. He made his final career move into real estate and continues to thrive in that field. Barbara is an interior decorator and has a wonderful career helping people in decorating their homes and businesses. They are both active members of their church, where Don Ray serves as a deacon.

They have one daughter, Meredith, who has been very active in Dallas business and civic activities. She married Matt Mosley, a well-known sportscaster and ESPN contributor. They have one daughter, Parker, who is the delight of their lives.

Carol Ann sixth grade with her doll Jimmie Lee

Carol Ann seventh grade

Finish and Lucille Floyd, Carol Ann's parents

SAN ANTONIO ROSE

Don Ray, Mother, Carol Ann & Dad

Carol Ann High School Graduation

Carol Ann

Lucille Huffhines, Carol Ann's mother

Carol Ann 17 years old

WHO BUT GOD! RIDING THE WHIRLWIND
JIMMY AND CAROL ANN DRAPER

Carol Ann
Wedding Day
July 14, 1956

ROMANCE, MARRIAGE AND BAYLOR

In the summer of 1955, I preached revivals every week except for one—the one when I officially met Carol Ann. I was already looking forward to a week off from the grueling schedule I'd kept up all summer long. Apparently, the Lord had other plans for me.

While preaching at a church in Houston, I was approached by an older minister after one of the services. He had just finished serving as interim pastor at First Baptist Church Lake Jackson and had come to the revival to see his granddaughter baptized following her conversion earlier in that week.

The new pastor of First Baptist Church of Lake Jackson was Johnny Beard. When he arrived in Lake Jackson, he soon learned the church had scheduled a revival for the third week in August, and several weeks earlier, the scheduled singer had canceled. Johnny Beard was new to the state and new to the church and didn't know where to turn to find a singer at such late notice, so he turned to the minister who had just served as interim pastor, Bro. McIntyre.

WHO BUT GOD! RIDING THE WHIRLWIND
JIMMY AND CAROL ANN DRAPER

Bro. McIntyre visited with the singer at the revival first, but when he told him he had a full-time job and couldn't do it, he suggested me for the position. He asked me if I would lead the music for the revival in Lake Jackson, and when I agreed to do that, he recommended me to Bro. Johnny to come and lead without knowing anything else about me—including whether I could actually sing!

But the Lord knew and set the stage for me to meet Carol Ann. She was a beautiful girl, popular in the church, and in her school. Everyone else also thought she was beautiful, too, as she was voted the most beautiful girl in school her senior year. For me, meeting Carol Ann was love at first sight! I just didn't know if or how we could make this thing work. She was a senior in high school living in Lake Jackson, and I was entering my junior year at Baylor. I had a car now, but the two cities were 200 miles apart, and no major highway connected the two cities, only small farm-to-market roads.

A funny thing happened during that revival. Bro. Johnny introduced the week's evangelist, Harold Proctor, to me as 'Andy' instead of his real name. Since I didn't realize he was kidding, I called him 'Andy' for much of the revival. When I finally found out his real name, I began to call him Harold, except in one memorable instance. I had gotten up to sing a solo before he preached and said, "Now before Andy comes to preach, I want to sing…." I didn't even notice I had called him Andy, but the audience did. There was a muffled laughter that went through the crowd because they thought I had mistakenly called him by the wrong name, but I went on to sing and exited the platform. When Harold got up to preach, he cleverly said, "Thank you, Herschel," and the crowd released their muffled snickers and roared with laughter. After that, Carol Ann and I named my car

ROMANCE, MARRIAGE & BAYLOR

'Herschel' and regularly referred to it by name in the letters we sent back and forth to one another.

The romance blossomed quickly. Letters flowed daily between the two of us, and when I was not preaching, I would travel those 200 miles for weekends in Lake Jackson. Our romance was a whirlwind itself! I bought Carol Ann a ring in November, and after asking her dad for his permission to marry her, I gave the engagement ring during the Christmas holidays.

In the early spring of 1956, I preached a revival in Central Baptist Church in Baytown, Texas, where John Osteen was pastor. He was a highly successful Southern Baptist pastor. He had asked me to come supply preach for him in late May. A few days before I was to preach for him, Carol Ann called to tell me that she had a case of the three-day measles and that I might have caught it from her.

The day I preached for John Osteen; I did not feel well at all. When I got home, I told my parents how I was feeling, and my mother told me to take off my shirt. I was certain it wasn't the measles and told her I'd pay her a dollar for every measles spot she found on me. I'm glad she didn't take me up on that offer because I was covered in measles. Not long after, I had to wear sunglasses to Carol Ann's graduation ceremony because my eyes were so sensitive, and the ceremony was held in the outdoor at Hopper Field, the football field for Brazosport High School.

Several years later, John Osteen left Central Baptist and founded Lakewood Church in Houston. It is now pastored by his son, Joel, a very popular charismatic preacher and television personality. Lakewood is now one of the largest churches in America.

WHO BUT GOD! RIDING THE WHIRLWIND
JIMMY AND CAROL ANN DRAPER

The school year passed quickly for both of us, and on July 14, 1956, we were married with both Carol Ann's pastor, Johnny Beard, and my dad sharing the ceremony. It was unforgettable! The humidity and temperature were both extremely high, the church had no air conditioning, and we were all decked out in formal attire. The middle of July on the Texas coast is not an easy time to have a wedding, but nothing could spoil our joy and happiness!

Since we had no money for a honeymoon, we had to improvise. I had made arrangements with family friends in Jacksonville, Texas, the Holman family, to borrow their cabin on Club Lake, just outside town. After a night at the famous Shamrock Hotel in Houston, we headed to Jacksonville for our honeymoon with $20 in our pocket for the week.

As a special wedding gift, the Holmans had prepared for us in every way. When we got to Jacksonville, plans had already been made for us to eat at Sadler's Restaurant in town anytime we wanted, and all we had to do was sign the ticket. They also invited us to eat with them any other time throughout the week, and they had stocked the refrigerator with enough food to feed a small army. We felt like we were being treated like royalty!

Every night that week, we went into town and attended the annual Youth Revival at Central Baptist Church. It was a good time for me to get used to introducing Carol Ann as my wife! The week was perfect except Carol Ann said she never got to see the lake! When we stopped by the Holman's on our way out of town to thank them for their generous hospitality, they gave us another wedding gift—a $20 bill. We came with $20 and left after a wonderful week with $40. It was a special way to begin our marriage.

ROMANCE, MARRIAGE & BAYLOR

I preached two revivals the two weeks after the honeymoon, one in Houston and the other in Brazoria. I received the two largest love offerings I had ever received from each of those revivals—$200 each. From there, we headed to Waco to begin my senior year at Baylor. We now had $400 from our two revivals and $250 from a cashed-out Savings Bond Carol Ann's dad had bought for her when she was born, and we were ready to tackle the world!

Our first home was in the Kate Ross Apartments in Waco, a government housing project just as few blocks from Baylor. It was a large cluster of concrete two-story apartments with no air-conditioning. Our rent was $35 a month and included electricity.

We'll never forget our first night there. It was so hot that we got up around midnight and went to a motel to spend the night even though we were watching every dollar. The next day we bought a window water cooler unit that brought us some relief.

Carol Ann took several classes that year and worked on campus part-time. I made straight A's that year since I wasn't running around with my friends or spending my weekends driving to and from Lake Jackson. I graduated May 1957 and our class yell was, 'We're the angels sent from Heaven! We're the class of '57!' It wasn't a very accurate description of us, but it's the best we could do to rhyme with heaven!

WHO BUT GOD! RIDING THE WHIRLWIND
JIMMY AND CAROL ANN DRAPER

Carol Ann Houston

Jimmy and Carol Ann dating

Jimmy at rehersal dinner

Rehersal dinner

ROMANCE, MARRIAGE & BAYLOR

Jimmy's first car

Jimmy & Carol Ann
Wedding day

Carol Ann with her
mom and dad

WHO BUT GOD! RIDING THE WHIRLWIND
JIMMY AND CAROL ANN DRAPER

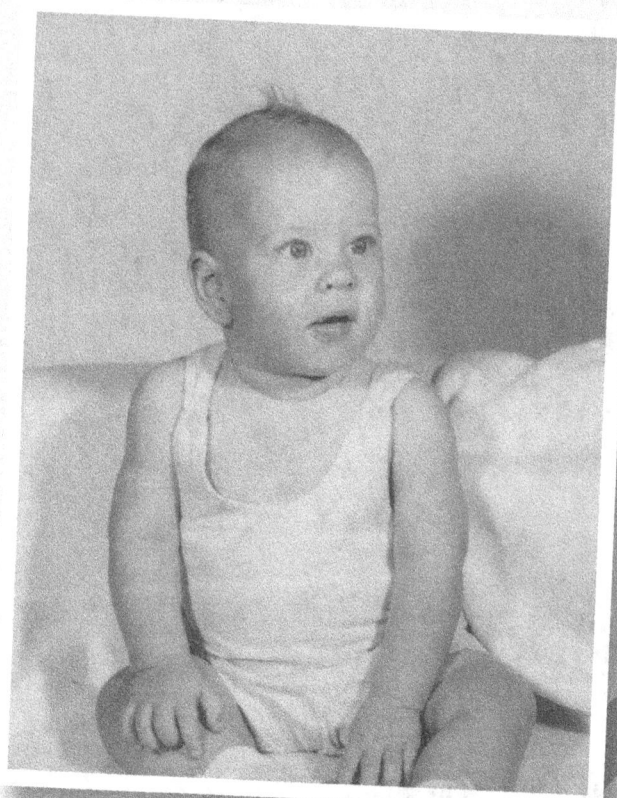

Our first born, Randy
9 months old

LIVING IN AGGIELAND

SAINTS' REST BAPTIST CHURCH

The first church we pastored as husband and wife was located just outside of the Bryan/College Station area, home of Texas A&M University. The Saints' Rest Baptist Church was in the Steep Hollow community just three miles east of A&M. It was only one month after we were married when we were called to serve this wonderful church. They had called a brand new 20-year-old pastor and his newlywed 18-year-old wife from Baylor to the heart of Aggieland. I remember joking that children in that area thought you said 'A&M ' after prayers! I used to have to keep our car locked every day, or else they would put Aggie stickers inside on the windows.

The Saints' Rest Baptist Church had a long history. They held their first meeting in 1873 with 33 charter members under a large tree on the site. Years later, the Steep Hollow Community Center was built on the church's five acres.

WHO BUT GOD! RIDING THE WHIRLWIND
JIMMY AND CAROL ANN DRAPER

How we got to Steep Hollow is a wonderful example of God at work in our lives and in the life of that church. When my dad was pastor at First Baptist Church Bay City, one of the teenagers in the youth group, Justice Anderson, surrendered to preach and my dad had the privilege of leading the church to license him to the gospel ministry. He later served as pastor at First Baptist Church in Franklin, Texas.

Justice and I became strong friends during our seminary days, even though he was six years older than I. He was completing his Ph.D. when I was just starting. The day he passed his oral exams to complete his doctorate, he came by our little apartment. He said, "because I just had to tell someone!"

During his days as pastor in Franklin, Justice had a big dog, and his neighbor had a much smaller dog. One day Justice's big dog nearly killed the neighbor's little dog, so Justice and his neighbor took the dog and raced off for Bryan, some 30 miles away and the closest veterinarian. The veterinarian who treated the little dog was Howard Cargill, a deacon at Steep Hollow Baptist Church. While Howard was mending the dog, Justice mentioned in passing that if they ever needed a pastor to let him know because he had someone he wanted to recommend to the church.

A few months later, Howard followed up and wanted to know who Justice would recommend. Justice gave him my name and his endorsement. The church never had a pulpit committee. Howard's dad, George was the chairman of the deacons and responsible to find a new pastor. He called my parents' to invite me to come to preach. My dad told him that we were on our honeymoon and that I had two revivals to preach when I got back and would not be free to preach for them for a month.

LIVING IN AGGIELAND

George told him that they would just get someone local to fill in and would wait for me to preach before looking at anyone else. After I preached on August 17, 1956, the church voted unanimously to call us to be pastor and wife.

I still had one revival to preach at Baptist Tabernacle in Little Rock, Arkansas, before we moved. This revival was special to me because their pastor had been a close friend of my grandfather's, and we were able to bring back the books from Grandad's library that he had promised to me just before he died two years earlier.

We began our ministry on August 26, 1956. It was my father's birthday and exactly six years since the night I had surrendered to preach. When I was called to Steep Hollow, my dad gave me some pastoral advice that has stood with me all these years. First, he said to be kind to everyone because everyone is having a hard time! Maybe we know what troubles they have, maybe we don't, but we can be sure everyone is facing something. Second, he told me not to be threatened if people loved their former pastor because it meant they had the capacity to love us as well. Third, he told me if someone wanted to do something for us, to let them do it and not rob them of the joy of providing something for us. Fourth, he told me never to make a decision if I was discouraged or depressed. He warned me, "You will likely make the wrong decision in these circumstances." And fifth, he told me that doubt never meant 'yes,' but always meant 'no' or 'wait.' All five of these insights have been vital in our decision-making process throughout our marriage and our ministry.

Soon after beginning our ministry at Steep Hollow we purchased our first new car. It was sitting on the showroom floor of a Chevrolet dealer on Harrisburg Street near Park Memorial Baptist Church.

WHO BUT GOD! RIDING THE WHIRLWIND
JIMMY AND CAROL ANN DRAPER

Elbert Naylor was the sales manager for the dealership, a deacon at Park Memorial, and a close friend to our family. It was an aqua blue and white Chevrolet Impala. Aqua blue was our favorite color and we loved that car!

A parsonage was being completed just as we were called, so we were the first family to live in it. During the few weeks before the completion of the parsonage, we stayed every weekend with Elmer and Iva Bullock. What wonderful encouragers and friends they were for us. Once the parsonage was completed, we would still stop by their house when we arrived at Steep Hollow to get fresh water to take to the parsonage. When we turned on the faucet, the well water was so rich in iron that the water ran red and was completely undrinkable.

Since the parsonage was new, we also had lots of new critters around. Scorpions seemed to pop up everywhere. One day over lunch, I noticed what I thought to be crumbs floating in my milk. When I looked a little closer, I realized it was a scorpion that had fallen into the glass while in the cabinet. Ever since then, we have stored the glasses upside down!

As is common with many country churches, a cemetery was right across the farm-to-market road from the church. Each year the church held a homecoming mostly for folks who had plots in the cemetery to clean and spruce up the cemetery and to rejoice along with great Southern Gospel music and dinner on the grounds. It was always a sweet time of fellowship and a way of honoring those already with the Lord.

The name of the church was changed somewhere around 1960 to Steep Hollow Baptist Church. It was a great church full of wonderful people who prayed for us for decades. Twenty-one years after we left, I preached a revival at First Baptist Church in Bryan. The Steep Hollow Church canceled the Sunday evening service, and over 50 of the members came to hear me preach!

It has remained a strong country church over most of the years since we left. We loved so many of the people there that when I was elected president of the Southern Baptist Convention, Steep Hollow was the first place we went for a time of fellowship and celebration.

We served at Steep Hollow for two years. During our first summer there, Carol Ann was the principal of our Vacation Bible School. I was actually bi-vocational at that time, working at a clothing store in Bryan to make ends meet. It was challenging holding down two jobs at once, but it gave me a great appreciation for pastors who maintain two jobs so much longer than I did. Since I could not be at VBS, Carol Ann was in charge of the whole program, and she was seven months pregnant. Not surprisingly, that summer, the VBS program was a great success.

Other than her excellent leadership for the VBS program, the summer of 1957 was hot and challenging for Carol Ann. Besides being pregnant in the heat of a Texas summer, we had no phone, and she had no access to a car because I needed it to get to work every day in Bryan. This left her alone much of the time. On top of all this, she still viewed her role as a pastor's wife to be an impossible assignment, one for which she felt very inadequate. But her hunger to know God's Word, to hear His voice, to receive his promises, and to be obedient proved to be very fruitful. It was during these days she learned to live in the awareness that God chose her to walk in this calling with Him and in His strength and ability. She came to realize that God always equips those He calls, and she grew steadily in her faith and special calling.

During her 'alone summer,' Carol Ann came to understand a great principle of following the Lord: she learned that God doesn't want us just to do something for Him, but that He wants us to build a relationship with him and to be obedient to Him. She learned to hear His voice and discover that the Lord always listened to her voice!

Carol Ann was lonely but not discouraged or depressed as her relationship with the Lord continued to strengthen. She had come to rely on Jesus as her constant companion. Though she did not play the piano well and had no formal training, God equipped her generously. She began teaching our Junior High youth. She loved it, and they loved her. These new adventures also gave her the opportunity to fully grow into her life verse, Philippians 4:13: "I can do all things through Christ who gives me strength." Every challenge she faced was an opportunity to ask herself, "Do I really believe God can do all things?" Each time she asked, God proved himself faithful.

Our first wedding anniversary the next summer was memorable for several reasons. I surprised Carol Ann with a Singer cabinet sewing machine, much like the one her mother had taught her to sew on. It was a great surprise for her, and I also presented her with six yards of plaid material for her to make a skirt for herself and a shirt for me. Naively, I thought she could have both made by the next day for our church softball game. I was so excited to give it to her; I didn't even think about her being pregnant. Carol Ann did manage to get my shirt made by the next day and continued to sew for many years afterward—especially when she wasn't pregnant!

LIVING IN AGGIELAND

We had one other memorable and somewhat foolish adventure that summer before we became parents—we went roller skating! We had a great group of young people at Steep Hollow and thought it would be fun to take the group roller skating. We made arrangements to skate in the gym of a nearby high school. We didn't give it much thought when Carol Ann laced up some skates and joined in the fun. Looking back, we can only chalk this lapse in judgment to youth and foolishness!

The day before our firstborn son, Randy, was born, started out uneventful. We had been enjoying the afternoon eating watermelon at Jack and Jessie Jones' house when Carol Ann's water broke. We didn't waste a minute in calling the doctor and heading to the Bryan City Hospital. That Saturday afternoon became evening and eventually early Sunday morning before Randy made his arrival at 3:30 a.m. September 8, 1957. I got to spend some special time with him, Carol Ann, and her mom before racing off to preach that morning and having the privilege of announcing his arrival at church.

Even though we had no experience at being parents, we learned very quickly to trust in the Lord and in His Word. We also thanked the Lord daily for our own godly parents who had set such a remarkable example for us as we were growing up. Both of our moms came to help us for two weeks each, and we were very grateful as we adjusted to life with a newborn. It was a sad day when they had to go home! Because our mothers never lived close to where we lived, we were on our own soon enough after we became a family of three.

Carol Ann learned to nap while Randy was sleeping during the day so she could make it through the nighttime feedings. We both grew up a lot during those early days with a newborn baby. We also learned so much from the precious church families who came alongside us as we learned to nurture Randy in those first months. It was also during these sleep-deprived days and nights when we came to experience the truth that God specializes in doing the impossible and fulfilling His promises to His children.

In spite of not knowing what we didn't know, God blessed our adventures in parenting, and today Randy is a great Christian man, a deacon, and a lay preacher. He consistently models his great love and devotion for the Lord! He has a positive, 'Happy to do it!' attitude and is a constant encourager for all whose lives he touches.

We had five acres of church property, so we put in a softball field complete with lights courtesy of the county. We had more fun than victories, but it was a great memory for us—especially since they let me play first base. I remember just before we left Steep Hollow, one gentleman said to me, "Preacher, we'll miss your preaching, but we will really miss you as our first baseman!" He also went on to add, "You can go, but Carol Ann has to stay!" That has been the story of my life and rightly so! Everywhere we've served, Carol Ann has always been the one who was loved the most, and that is as it should be as that is her place in my heart too.

In our early days at the church, one of the deacons, Alex Garner, and his wife, Gertrude, invited us to dinner at their home one evening. Gertrude was said to be the best cook in the church, so we were excited to spend the evening with them. We arrived around 6 p.m. hungry and looking forward to dinner with them. Imagine our surprise when we arrived, and Gertrude hadn't even begun to prepare the meal. Three hours later we finally sat down to a terrific meal, but we did have a good laugh on the way home because just about anything would have tasted good to us at that point!

After we left Steep Hollow, my brother, Charlie, was called to be Youth Minister at First Baptist Church in Bryan. After one pastor followed us, Steep Hollow called Charlie and Retta to be their pastor and wife. Several years later, Charlie and Retta moved to Honolulu, Hawaii, where they served at the Pearl Harbor Baptist Church for five years. During their time at Steep Hollow, they had become very close friends with Alex and Gertrude's children. When Alex died, Charlie and Retta were asked to return for the funeral service—a service that quickly became more than for one person.

Minutes after Alex died in the hospital in Bryan, Gertrude came out to tell their children and friends who had gathered. As she did, she had a massive heart attack and died just a few minutes later—literally just minutes after her husband had passed away. A few days later, their joint funeral was a remarkable celebration of both their lives and provided closure in a special way to their friends and family. Ever since then, Carol Ann and I have felt that the best way for us to die would be together, much like Alex and Gertrude did. They were together in life and soon together in Glory!

Another special memory from Steep Hollow was a classic case of misunderstanding. I found out two of our deacons, George Cargill & Esker Martin, appeared to be at odds with one another, yet no one knew why. For some unknown reason, Esker had suddenly stopped speaking to George. When I asked George why Esker wasn't speaking to him, he didn't have a clue. So I paid Esker a visit and asked why he had quit speaking to George. He told me that the Sunday School lesson one Sunday dealt with the issue of those incarcerated in prison. As his grandson had recently been sent to prison, he assumed George was directing the lesson specifically at him.

I asked him if he would tell George what he told me, and he agreed. I told him I'd be back soon and not to go anywhere until I returned. I raced to pick up the chairman of our deacons, Jack Jones, and together we went to pick up George and asked him to come with us as we all headed back to Esker's.

Inside the 10' x 10' living room of that small house, I sat across from Jack while George and Esker sat opposite of each other. I asked Esker to tell George what he told me, and he did. George's response was clear and emotional as he told Esker that he did not know about his grandson and was simply teaching the prescribed lesson from the Sunday School Board. He apologized, and with tears in both their eyes, those two older saints embraced one another in forgiveness. That single moment—whereby two saints were fully reconciled and restored to fellowship—is the single most cherished memory I have today of our time at Steep Hollow. It just doesn't get any better than that!

With Randy's birth in early September, we decided to wait until the spring semester for me to begin seminary. We began our seminary journey in January 1958. J. Howard Williams was the seminary president and a close friend of our family. When we came to enroll, Randy was just four months old, and Dr. Williams got down on his knees to play with and talk to Randy. We never forgot his gracious reception. Sadly, Dr. Williams died suddenly just two months later.

After Dr. Williams' passing, his successor was Dr. Robert Naylor, then-pastor of the Travis Avenue Baptist Church in Fort Worth and chairman of the Board of the Seminary Trustees. Dr. Naylor came

LIVING IN AGGIELAND

to the seminary with a pastor's heart and quickly won the hearts of all of us. He never introduced any meeting he presided over without quoting Scripture. What a great example he was for all of us.

During that first winter in the new parsonage, we faced one serious crisis in the early hours of the morning. We only had some city electricity at the church and parsonage. We had a septic tank and well water rather than city water. The gas was propane, not natural gas. Early one very cold winter morning, the propane tank at the parsonage went dry, and we found ourselves with a very young baby, no heat, and no way to heat his bottle. We tried to stay warm and comfort Randy, but eventually had to find warmth somewhere fast.

We headed to George and Stella Cargill's house somewhere around 3:30 a.m. George was a rancher and used to getting up well before sunrise, but 3:30 a.m. was a stretch even for him! Before long, though, Stella was up and cooking a huge ranch breakfast for us all with biscuits and gravy, eggs, sausage, and bacon. That wonderful breakfast—as early as it was—made being that cold just about worth it!

One weekend our 'new car' threw a rod going on a trip to Bryan. It just rolled completely dead about half a mile past a local tavern. We were stranded two miles north of Hearne and about 25 miles from Steep Hollow. We had no cell phones, so I walked back to the 'honky-tonk,' the only thing near us. They allowed me to call someone at Steep Hollow to come and get us and take us to the parsonage.

We left the car in Hearne to be repaired over the weekend. That Sunday night the church surprised us by voting to raise our salary from $35 to $45 each week. That's the kind of wonderful people they were—always generous to greatly bless us. We still stay in contact with some of the kids who grew up there and remain in the area, as well as a few of the adults who are still alive.

Our first year at Steep Hollow, our area was in a deep drought. We really needed rain, but none came. One Sunday, after months of no rain, as we were eating lunch with Howard and Irene Cargill and their family, it became evident that it was about to rain. Because we had been so long without rain, we always left the windows open at the church on Sunday afternoon and thought nothing about it. But with the rain finally approaching, we jumped in our car and raced back to Steep Hollow. When we arrived, the rain was coming down in sheets and the church flooded through every open window.

I had said with quite some authority, that it always rains straight down, so rain should not be a problem at the house. However, with the wind was howling as the rain came down, we not only had water everywhere in the church building, but also at our parsonage. We were thankful the drought had broken, but I had proven once again that I could not forecast the weather!

The church building at Steep Hollow was built like a big cross with an alcove on each side of the pulpit stretching wider than the main portion of the auditorium. In the corner to the right of the pulpit area, there was an open flue where a potbelly stove had once been connected. Even though the potbelly stove was gone, the flue was still open to the auditorium. As I was wrapping up my first Easter sermon at the church, a bird flew out of the open flue and made several flyovers above the congregation before making a fast exit out of one of the open windows. One of our members seemed to think I must have planned the dramatic finish because on his way out he stopped to tell me, "Preacher, that was really good of you to have that bird come out in your sermon to wake everyone up!"

We had several more unexpected (and uninvited!) visitors that showed up one Wednesday evening as we were gathered for prayer meeting. Before we knew what was going on, the children in the auditorium began to shriek and stomp their feet and cause quite a commotion. It turned out, a whole herd of small mice had come out and were chasing one another around the auditorium. Needless to say, the mice won out over prayer that night.

As I was beginning seminary, Carol Ann also had plans for her seminary training. She envisioned me returning home as soon as classes were over, having dinner together, and then I would share everything I had learned that day with her. It made perfect sense to her at the time. When I explained that I had a part-time job, sermons to prepare and preach every weekend, books to read and papers to write, and that I just could not do that, she got mad. She was mad at me, mad at God, and mad at anyone else she could think of to be angry with.

When she complained to the Lord that she was not going to have a chance to learn all that I was learning and would forever be less educated, the Lord most certainly honored the longings of her heart. "God wrapped His arms of love around me and spoke to my heart," she remembers. "And then He said, 'My Child, I am the greatest teacher ever, and if you will show up daily with My Word with open ears to hear and a heart to receive, I will guide you into wisdom, truth and understanding.'"

"My class with The One who wrote God's Word was exciting and blessed," she says. "It was at His feet that I learned to read and to heed

God's Word and to lean on Him for every provision I ever needed. It wasn't how I imagined I would grow in my understanding of the Lord, but looking back, I'm thankful for a stubborn husband who helped me learn to spend the day in the lap of my Savior and come to realize He would always there for me."

When we first arrived in Fort Worth, Carol Ann first worked as the secretary for Dr. Carl Clark, a Christian ethics professor. He and his wife had been friends of our Draper family for years, and we had much in common. Like my mother, Dr. Clark had also had polio and was cripple throughout his adult life. He walked with specially made crutches and was always a wonderful Christian gentleman. The friendship we shared helped make that a special time for Carol Ann as well as provide a generous salary of $119 a month!

The duplex we lived in during our first year in seminary was tiny. With only kitchen, bedroom, small living room and one closet in somewhere around 900 square feet, I used to joke that it was so small, we had to go outside to change our mind!

In the Spring of 1958, I was invited to spend the summer preaching youth revivals by the Student Department of the Baptist General Convention of Texas. I had been preaching in Youth Revivals since 1953 and had preached over three dozen revivals during those years. The Student Department was training revival teams of young ministers and then sending them out to the churches in the state. Carol Ann and I prayed about whether to accept the invitation or not, but ultimately did so when we came to understand that few preachers were asked to do more than ten revivals all summer long. We made the decision to ask God to give me at least ten revivals for the summer, and we would know it was God's will for me to commit to do that in the summer months. Several years later, while we were in San Antonio, we learned that it is not a good idea to 'put out a fleece' when making decisions. More about that later. When the answer came for assignments, I had been given 12 revivals to preach that summer.

Next, I had to tell the deacons at our church that I would be gone most of the summer. I proposed to them that I take a leave of absence for the summer and then return in the fall to continue serving at Steep Hollow. All the deacons but one agreed—Melvin Hartsfield, one of our best friends of all the deacons. Melvin had the courage to say to me and the entire deacon body, "Brother Jimmy, I love you, but if that is what God has told you to do, you need to do it and let us find another pastor." In the end, Melvin was exactly right, and we resigned in May before the summer started.

Since I was booked every week of the summer, Carol Ann and Randy moved back to Lake Jackson while I traveled the state preaching revivals. Since we saw one another only two times that summer, Carol Ann remembers spending much of her time explaining to people that our marriage was fine, and I was away preaching just for the summer. We each were blessed many times over during that summer, but it was still a long time to be apart. Needless to say, we all rejoiced greatly when that summer ended!

WHO BUT GOD! RIDING THE WHIRLWIND
JIMMY AND CAROL ANN DRAPER

Randy and Carol Ann

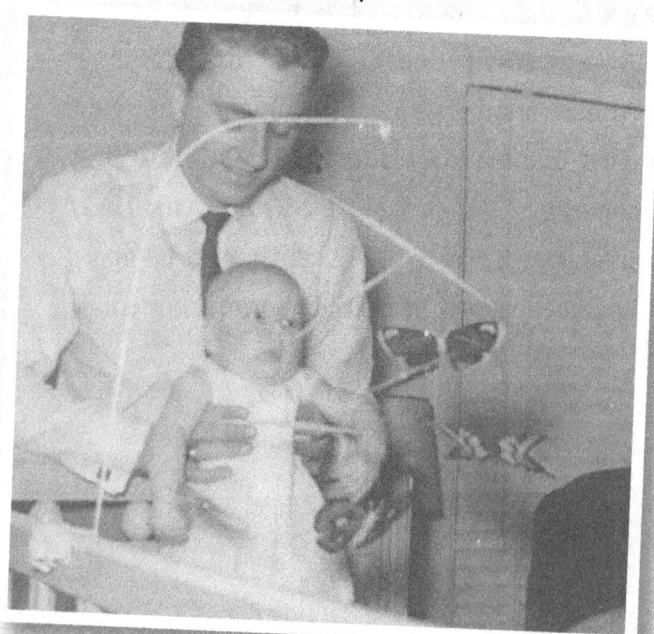

Jimmy and Randy 2 1/2 months

LIVING IN AGGIELAND

Jimmy and Randy 1968

Randy 14-years old

Randy 20-years old

WHO BUT GOD! RIDING THE WHIRLWIND
JIMMY AND CAROL ANN DRAPER

Jimmy, Carol Ann & Randy

SEMINARY, INTERIM PASTOR & PART-TIME JOBS

As summer ended, we were glad to get back to the regular rhythm of a new semester at seminary. However, not having the responsibility of serving a church full-time also meant we didn't have a full-time income either. To make ends meet, I worked as the janitor in Barnard Hall, the only women's dormitory at the seminary. Later I worked at the TCU Library before moving on to the Fort Worth Public Library in the Bookmobile Department. I filed book cards in the massive index the library maintained and drove one of the library's bookmobiles out to satellite locations.

Besides the loss of a steady salary, I was missing something just as important to me—the opportunity to preach to a church family. It was a difficult time for me that lasted the nine months of the school year. Carol Ann likened my unrest during these months to being like a caged lion with no place for me to preach.

We also did not have very much social life during our seminary years. We had little spare time, a whole lot of work for both of us and studying on my part. Both of us gave full-time attention just trying to make ends meet and survive. The friends we did make during these years have turned out to be wonderful lifelong friends. When we did manage to get together, it was either for dinner and dominoes at someone's house or to get our kids together to play and fellowship for the parents. Probably the most significant lesson we both experienced from these years of very limited fellowship with other couples and families was the realization that our strength and wisdom for each day came from the Lord. This was a great truth for us to learn in those early years of family, seminary, and ministry.

Also, during these years in seminary, Carol Ann began to work for Plastalite Engineering Company. Her older cousin was the company owner and paid her $179 a month—a nice contribution to our floundering finances. Unfortunately, on the way to her first day of work, she inadvertently ran a stop sign and was broadsided by a post office delivery truck. She thought it was his fault until she got out and saw the stop sign that she had run. When the police arrived, he told her she was very fortunate not to have been hurt seriously, but she was still very upset by all the damage done to the car.

Through buckets of tears, she finally got in touch with me to tell me what had happened. She was so upset because the car had suffered so much damage and we had no money to make the repairs. I did my best to console her and assured her the most important thing was that she was all right. I knew, even with our very limited funds, that the damage to the car was of no consequence as long as she was unhurt. It was also a good reminder that even though God

SEMINARY, INTERIM PASTOR & PART-TIME JOBS

does not keep trials and challenges from touching our lives, He is always present to teach us more about His love and provision for us.

Around this same time as I was juggling several part-time jobs, I was asked to be interim pastor at the Calvary Baptist Church in Talco, Texas, just a few miles north of Mount Pleasant, Texas. Even though it was three hours away from our home near the seminary, we were excited about the opportunity for me to preach and for the additional salary in provided for our growing family.

Talco was a small town near an oil company town built for employees of Humble Oil Company (now Exxon). The oil company town had been shut down, but the town of Talco still had a full slate of schools and businesses there. We were there for nearly a year in that church and loved the people. The church asked us to stay as pastor and family, but I knew we would never finish seminary if I dropped out of school, so we declined their gracious invitation.

Dad had been the Area Director of Missions for the District One in Northeast Texas; for five years but had recently moved to serve in the town where he was raised in Warren, Arkansas. My brother, George, had decided to move to Warren and live with my parents, so he came up to Fort Worth and rode with me to Talco, where dad met us and then took George home with him.

The church had a three-bedroom parsonage they made available for us for the weekends. Even though it had no furniture in it initially, the members came together with enough furniture to meet our needs while we were there. We would arrive in town on Friday nights, make visits in the area on Saturday, I would preach Sunday morning and evening, and then we would all head back to Ft. Worth arriving home around 2 a.m.

WHO BUT GOD! RIDING THE WHIRLWIND
JIMMY AND CAROL ANN DRAPER

Money was always a challenge for us during our seminary years, but God always provided all we needed. One night as we came back from Talco, we did not have the 40 cents required to return from Dallas to Fort Worth on the turnpike. Between the two of us, we had just enough to go as far as Arlington, and then we had to get off the toll road and drive into Ft. Worth on Highway 80—that's how important every cent was to us back then.

Randy would almost always be asleep on his mattress in the back seat when we arrived home. We lived across the street from railroad tracks and the train usually arrived about the time we got home, so we would carry him inside with a small pillow over his ears so he wouldn't wake up.

It made for a short night's sleep for Carol Ann, who had to be at work by 8:00 a.m. We did not have Monday classes at seminary, so my schedule was not as demanding on Mondays. I had a little more time for sleep than Carol Ann. We kept up this schedule of school, work, and interim preaching until May 31, 1959, when I preached my last sermon in Talco.

To keep our finances straight, we used an envelope system as a way of handling the money as we received it. This worked well for us since we paid for most things in cash and didn't write many checks at the time. We had envelopes for all the bills we regularly paid and even for those that weren't regular but were expected. We had envelopes for our tithe, groceries, cleaning supplies, gas, miscellaneous and so on. On paper, it never appeared as if we would have enough to pay all our bills, but in reality, we always had enough to pay them all and on time. It was God's math that allowed us to always honor the expenses we incurred with the money we had earned.

SEMINARY, INTERIM PASTOR & PART-TIME JOBS

About a year after starting work at Plastalite, Carol Ann heard of a new job possibility with an oil company that paid $250 per month—a sizeable increase over her current position—so she didn't waste any time in applying for it. Naturally, she did great on the preliminary tests and the interview, but there was one more hurdle to clear before the job could be hers—the physical exam. When her blood work revealed she was pregnant again, her availability for the position quickly disappeared. Fortunately, she was able to maintain her position at Plastalite Engineering until we moved to our next adventure...Iredell, Texas.

Randy 1-year old

Carol Ann & Jimmy
1958

Carol Ann, Randy & Jimmy

WHO BUT GOD! RIDING THE WHIRLWIND
JIMMY AND CAROL ANN DRAPER

Iredell Baptist Church

8

SNUFF CITY AND IREDELL BAPTIST CHURCH

On August 2, 1959, Carol Ann, Randy and I went to preach in view of a call at Iredell Baptist Church. They extended a call to us, and we moved to Iredell shortly thereafter. We were both excited about the prospect of our first full-time church. The downside is that it also left Carol Ann isolated from established friends and pregnant with our second child. We had moved from the big city of Ft. Worth to the small rural town of Iredell in central Texas.

The town was founded in the late 1850s and became known as 'Snuff City' when a traveling tobacco salesman declared that there were more people who dipped snuff in Iredell than in any other place in his territory. When we arrived in Iredell, the population was 366; I had 21 funerals in the nearly two years we were there.

The town had its own Independent School District for all 112 students in grades 1-12. They played six-man football, and I was the announcer for all the team's home games. Probably the most memorable game was against a team from Flat, Texas. We had had torrential rain throughout the first half, and by half-time, the field was six inches deep in water as the nearby Bosque River had far surpassed its banks. We were happy to end the game under those circumstances—especially since we were ahead 50-0!

Iredell also had both boys and girls basketball. I refereed basketball for the Southwest Basketball Officials Association to put food on our table. Richard Jackson was my referee partner in most of the games I officiated that winter. Richard went on to serve as pastor in North Phoenix Baptist Church in Phoenix, Arizona, which became one of the largest Southern Baptist Churches in the west. We each got paid $6 for one game and $10 for two, plus six cents for every mile we had to drive to get to games. We usually officiated a girls' game and then a boys' game. We didn't get rich refereeing, but it helped, and we had a lot of fun doing it too! I also learned that just because the kids were playing in smaller country schools, it didn't diminish their fight to win.

I even refereed one girls' basketball game in Iredell by myself between Iredell and Hico. Hico was a much larger school and Iredell rarely, if ever, had defeated them in a team sport. Iredell won on a free throw after time expired. I don't know what I was thinking by making that call, but I managed to escape the potential riot that could have followed!

Out in those country schools, the competition was fierce. Many of the gymnasiums were not full-size meaning the walls under the basket were actually the out of bounds line! This made for some rough activity under the baskets!

We had some wonderful families involved in the Iredell sports

SNUFF CITY AND IREDELL BAPTIST CHURCH

programs and saw many of the schools' students come to know the Lord while we were there.

During this time, we also met George and Lynda Harris, who have been among our very best friends for 60 years. George served at First Baptist in Hico, Texas, just 9 miles up Highway 6 while he was still attending Southwestern Seminary. Because their kids were close to the same ages as ours, our families spent lots of time together during those years. Hico was bigger than Iredell and home to our favorite burger place when we treated ourselves to eating out. It was also the closest hospital to us—all 22 rooms!—and where Bailey was born.

Randy learned to get around in the house in his walker before he learned to walk. He particularly enjoyed watching our old black and white television, complete with foil on the antennas, that allowed us to get a few stations. His favorite show was 'Dick Clark's American Bandstand.' Whenever it was on, he would go all out dancing up and down to the beat of the music and stop when the music stopped.

Randy was known and loved by just about everyone in town—especially the folks in our tiny downtown area. Our friend, Bill Clanton, owned the corner drugstore, which was complete with an old-fashioned soda fountain. Every time we came in the store with Randy, Bill would give him a small paper sack and let him go behind the counter and pick out whatever candy he wanted and put in the sack. He never charged us for that candy, and he always had a silver dollar ready to give to Randy. It was a great treat for him and for us!

Later on, Bill's generous ways created some 'teachable moments' for us as Randy soon came to believe he could just go into any store, pick up what he wanted, and leave with it—for free!

WHO BUT GOD! RIDING THE WHIRLWIND
JIMMY AND CAROL ANN DRAPER

Iredell was a small town, but it did have one more place downtown – a pool hall that also doubled as a place to play dominoes. It was almost to the river on the north side of downtown.

One of our vivid memories of downtown Iredell started at the hardware store, but it didn't end there. Carol Ann and I had met at the hardware store to pick out some linoleum to put in the kitchen of the parsonage. After we met, Carol Ann drove on home, and I walked over to the church and then home. When we both got home, we realized we had left Randy downtown! We jumped in the car and headed back downtown. When we arrived downtown, we found Randy coming back from the town's pool hall singing, 'It was an itsy bitsy, teenie weenie, yellow polka dot bikini, that she wore for the first time that night.' He knew 'Jesus Loves Me' but remember American Bandstand!

Carol Ann learned the value of trust in a small town during our time in Iredell. One day, she heard a knock at the kitchen door. Since it was unusual for visitors to come to the back door, she cautiously checked to see who it was. When she saw a man in overalls with a scraggly beard and a long pole for a walking stick, she was a bit leery. Reluctantly, she opened the door and greeted him. She was relieved to find out it was one of our members we had not had the pleasure of meeting yet who had thought to stop by and bring some vegetables to his new pastor and his family.

In other ways, Iredell was a special blessing for Carol Ann. For the first time since we became parents, she got to stay at home with Randy and Bailey. Up until that time, she had always worked outside our home. She had always had a great love for children, and God taught her a lot about being a parent in those years when she was with

SNUFF CITY AND IREDELL BAPTIST CHURCH

them all the time. She describes what she learned as "unconditional love, patience, and contentment."

One of the most remarkable visits I ever made in Iredell was to Emma Houston. When I got to Iredell, I set out to visit every church family. I had waited until the very last to go see Emma. She had had both legs amputated at the highest possible place that would still allow her to have normal body functions. She had extreme arthritis and could not pick up anything with her hands because her fingers were stiff and unbendable. She could eat for herself if someone put the utensil in her hand for her. Frankly, I was afraid to go see her because I just didn't know what to say to her.

I will never forget driving out on the dirt road from Iredell to Cranfill's Gap, where Emma lived. When I pulled up to her house, one of the goats she owned was delivering a new kid. That was amazing to witness! I walked up to the house, knocked, and was greeted by a cherry, "Come on in," from within the house. As I opened the door, I entered one of the most transforming visits of my life.

When I entered, I saw Emma in a hospital bed in the living room with one of the biggest smiles you've ever seen on anyone. She was vibrant and vivacious to an extreme; she mesmerized me and made me ashamed that I had waited so long to come see her. We had a wonderful visit as we sang hymns together and read Scripture and visited about the church and Iredell. As we neared the end of our visit, she told me, "Bro. Jimmy, I will never get to come hear you preach and have no way of hearing one of your sermons. But I want you to know that you will never stand to preach in our church that I won't be praying for you!"

WHO BUT GOD! RIDING THE WHIRLWIND
JIMMY AND CAROL ANN DRAPER

I made many trips out to see Emma Houston during the two years I served in Iredell. Truthfully, I did it more for me than for her. She was a ray of sunshine that shone in a very unlikely place! I know she prayed for me because the last Sunday I was pastor in Iredell, I baptized 13 teenagers, and I'm confident her prayers were a major reason for that experience!

Our youngest son, Bailey Ray, made his grand arrival during our time in Iredell. Carol Ann began having labor pains early Tuesday morning, so we raced to the hospital, only to be told it was a false alarm on Wednesday morning. Since I did not have seminary classes on Monday, I had only missed one day of class. When we got home Wednesday we settled in for the night.

The labor pains started again very early Thursday morning, but this time we called a nurse in our church in the early morning hours and described to her where her pains were. She told us we needed to go to the hospital, so we headed back to Hico. It was an icy and windy day when we got to the hospital, and this time we stayed. Bailey was born later that morning of Thursday, February 11, 1960. I had already missed three days of school, so I decided to miss one more and not go on Friday. I missed the entire week of classes!

When Bailey was six weeks old, Randy caught the chicken pox. We prayed for both our boys and separated them as much as possible. Fortunately, newborn Bailey never caught them from his older brother. Bailey was a good baby and slept most of the time during the first months he was home with us. As both of our mothers had come when Randy was born, they each came again for two weeks when Bailey arrived. This was a great blessing for all of us!

We had two gardens that year—our first and our last! I did not

SNUFF CITY AND IREDELL BAPTIST CHURCH

know anything about how to plant potatoes. We put the 'eyes' of the potato, the part intended to produce new potatoes, so far down into the dirt, we couldn't get them out of the ground without using a tractor to turn the dirt! Definitely a rookie mistake! Later I found out that if we had just laid the eye on the ground and mounded the dirt over it, they would grow, and the potatoes wouldn't be so hard to harvest. Suffice it to say, we left lots of potatoes in the ground that year! We also found out that rabbits really like English peas—especially our English peas! We rounded out our garden with onions and carrots and learned another important lesson: you don't have to plant weeds; they spring up by themselves, and they grow faster than vegetables! For our family, we said, 'Never again!' to gardens.

I carpooled 85 miles each way four days a week to Southwestern Seminary. I lived the furthest away, so the carpool began and ended with me. Doyle Edson was the closest pick-up in Walnut Springs. Next, we picked up Bill Tomerlin, my college roommate, in Morgan, Texas. From there, we would get Ebby Smith, who was also pastoring at First Baptist Church in Blum. The last one we picked up was Leon McBeth, who was a pastor in Rio Vista. I would leave every morning around 5:30 a.m. and return about 7:00 o'clock in the evening. They were long days of learning and driving that kept me away from our family much of the time.

During this time, both Ebby and Leon were completing their PhDs at Southwestern. Ironically, Leon was my church history professor one semester while we carpooled. Ebby became a Southern Baptist Missionary before returning to Southwestern to teach. Leon became the premier Southern Baptist historian of his generation and remained at Southwestern until his retirement. It was a fun group of men I admired and learned from. We regularly discussed theology, methodology, strategies, and more on our drives. Truth be told, some days, I think I learned more from my carpool discussions during the two years we drove together than I did in the seminary classes!

It was near the end of my seminary and carpooling days that the Fort Worth Star-Telegram ran an article about my commute to school. The best guess was that I had traveled over 10,000 miles driving back and forth from Ft. Worth to Iredell in my last two years of seminary. The article was a gracious story of my commitment to finish my formal training while serving the people of Iredell as well as my growing family and included a picture of me sitting in the driver's seat reading a book.

Bailey was about seven months old and Carol Ann decided to get outside and enjoy a beautiful late summer day. She put Bailey in his stroller and Randy walked with her the three blocks to town. The first stop was to Bill Clanton's drug store on the corner of the main street. He offered them all an ice cream cone—an offer too good to refuse! Bailey had never had an ice cone until then. When Bailey took the cone, he immediately bit the bottom end out of the cone which meant ice cream started running everywhere! It made a mess, but also a delicious memory.

We had two dogs while we lived in Iredell. The first one was run over and killed by a neighbor when he was just a puppy. The other one was a young dog who got into the bad habit of chasing our neighbor's sheep. One day the neighbor came to tell me that our dog had killed one of his sheep and that he had to shoot the dog. He explained that once dogs killed another animal they would continue to do so and had to be put down. Apparently, it just was not meant for us to have a dog at that time.

When I wasn't driving carpool, I regularly drove a school bus to take our church youth to Baylor football games and other places. On one of those trips we went to the county fair. I brought back seven live chickens as a gift to Carol Ann. I was so proud of those prize chickens I had gotten for $1 each, but Carol Ann was not nearly as excited as I was—especially because not long after I brought them home, I had to leave them with her and drive the bus to Waco for a Baylor football game.

I had forgotten that someone had to kill those chickens, pluck the feathers, and cut up the meat. Carol Ann did not have a clue how to do any of that...or want any part of it! Thank the Lord, my mom was there and knew what to do after our next-door neighbor, Mrs. Hudson, came over and wrung the chickens' necks. Needless to say, Carol Ann was not a happy camper—especially after she learned she could have gotten the chickens prepared to cook for 25 cents each at the grocery store in Hico.

Just as Mrs. Hudson had helped Carol Ann, Mr. Hudson was also very helpful to me. He and I got under our house and together we did everything necessary to get a new washing machine installed in one day. It took us eight hours of hard and hot labor, but we got it done. With children in diapers before the invention of Pampers, having a washing machine made using cloth diapers a whole lot more tolerable. The Hudsons were both tremendous blessings to us during our days in Iredell.

The church did not have a nursery for children during the worship services, so each child had to be picked up by their parents before the service. One Sunday morning, Randy was getting impatient for Carol Ann to come and get him and asked the teacher, "When is my mother coming?" He asked that several times and each time the teacher would say, "We just have to wait till Carol Ann gets here."

When Carol Ann did arrive, she told him, "Come on Randy, we get to go to church." Randy didn't miss a beat and said, "I have to wait for Carol Ann to come!" He had never heard anyone call her 'Carol Ann' before; it was always 'Mrs. Draper' at church. And I had my own nicknames for her such as 'Sweetheart,' 'Honey,' 'Sugar,' and many more. When Randy kept calling her 'Carol Ann' for several days afterward, Carol Ann finally quit responding to him until he called her 'Mother.'

Money remained a very real challenge for us in our early years of marriage. There were times when we just ran out of funds. One of the early times we were running short was also one of the best examples of the Lord's faithfulness to each of us. When it came time for us to give our tithe to the church one month, we were running extremely low—so much so that if we tithed, we would only have $.25 left for the remaining two weeks of the month. We talked about it and decided we had never failed to tithe in the past and were not starting then. In faith, we trusted God to provide the funds to help us survive, and we gave our tithe to the church.

Two days later, we received a strange-looking envelope from a doctor in Oklahoma. Even though we hadn't been in Oklahoma, it looked like a bill of some sort. Curious, we opened it to find a $10 check made out to me. We soon learned that Carol Ann's dad had been on one of his frequent recruitment trips to college campuses looking for employees for Dow Chemical Company and had found a

SNUFF CITY AND IREDELL BAPTIST CHURCH

doctor's wallet in a restaurant restroom. The wallet was full of cash and credit cards, as well as the contact information for the doctor.

When Carol Ann's dad called the doctor to tell him he'd found it and wanted to return it to him, the doctor wanted to reward his honesty and goodwill. Mr. Floyd refused to accept anything for himself, but told him, "My daughter and her husband are in seminary in Fort Worth and serving in a small-town church south of Fort Worth. If you want to do something, please send it to them." And he did! It was just one of the many and unusual ways God has found to provide for us time and time again all throughout our lives, generously and always in the nick of time.

It only snowed occasionally in Bosque County, but it came in a big way one Sunday in January 1961. We had 7 inches of accumulated snow that morning, which meant most of our congregation had to be out and about taking care of their livestock that morning. I knew and understood that, and so, with only 20 present for service, I moved the lectern down to the floor level and asked those present to sit in a small group all together on one side of our small auditorium. Just as I was about to begin, five strangers walked in, all dressed in their Sunday best and standing out like sore thumbs. We discovered they were the pulpit committee from Temple Baptist Church in Tyler, Texas.

Since it had not been snowing when they left Tyler, they had no idea about the snow in Iredell. We didn't expect to ever hear from them again since we were such a sparse crowd that morning, even though we explained why so many were absent. But sure enough, a few days later, they called asking us to come in view of a call to Temple Baptist Church in Tyler. We preached in view of a call on February 12, 1961, and soon were on the move again.

WHO BUT GOD! RIDING THE WHIRLWIND
JIMMY AND CAROL ANN DRAPER

Iredell Parsonage

Carol Ann, Randy & Bailey

Bailey 1-year old

Bailey, our climber

SNUFF CITY AND IREDELL BAPTIST CHURCH

Bailey 3-years old

Bailey 8-years old

Bailey 13-years old

Bailey 19-years old

WHO BUT GOD! RIDING THE WHIRLWIND
JIMMY AND CAROL ANN DRAPER

Temple Baptist Church

DEEP IN THE HEART OF TEXAS

TEMPLE BAPTIST CHURCH TYLER, TEXAS

Tyler was incorporated as a city on January 28, 1850. Earlier on April 11, 1846, the Texas Legislature created Smith County and chose Tyler for its county seat. It was named for John Tyler, tenth president of the United States, who had advocated for the annexation of the Republic of Texas into the United States.

By 1860 there were over 1,000 slaves held in Tyler. The agriculture around Tyler was 80% cotton and relied heavily on slave labor, so naturally, Tyler gave great support to the Confederate Army during the Civil War. Just outside of Tyler, Camp Ford was the largest Confederate POW camp west of the Mississippi River during the Civil War.

Peaches were the chief fruit crop in the area, and roses were the most famous export. By 1920 most of roses supplied in the United States came from Tyler. It became known as the Rose Capital of the United States. The largest rose garden in our nation is in Tyler; it spreads out over 14 acres and contains 38,000 rose bushes and 500 different varieties. Tyler is also home to the famous Azalea Trail in the spring and the annual Tyler Rose Festival.

Temple Baptist Church was a small church with close to 150 regular attendees each Sunday. We were very excited about the move to Tyler because it was such a great place to raise a family. Carol Ann was pregnant again and soon to deliver within two months of making the move.

This was a special church for us, even though it was fairly small. It was a neighborhood church filled with terrific people. The people welcomed us with open arms as we settled in for what we expected to be a long pastorate. For the first time since we had been married, I had no more commuting and no punishing schedule to maintain. I was ready to jump headlong into the ministry at Temple Baptist Church.

The church parsonage was just one and a half blocks from the church. It was a big house that suited our growing family well. The rooms were big, and the kitchen had lots of wonderful cabinets. Being so close to the church, we walked to church when the weather permitted. We only had one car when we got to Tyler; it had neither seat belts nor car seats, but we lived through it all with no serious accidents.

Terri Jean was born on April 13, much earlier than her expected due date of May 10. We were blessed by all the space, especially with three small children under the age of four. But with two kids still in diapers, we needed not only a washer, but a dryer as well. Even with all our modern conveniences, keeping up with the diapers was a daily task that could not be overlooked. For all the work of three small children, life was good, and we knew we were incredibly blessed. Carol Ann was the keeper of our home. She loved being a mother and seemed to love all that came with each age for them. Although they were sometimes a handful, she recognized early on that being a mother was a great privilege and the opportunity to mold the lives of our children every day.

Still, our first year in Tyler was a year of survival for Carol Ann. There was never a dull moment for her. Her days seemed to run together; they were a continual blur of changing diapers, wiping noses, fixing bottles and meals, washing diapers, and speaking in three-word sentences. She knew that was her calling and loved it, but she was starved for an occasional adult conversation.

I regret that I failed to realize this and to provide it because I was so focused on settling into my new responsibilities at church. It was a moment of reckoning one day when she told me, "You would be better off without me. You could just get someone to take care of the kids if I was gone." That was a wake-up call for how neglectful of her I had been for the better part of that year.

She later said that she had listened to Satan too much and allowed him to become the guest of honor at her own pity party. In return, she felt unappreciated, neglected, and of no use in the ministry—just the way Satan wants us all to feel. Besides the mental and emotional exhaustion and fatigue that comes with three small kids, the endless physical demands of her days left her perpetually tired and worn out by day's end. She did battle with Satan every day that year. She faced this discouraging time in her life by leaning on the promise of Isaiah 40:29-31: "He gives strength to the faint and strengthens the powerless. Your youths may become faint and weary, and young men stumble and fall, but those who trust in the Lord will renew their strength; they will soar on wings like eagles, they will run and not become weary, they will walk and not faint."

The Lord spoke to her heart, and she heard Him to say, "Oh, Carol Ann, how can you say that the Lord doesn't see your troubles and isn't being fair? Don't you know that the everlasting God, the Creator of the farthest parts of the earth, never grows faint or weary? He gives power to the tired and worn-out and strength to the weak." When she placed her name in the promise of God, she was comforted and strengthened. This practice has been a constant practice throughout her life.

When Terri was four months old, Carol Ann had an outpatient medical procedure. When the procedure was over, I brought her home and went to the office. When I came home around 5 p.m. from the office she was still on the sofa and had slept all afternoon. I called her mother and asked her to come up to help us and give her some relief. She happily agreed and rode the train from Houston to the closest train station in Troup, Texas, about 15 miles from Tyler. She was a lifesaver for us!

Carol Ann's testimony of that year was that as she focused on the Word of God and sought His presence, He brought her through it as she listened to His voice. Her prayer for help changed from, "God, make Jimmy to become the husband I need him to be," to "God, to make me the wife he needs me to be. I will be loving, supportive, prayerful, content, and with no nagging. I will be happy and excited that he comes home every day. I know that he loves me, and this is a time of change for both of us."

DEEP IN THE HEART OF TEXAS

To my shame, I failed miserably during this year in Tyler to provide her what she really needed from me. But thanks to a loving church family and the wonderful support of her mother, God provided for us far beyond what I deserved or expected. In spite of me, we were blessed with a growing church and saw many people saved.

Because of my experience in leading youth revivals, I brought in a young teenage evangelist, Richard Cheatham, for our revival services. Even though he was only 15 years old, he was a wonderful preacher whose coming refreshed so many significant memories of my own youth revival days and served our church youth so well. Following the revival, our part time Youth Minister, Bobby Dusek, scheduled a retreat for our young people and the attendance grew three-fold from the previous year.

We loved being in Tyler. Some of our special friends were the families of two brothers whose last name was Stanley. One brother owned a plumbing company, and the other owned Stanley's Barbecue, which is still in operation today. Some of our other friends included the families of Glen York, Les Axtell, Bill Satterwhite and E.V. Baldridge. They all opened their hearts to us in a special way. E.V.'s daughter, Beverly, was the pianist at the church at the time. We fell in love with her and were thrilled years later when she became my sister-in-law when she married my brother, George.

Our part-time music minister was O.Z. Walton. One Sunday, when the organist could not play, Beverly played the organ, and Carol Ann was asked to play the piano. O.Z. announced the hymns, and Carol Ann quickly realized they were all written in sharps. She knew how to play in flats, not sharps, but tried anyway. The sounds clashed so bad O.Z. started over three times, but each time Beverly played in sharps, and Carol Ann played in flats. Finally, the third time, Carol Ann chose not to play, and they finally finished the song!

While we lived in Tyler, I joined the Key Club, a service organization in Tyler made up mostly of businessmen. This gave me a vital point of contact with the community outside the church. One of the highlights was the annual patriotism essay contest we held for high school students. The year I chaired the contest, we received one essay that was so good, I thought it was worthy of national exposure. I sent it to Paul Harvey, who, at the time, had a daily radio program that was broadcast nationwide. He was so impressed with it that he accepted it and shared it on his broadcast.

I learned an important lesson that year that applied to lots of areas of my life. Each week, I drafted a Sunday bulletin using our mimeograph machine that involved a stencil with engraved lettering for special effects. I would type the order of service and announcements and run the copies on the mimeograph machine. One week, however, I was having trouble with the machine and decided to fix it—first by disassembling it and then putting it back together again.

It was really easy to take apart, but the problem came when I couldn't figure out how to put it back together again. I finally had to call a repairman who promptly came and fixed what I had taken apart. When he finished, he turned to me and jokingly said, "If you ever need a job, you are really good at tearing something down!" His words helped me to realize that anyone can tear something down, but the real key is being able to put it back together again. This simple comment helped me to see that's the way it is in church too. Anyone can tear up a church, but there is no spiritual value in that. God wants to keep all of us in His family together!

Our plans to settle down for a long ministry in Tyler soon changed. My Baylor roommate, Bill Tomerlin, was the Baptist Student Union Director in San Antonio and also the interim pastor at University Park Baptist Church. The recently retired pastor of the church was Hal Wingo, whose son, Hal, Jr., was one of our classmates at Baylor. Bro. Hal had been there for many years and had recently retired. Bill thought we should be considered to replace him, so he recommended us to the committee.

One year from the day we moved into Tyler, we moved to San Antonio, Texas. The pulpit committee from the University Park Baptist Church in San Antonio came to visit in early February, and by the last of that month, we were on our way to San Antonio.

The call itself was remarkable in that the pulpit committee had decided not to call anyone under 40, and I was just 26 at the time! We had been warned by older ministers that San Antonio was unlike any other part of Texas and that we should not go there because many pastors had gone before us and were never heard from again. The warnings went unheeded because God had called us, and we were off to San Antonio.

WHO BUT GOD! RIDING THE WHIRLWIND
JIMMY AND CAROL ANN DRAPER

Temple Parsonage

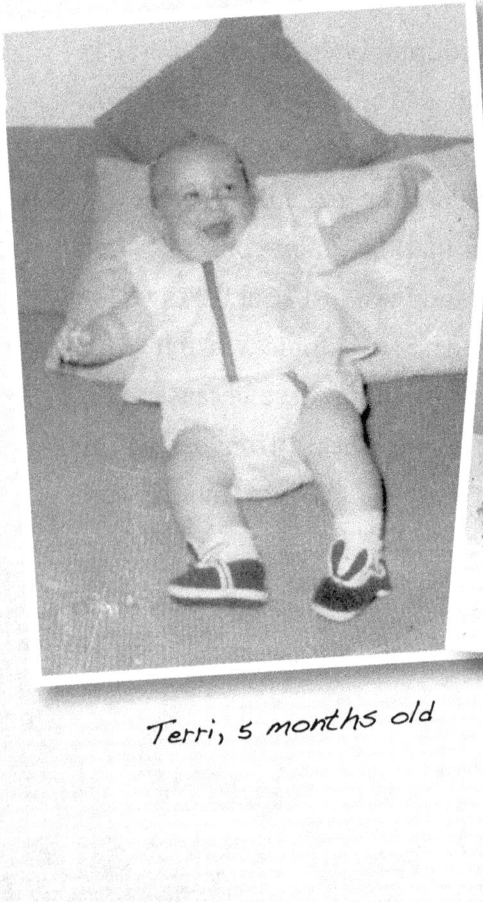

Terri, 5 months old

Terri 1-year old

DEEP IN THE HEART OF TEXAS

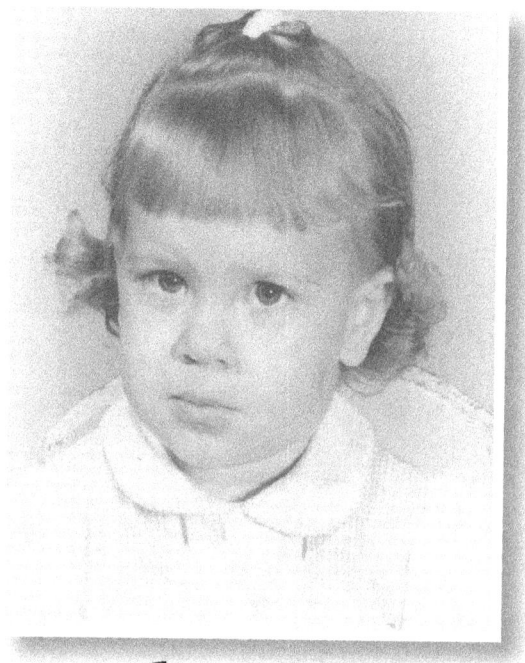

Terri 2-years old

Terri 14-years old

Terri 23-years old

WHO BUT GOD! RIDING THE WHIRLWIND
JIMMY AND CAROL ANN DRAPER

Bailey in front of University Park Baptist Church

REMEMBER THE ALAMO

UNIVERSITY PARK BAPTIST CHURCH, SAN ANTONIO, TX

The call to University Park was not without challenges. I had spoken at a sweetheart banquet in Gatesville the night before we were to preach in view of a call. Then we headed out the remaining 100 miles or so to San Antonio. Our car died and rolled to a stop on the side of the road about 40 miles out of San Antonio.

There we were, in the middle of the night, Carol Ann, three small children, and me on our way to preach in a new church. Since we had no way to call for help, I began to try to flag people down. Finally, an eighteen-wheeler stopped and offered us help. He suggested that he take Carol Ann and the children into San Antonio and send help back while I stayed with the car and all we had brought with us. As he drove off and I waved goodbye to my family, it suddenly struck me—I had let my entire family drive off with a total stranger in his truck! What on earth had I done? What if he did not keep his word?

I imagined all sorts of things during the several hours I waited for help to arrive.

Eventually, help did come, and I was able to get to San Antonio and in bed by about 4 a.m., just hours before I preached in view of a call to a new congregation. Our hosts for the weekend were Charles and Patsy Martin. We became fast friends with them and their kids and have remained close to them since. Patsy passed away several years ago, but Charles is still going strong. The Martin were genuine believers and wise parents who were patient and kind. They had a loving home and readily shared it with others.

One of our strongest memories from our many good times with the Martins occurred when Bailey and the Martin's son, Alan, were outside playing…or so we thought! Without us knowing what they were doing, they had begun to shoot pellet guns at cars as they passed by. They hit one of the cars and shattered the left rear door window. Charles and I apologized to the driver and gave him the necessary insurance information to have the window replaced. Suffice it to say the boys learned a very expensive lesson that day.

Ironically, a similar thing happened to me when I was about seven years old. Our family had gone to Bay City, Texas, for dad to preach in view of a call to the church. I joined several boys from the church playing with BB guns, and I shot one of the boys. Even though he was not injured, the pulpit committee still discussed my behavior. I'm not sure where it would have ended up otherwise, but one of the older members finally said, "We are not calling his son, we are calling a new pastor." That settled them all down, and they moved forward with the call.

REMEMBER THE ALAMO

In spite of the challenges of just getting to San Antonio, I preached the morning and evening services at University Park, and the church extended a unanimous call for us to come and serve their church. Believing God had opened that door, we went back to Tyler to close down our ministry there and make the move to San Antonio.

University Park was situated in northwest San Antonio, just one block away from General McMullen Drive, which led to Kelly Air Force Base. There were six military bases in San Antonio at the time and very much influenced the culture of the city. The church was centrally located between St. Mary's University, a Roman Catholic university, and Assumption Seminary, a Roman Catholic seminary. Catholicism was far and above the most prevalent religion in San Antonio and remains so still. One of my more unique experiences while at University Park was the opportunity to speak on the subject of baptism at St. Mary's University to the Catholic Brothers, the unordained clergy for the Roman Catholic Church. It was a class of about 50 students, and the professor even admitted that emersion was the original form of baptism!

After we arrived in San Antonio, I heard from one of the pulpit committee that there had been a lot of concern for the day I preached in view of a call. One of the women on the committee, Buna Burnett, was having a personal feud with one of the deacons in the church. They apparently didn't like each other and were actively engaged in verbal warfare. The deacon was Gene Burroughs, a working CPA whose office was in South San Antonio. The church itself was largely blue-collar workers, but Gene was a very impressive member who had just won second place in the National Toastmasters' competition.

Gene was a remarkable Christian and leader in the church. He always dressed more formally than most of the congregation, usually in navy blue suit and tie. His ability to speak effectively also made him somewhat intimidating to some in the church. The Pulpit Committee was afraid that Gene might come to the service that night when the church voted on us and try to derail our call to the church. The committee had actually met that afternoon to decide how they would respond to any confusion he might create. Since he didn't come the evening the church voted, I met him the first Sunday I preached as pastor. He shook my hand and said, "I just came to see if the pulpit committee did a good job." He must have approved because he didn't mention it again.

I called him the next week and asked if I could buy his lunch. When he said he never turned down a free lunch, we set a date. Even though I had no entertainment budget from the church, I paid for it out of our still-meager funds because I thought it was important enough to get to know him.

On the day we had lunch, we met at a Mexican restaurant near his office on the southside of San Antonio. We sat and visited till the waiter took our order. After the waiter left, I told him about the pulpit committee's concern and actions the day I came in view of a call. He indicated that he was not aware of that happening. Then I told him, "Gene, I am here to be your pastor and to love you and your family, but I am not afraid of you!" At that point, he just threw back his head and laughed and said, "Oh, preacher, I never have eaten very many people alive who came straight to me!"

We both had a good laugh and shared a long friendship. He and his family remained great members and friends during the time

REMEMBER THE ALAMO

we were there. Gene would sing each week in the choir and when needed would fill in leading our music in the worship services as needed. It was my privilege to perform the wedding ceremonies for all three of his children. He and his wife, Pauline, were some of our very best friends. She died many years before he did, but he kept in touch with us through those years. Even when he drifted into Alzheimer's Disease, he would sometimes call late at night and say, "I was just sitting here going through Pauline's address book and saw your name. Now tell me how I am supposed to know you." We continued having these conversations until he died.

I returned to San Antonio one more time before we moved and found a house for us to rent. It was just a couple of blocks from the church and seemed to be a good fit for our family. Even though the house was very small, it had some interesting characteristics. After we moved in, we realized that the floor sloped from the kitchen, all the way through the dining room, and on to the front of the house. We would never have known that had something not happened after we moved in that we still laugh about today.

Carol Ann was trying her best to take care of Randy (5), Bailey (2), and Terri Jean, who was just eight months old. Believe me, these three together at those ages was a true test of Carol Ann's patience and perseverance. To get her through these challenging days, she made an effort to focus on Ephesians 5:20, particularly the command that read, "in all things give thanks." She did well so much of the time, but that tiny word, 'all' was so encompassing, and there were just some things involving three small children that made it hard to give thanks.

WHO BUT GOD! RIDING THE WHIRLWIND
JIMMY AND CAROL ANN DRAPER

It wasn't an easy lesson to learn, but God was patient as Carol Ann came to appreciate that 'all things' truly meant 'all things' including what was good, bad, funny, hard, or painful. The test for fully understanding this verse came when she had Terri in one arm while she tried to get a glass gallon of milk out of the refrigerator. The jug had no handle, so when she grabbed it and swung it out of the refrigerator, it slipped and fell on the floor, shattering into a thousand pieces. Not only did the glass go everywhere, but the milk ran down the incline of the floor, into the dining room, and all the way under the piano on the outside wall.

Her first thought in the middle of the mess was to talk to God. "Lord, surely You don't expect me to give thanks for this!" she said. And God's answer is what convicted her: "No, my child, I don't want you to give thanks, unless you want to be obedient." Obedience had always been a priority to Carol Ann. All through our seminary days and the birth of our children, she had always strived to be obedient to the Lord. She wasn't about to let a broken milk jug cause her to stop now. So she gave thanks for the mess and even entertained hopes of an angel appearing to clean up the mess. No angel wiped the floor clean, but Carol Ann's commitment to be obedient remained intact.

The good news was that Terri had quit crying because the crash was louder than she was, and there was a neighbor nearby whom Carol Ann could borrow milk from to fill one last bottle for bedtime. It was another reminder that God is always good to make provision before we know we need it.

Sometime after we got to University Park, we had evangelist Paul Carlin come for a revival meeting. Originally scheduled to come to Temple Baptist in Tyler, Paul agreed to move with us and preach at

REMEMBER THE ALAMO

University Park. I baptized 26 people on the last Sunday night of that revival. It was a wonderful way to begin a new pastorate!

The first baptism there was also the first time I had the opportunity to wear waders when I baptized. Before that, I had just baptized with jeans on and then changed into my dress clothes afterward. I learned the hard way that you should never fully cinch up waders because it creates a vacuum inside that makes you very buoyant and unable to stand upright. That first time, I almost floated the whole time I was baptizing people. I bounced up and down like the moonwalks at amusement parks. Thank God I could hold on to those I baptized to help keep me grounded!

Paul stayed with us during the revival week and always had toast and coffee for breakfast. Bailey wanted to eat with him and wanted to drink coffee too. Carol Ann put a little coffee with milk, and he was satisfied. A few weeks after the revival, I took Bailey to church with me one morning until lunchtime. My secretary, Martha, called Carol Ann several hours later to see if Bailey had taken a nap. She said, "He might not be sleepy because I gave him three cups of coffee before I realized what I had done." To this day, Bailey is the only one of our children who drinks coffee, but he enjoys it every morning.

Carol Ann and I visited prospects on Saturdays while Carmen and Lonnie Peters kept our three children. Their friendship was a blessing for us during those years because it gave Carol Ann and me a chance to do ministry together, which was greatly needed after my failures in Tyler. Besides all she did at home, Carol Ann also taught teenagers and directed the children's choir. Wherever we ministered, Carol Ann has given great support to every phase of our church life.

WHO BUT GOD! RIDING THE WHIRLWIND
JIMMY AND CAROL ANN DRAPER

Late in our first year there, Terri began to cry every time we got in the car to go to church. That broke our hearts as we wanted our children to love going to church. As we looked into what had happened, it all revolved around our paid nursery worker, Mrs. Hinch. She ran the nursery like a boot camp. She allowed no toys, just some chairs and a few books. When we realized what was going on, we began to pray that God would change Mrs. Hinch and make her understand that children needed to have fun things to do as they learned about the Bible. But Mrs. Hinch was not there to provide a positive and happy atmosphere for the children.

Carol Ann prayed earnestly for God to change Mrs. Hinch. One day she sensed the Lord saying to her, "Carol Ann, why don't you pray for Carol Ann instead of Mrs. Hinch?" That still small voice spoke to her three times before she obeyed. When she began to pray for herself, she realized the critical spirit she had toward Mrs. Hinch. She realized she was the one in need of change and confessed her attitude and asked forgiveness. Then she told the Lord, "Lord, I can't love her, but I want You to love her through me."

The Holy Spirit was waiting patiently for her to agree with Him so He could flow through her. It was a great lesson for us both to learn—that each of us has to cooperate with the Holy Spirit in us so He can live through us for God's glory.

Carol Ann realized she could love Mrs. Hinch just like she was even if she never changed because she had changed how she saw her; the Lord just wanted Carol Ann to develop to the right attitude. When she confessed that she could not love Mrs. Hinch the way she should, but wanted the Lord to love Mrs. Hinch through her, she got victory over her own attitude. This experience greatly impacted our young lives and was a significant step toward the maturity we needed to be the instruments God was molding us to be.

Carol Ann still thanks the Lord for Mrs. Hinch "and the miracle You did through me" in learning to yield to the Holy Spirit. Mrs. Hinch never changed, but Terri did stop crying in the nursery when Carol Ann realized that her critical attitude toward Mrs. Hinch was the main source of Terri's tears. Once that got straightened out, the church became a happy time for Terri again.

One of Carol Ann's most time-consuming tasks was to iron the clothes when they finished washing and drying. But what had been a cumbersome chore became something more when she began to see the ironing as an opportunity to pray for the person whose garment she was ironing. This simple change in perspective turned the task into a prayer and praise time with the Lord and made a huge difference in her life and disposition. It was such a simple way of putting into practice the Scripture that commands us in whatever we do, to do it, "as unto the Lord!"

Another real challenge for us was the summer my 13-year-old brother Charlie spent with us so he could to summer school. God used that summer of living with a young teenager to show her she needed to pray for our children when they were younger in order to better understand them as they grew older into their teenage years. With Charlie as our summer houseguest, we gained a great insight into what life with a teenage boy would be like.

My 19-year-old brother George already lived in San Antonio and was also frequently in our home. One night while he was spending the night with us, he walked in his sleep. The bedroom where he usually slept had a door opening to the front porch. When his feet touched the front porch, the cold concrete woke him abruptly, but not before the door behind him closed and automatically locked, leaving him on the porch at 2 a.m. in his underwear.

Fortunately for him, we never locked the door from the driveway into our den, so getting back in was no problem—except when he came back in through the den in the middle of the night, we all woke up and had a good laugh at his expense. During times like these with my brothers, we realized God was teaching us how to build and maintain relationships with family and church members.

We were blessed with a wonderful ministry at University Park, and we grew in the Lord, His Word, and His ways. We both learned we are not to live by feelings, but by God's Word. And if we wanted to hear God's voice, we had to know what He says in His Word.

One real tragedy occurred in our church shortly after we got there. Previously, on my trip to San Antonio to find a place for us to live, I met Maureen McLane and her daughter, Lynda, as I came out of the church. Lynda was about to be married, and they were looking for a place to have the wedding. I went back inside and got with Martha Aaron, our church secretary, and we made arrangements for them to have the wedding at University Park soon after our family moved to San Antonio.

Maureen's husband, Glen, was a retired colonel in the Air Force and had been a career military soldier. Now in retirement, the McLane's had settled in San Antonio as many other veterans did. In addition to their daughter, Glen and Maureen had a brilliant son named Jerry, a high school senior. He had already received a full scholarship to Southern Methodist University.

REMEMBER THE ALAMO

The McLane family had visited our church several times in the months following the wedding in March but had not joined yet. By now, it was late May, and graduations had occurred, the school year was over, and summer was just getting started. I was making some visits and came upon a bad accident not far from our house. The first responders had arrived as well as many onlookers, and I noticed a motor scooter in the concrete drainage ditch that ran under the main road.

When I stopped to find out more about the accident, I was told a drunk driver in a car had run a stop sign and plowed head-on into the scooter and its driver. And then I learned the scooter driver's name was Jerry McLane, and that he had suffered life-threatening injuries and been taken to the hospital.

San Antonio is now, and certainly was then, a large city, which meant there were lots of hospitals. I didn't have a clue where they had taken Jerry. I raced home and started calling hospitals as fast as I could, trying to locate Jerry. I eventually spoke with a nurse at Santa Rosa Hospital in downtown San Antonio, and when she learned I was the pastor, she asked that I come to the hospital as they had not yet been able to locate Jerry's parents.

As soon as I got to the hospital, I was taken to the room where Jerry was being held. That's when I learned he was already dead, and I was needed to identify him and tell his parents. Not long after, Glen and Maureen arrived at the hospital, and I had to tell them about Jerry. It was a devasting night for all of us.

The Sunday before the accident, I had preached to our graduating seniors specifically. It was like our own baccalaureate service just for our 12 seniors. Jerry had gone home from that service and told his folks that he felt like I was preaching to him, and he was going to make his decision for Christ public on the following Sunday. His death came before he would have another opportunity to make his decision public, but what he shared with his family was life-changing. The Sunday after the accident, four people made professions of faith at University Park—Glen and Maureen McLane and their newlywed daughter, Lynda, and her husband, Gary. All of them became part of the fellowship of our church. While this was a cause of rejoicing, the sadness that Jerry was not among them was strong.

A few weeks later, as I was leaving after the morning service to preach a revival at another church, Maureen came out to the vestibule, where I always stood after services and grabbed me by the collar of my coat. Pulling me down to her face, she said, "Tell them about Jerry. He was going to make his decision, but he waited too late!" With that, she turned and walked away. I have never forgotten the urgency of her words. That is why I always preach that for every individual, there comes a time when the Holy Spirit draws them to be saved. It is never safe to wait to make that decision, like Jerry, and risk being too late.

Sometime later, Carol Ann's mom became ill with breast cancer and faced a mastectomy in a Houston hospital. Carol Ann went down to be with her, and as they waited for the medical staff to come get her for the surgery, she said to Carol Ann, "I can't let them put me to sleep until I confess something to you." Carol Ann wondered what her mother could possibly confess to her because her mother was the best Christian she knew.

REMEMBER THE ALAMO

Before she was taken back to surgery, she confessed to Carol Ann that she and her dad watched their very young teenage daughter falling in love with someone they didn't know. And it was all happening through the letters she received every day. Then she confessed, "Your dad and I read all your love letters!" Carol Ann laughed with relief and exclaimed, "Mother, if I had known you were interested, I would have read them to you myself!"

Carol Ann loves telling that story when she speaks to women around the world. She does so because she urges them that if they want to fall in love with Jesus, all they need to do is to read His love letters—the Bible. She always picks up her Bible and tells them, "This is His love letter to us." She goes on to explain how she has always made reading these love letters a personal experience, "To deepen your love for the Lord, stay focused on His Word. Put your name in Scripture so it will speak directly to you. For instance, in I Corinthians 13, where it says, 'Love is patient, love is kind, love does not envy...', put your name in place of love.' You'll be amazed at how much more personal the Bible becomes."

University Park had a remarkable fellowship that accepted us immediately. The church was a blend of Anglo and Hispanic families. At the time, the language of the streets in San Antonio was Spanish, so it was a great benefit that our staff was partially Hispanic. Our Minister of Music was Lloyd Garcia, and the chairman of the deacons, Napoleon Arredondo.

I always made it a habit in our earliest churches to visit on Tuesday evenings with the chairman of the deacons of our church. One year our chairman was Warren Wessley, a 6'8" gentleman who owned a commercial hardware company. As we were visiting one evening, he asked me if I would like to know how he was saved. Naturally, I was eager to hear his story.

He explained that when he first met the woman who would later become his wife, Louise, he was not saved and wanted nothing to do with church. When he finally asked her out, she agreed on one condition: that he would go to church with her. Even though he didn't want to go to church, he wanted to date Louise. He agreed and went to church with her at South San Antonio Baptist Church.

Warren clearly remembered the church's auditorium was located on the second floor of the building and required everyone to walk up 25 steps just to get inside. As time went by, they fell in love, and he asked Louise to marry him. She accepted his proposal, again with a condition: he would have to continue to go to church with her after they were married.

He still did not want to go to church, but again, he wanted to marry Louise. They remained at the same church after they were married, and a strange thing happened: the more they attended, the more the Holy Spirit worked on Warren—to the point of him feeling under conviction to be saved. Looking back, Warren remembered every Sunday as they climbed the stairs to the auditorium, there was a man who handed out bulletins at that entrance. The man always greeted them with a big smile and a warm welcome. Warren said that he got to the point where he looked forward to seeing that man who always met them at the door. This man made such an impression on Warren that the day he was saved, he doesn't remember what the preacher preached or what the choir sang, but he still remembered the man whose warm handshake and consistent smile always made him feel welcome.

Since then, I've thought a lot about that man. Even though Warren didn't know it, the man was an usher or a greeter. Most times being an usher isn't thought of as being an important part of Sunday's service, but Warren's story is a great example of how every job within the church is important to the people we serve just as every member of God's family plays an important part. I am reminded daily of the importance of everyone who, through faith in Jesus Christ, becomes part of the family of God. It's one of the greatest things about Christianity—in Christ, everybody is somebody special!

One special family at University Park was Doc and Myrtle Hodges. He was a retired home builder, and together, they took our young family under their wings to protect and encourage. One year as we were about to leave for vacation, Doc pressed a bill into my hand when we shook hands. I soon discovered it was a $50 bill that he wanted us to have to help with our trip.

One of the exciting things about University Park was that I got to lead my first bond program and build a new educational building. Both were highly successful, and the church began to grow quickly as a result. We also remodeled our church offices during those years and had great fun getting to tear out the walls and helping with the other demolition that had to take place before we could begin the rebuilding process.

I was very involved in our San Antonio Baptist Association and served as chairman of the New Work Committee. At one point, I also taught a Seminary Extension class on the New Testament for fellow ministers and laymen in the area. The years when all this was going on were some of the busiest and most satisfying years we had in San Antonio.

One of the unique things about University Park was that we had the largest kindergarten in San Antonio. Since the public schools did not offer kindergarten back then, many people turned to church-sponsored kindergartens. Ours was so well-received, it became the largest private kindergarten provider in the city. It was a tremendous outreach tool because, in serving 120 children each year in kindergarten, we also reached many of their families. Upon our family's arrival in San Antonio, the kindergarten teachers announced to the children that the "new preacher had come to the church." Later on, we heard that one of the children went home and reported, "They have a new creature at the church!"

Our kindergarten director, Dixie Marty, had an effective way of encouraging the children to cooperate during class time. If a child ignored her warnings to cooperate and became disruptive during class, she would have them sit in a chair in the corner called 'the lonesome chair.' She even wrote a song for the children to sing if they were sent to 'the lonesome chair.' Not surprisingly, Randy had his day in the lonesome chair from time to time, but it was never an experience he wanted to repeat.

One of the funny things that happened at University Park centered around cutting down a tree in front of the church building. The front of the auditorium had a steep high-pitched roof with the name of the church about 25-feet up the face of the building. The problem was a tree growing right in front of the building that obscured the name so it couldn't be seen. When I mentioned that we needed to cut the

REMEMBER THE ALAMO

tree down so the name could be seen clearly, some of the ladies in the church were very upset. One of the even commenting, "How dare you cut that tree down!"

This was before the time when cutting trees down on one's property had to have the approval of city officials, so it was up to us to leave it or cut it down. Without saying anything further to the ladies who had spoken against cutting it down, several of the men got together one day and cut the tree down. The funny thing is no one even noticed it missing at first. It was weeks before anyone realized it was gone!

One of our more special memories of our time at University Park centers around Murray and Virginia Barr, and the morning Murray was saved. Virginia had joined the church, but Murray had not yet become a believer. Even though he was not saved, he regularly attended with Virginia.

I remember a bright sunshine greeted folks as they came to church that day. I was particularly excited because I had prepared a special sermon. My primary Scripture reference was on Acts 5:25-32, particularly verse 32: "We are his witnesses of these things; and so is the Holy Spirit, whom God has given to those that obey him." I just knew this would be the first sermon in the volume of books of my sermons that would one day be published. I imagined it would be similar to the many volumes of Charles Spurgeon's sermons in England! I was really proud of myself that day!

Midway through the sermon, I realized it was probably the worst sermon I had ever preached! The further I got into the message, the more embarrassed I became. By the time I finished the message, I wanted to run out the side door and not even give the invitation. If we had not printed the "invitation" in the Sunday bulletin, I would have done just that. But instead of leaving the service, I extended the invitation. As soon as I did, Murray Barr rushed down the aisle like he had been fired out of a shotgun. It was a glorious conclusion to what had been a prideful and very poor sermon. It was also a wonderful reminder that God does not use any of us because of us, but always in spite of us. He also showed me that He always honors His Word.

A highlight of our time there was a special mission trip to Detroit, Michigan, I took with my good friend George Harris and two of our deacons, Nap Arredondo, and Bill Strawn. Nap went with George to preach in Lebanon, Michigan, and Bill went with me to First Baptist Church, Warren, Michigan. It was a special time that strengthened the relationship between all of us. The weather was near zero as we were in the early days of February. In spite of that, we had a wonderful experience together.

The same year I flew to Chicago to do a revival with another Baylor roommate, Charles Leach, at the Lamon Avenue Baptist Church there. He worked downtown in the "loop" area of Chicago. I went with him every morning down to that area and really enjoyed exploring the "loop" during that week. The church itself was in a house on Lamon Avenue. Both trips were great ministry opportunities that have given me lasting memories.

One of the things that made living in San Antonio so special was being closer to Buckner Fannin, who was pastor of Trinity Baptist Church. Buckner was one of the preachers at the revival at Central Baptist Church in Jacksonville the night I surrendered to preach. Bailey Stone had been preaching that night, and Buckner was standing down front; he was the one who greeted me at the altar to hear my commitment that night.

Obviously Bill Tomerlin was another important relationship in San Antonio. We had been roommates and close friends at Baylor and were in each other's weddings. Bill was part owner of an airplane and had traveled around the state in that plane. About the time we moved to San Antonio, Bill crashed his plane and was severely burned. He survived and kept on with his ministry, but that was a scary time for all of us. Bill and his wife, Rue, were an important part of our lives during those years.

The annual evangelism conferences were our favorite meetings of the year. They were big, exciting, and inspiring, and we always came away from them recharged and ready to head back into the ministry of our church with renewed enthusiasm. One of the more pivotal conferences was held in January 1963. Dub Jackson was a missionary to Japan, and he issued a powerful appeal to everyone at the conference to come to Japan for what he called the Japan New Life Crusade. He electrified all of us to the point where more than 500 went to Japan later in the year for a life-changing crusade. By the time the crusade was over, other Asian countries got involved and there were more than 47,000 professions of faith, more than half of them from Japanese citizens.

Dub and his wife, Doris, served for 17 years in Japan with the Foreign Mission Board of the Southern Baptist Convention. Dub's passion for partnership missions with churches from the United States traveling overseas for crusades created such tension with the Foreign Mission Board leadership that Dub and Doris resigned from the field and came home. Upon their return, they founded the World

Evangelism Foundation and spent the rest of their lives promoting the concept of partnership missions between local churches and the Foreign Mission Board missionaries around the world.

It was my privilege to be chairman of the Board of WEF for many years and to continue our friendship with Dub and Doris for over 45 years. Doris passed away just before Christmas in 2015, and it was my privilege to preach her coronation service, along with a special testimony about our friendship by Carol Ann. Dub died on Feb. 12, 2020, at 95 years old, and it was my privilege to join Paige Patterson to share the service as Dub requested.

No man has had more impact on churches being involved with partnership missions than Dub. Without his tenacity and passion, it likely would never have happened. The conviction of the Foreign Mission Board leadership when Dub began World Evangelism Foundation was that 'tourists don't do missions.' As a result, the Foreign Mission Board did not make it easy for Dub to succeed with his passion for partnership missions. Though the opposition continued for many years, what is now the International Mission Board did adopt this strategy more than 20 years ago, and today over 100,000 Southern Baptists travel in such efforts annually. Partnership missions are a standard event for thousands of churches each year now with the full support of the International Mission Board.

My first experience flying in a private plane happened in the summer of 1963 when I preached in Hardin, Texas, just northeast of Houston for a revival. I was flown down in a single-engine private plane by a 17-year-old pilot! Needless to say, I was very glad and relieved when we made a successful landing on the grass runway.

REMEMBER THE ALAMO

We were living in San Antonio on the day that President John F. Kennedy was assassinated in Dallas. Like most people who were around then, I can vividly recall where we were on Friday, November 22, 1963, because it was such a tragic event. The Sunday following the assassination, I preached about what our response as citizens should be. I called the sermon, 'On the Death of John F. Kennedy.' Carol Ann was unable to come that Sunday morning and was actually watching the live coverage of the assassination on television when Jack Ruby shot and killed Lee Harvey Oswald on live TV. The entire weekend was unlike any other we had ever experienced.

In January 1964, while Carol Ann and I traveled to the Evangelism Conference in Ft. Worth, my mother came to keep the children. Because Randy and Terri were both running a bit of temperature, she gave them each a baby aspirin. Bailey wanted some, but since he wasn't sick, he didn't get any. When no one was around, Bailey climbed up on the kitchen counter, got the bottle of baby aspirin, and ate all the remaining baby aspirin in the bottle. When he told my mom what he'd done, she and a friend rushed them to the emergency room. They pumped his stomach and found a big wad of bubble gum covered with baby aspirin. That was the last time he swallowed any more bubble gum or took medicine without being told to do so.

While mother was still with the kids, she asked Bailey to grab a paper towel and wipe up some spilled water before anyone slipped. He looked at her quite surprised and said, "Don't you know, this is our plate for lunch," because we always ate our lunchtime sandwiches on paper towels!

WHO BUT GOD! RIDING THE WHIRLWIND
JIMMY AND CAROL ANN DRAPER

One of the funnier adventures with our kids happened on my watch. Carol Ann was out running some errands, and I was to watch the kids. I was also interested in watching a football game on television. When the kids were all quiet, I thought all was going well. I even managed to get everyone down for a nap. But when Carol Ann came home, she noticed 'fuzz' all over the floor of the boys' room. When everyone woke up, we realized Randy had given complimentary haircuts that day—a short haircut for Bailey and more of a random swatch taken from Terri. After that, scissors were banned from our kids.

One year we had a youth retreat at the Howard Butt Foundation retreat center in Leakey, Texas. It was a great place for our youth to get out of the city and really focus on their relationship with the Lord. The camp was in the hill country northwest of San Antonio with the beautiful Frio River flowing through it.

One of the unique things about the camp was how we got to our cabins. We had to drive across the river in the shallowest part between a set of poles to get from one side to the other. The system worked fine as long as you stayed within the poles, but definitely not if you didn't. We found this out one evening when one of our youth workers, Buna Burnett, knocked on our cabin door. She had accidentally driven off the side of the path, and her car had slipped into a deeper pocket of the river. She managed to climb out of her car and wade through the river to get to our cabin. In the meantime, she had gotten soaked head to toe. It wasn't funny to her at the time, but after we all managed to get the car upright and back on the right path, we all had a good laugh about it.

REMEMBER THE ALAMO

Part of that youth group formed one of the best basketball teams in the city's youth basketball program. Just for fun, the men in the church challenged the youth team to a basketball game. The church pitched in, and a big crowd gathered at the Woodlawn Community Center there in Northwest San Antonio. To add to the fun, our men's team all wore pink leotards under our uniforms. It was a big surprise to our members to see their pastor and deacons all decked out like that, but it was a lot of fun for everyone. The men's team played hard, but the youth were too good for us.

During that time, we sponsored a Spanish-speaking Mission Church. One night as I preached at the mission, a small child came up in the middle of my sermon and began to play around my feet and legs on the platform. That was not unusual in the regular services of the mission, so no one paid any attention to the child. I managed to make it through in spite of that unusual distraction.

Our family became involved in a new ministry while we were in San Antonio. I began sponsoring men in prison in order to help them readjust back into society when they were released. My introduction to this ministry came when my secretary, Martha Aaron, confronted me one day. Putting her hands on my shoulders, she said, "Please sit down, I need to talk with you." My pace of multi-tasking kept me going in and out without taking the time to often really talk with her, so I knew this was important to her. She told me about her brother, Billy Aylward, a prisoner in Leavenworth, Kansas.

After our conversation, I contacted the prison and began to communicate with Billy. One day he contacted me and asked if I would sponsor one of his friends out of prison. I agreed, and Dean

Foster came into our lives. The house we had bought after a year or so at the church had a one-room apartment attached to the garage. Dean came and lived in that apartment. We had no fear of danger and regularly left our doors unlocked and our windows open.

A few months after Dean arrived, a big, gold Cadillac came into our driveway and drove back to the garage. It was a Sunday morning, and I had already gone to the church, but Carol Ann was home with the children. Dean visited with the two men who were dressed in nice suits and ties, and then they left. We never knew what that was all about, but within a few days, Dean disappeared, and we never saw him again.

We did have one more pivotal event where God revealed to us in no uncertain terms what not to pray for! We had invited Carol Ann's pastor, Johnny Beard, to preach a revival at University Park. We had prepared every way possible for that revival. The spirit in the church was high, and there was no doubt we would have a great revival with Bro. Johnny leading the services.

Just before the revival, a church in Albuquerque had called and asked us to come in view of a call. I had always wanted to live in Albuquerque and was excited about possibly serving there with so much of my family close by. In a moment of utter foolishness, I prayed that if we were not to go to Albuquerque, to let the revival completely fail. I honestly thought there was no way that could happen. We were greatly prepared for the revival, and I never believed God would answer in the negative. That was when we learned the danger of 'putting out a fleece' for God.

The revival began poorly and got worse every day afterward. By Friday evening, there was hardly anyone there. It was a complete

REMEMBER THE ALAMO

flop, and we were terribly embarrassed for this to happen despite Bro. Johnny's efforts. Before all this happened, I had told Carol Ann to be prepared to go to Albuquerque, and I would pray. She had the wisdom not to pack and I came to learn a lot about prayer, specifically that it was not my place to 'put out a fleece' in order to try and bend circumstances to what I wanted to happen. It was a hard way to learn, but I've never forgotten it.

After four years, God began to orchestrate a contact that would open the door for our next pastorate. Bethany Baptist Church in Kansas City, Missouri, was a great church located just south of the Missouri River in an older section of Kansas City. It had planted a number of churches across the city. Bethany's strategy was simple: purchase five acres of land, build a building, and start the mission services. Red Bridge Baptist Chapel was the newest mission and had been started in 1963 about eighteen months earlier.

Luther Dyer had been the associate pastor at Bethany and became the pastor when the previous pastor, J.T. Elliff, resigned. Luther made the first contact with us. We were recommended by J. T. Elliff. He had never met us, nor had he ever heard me preach, but he was one of my dad's best friends for many years. J.T. wrote in his letter of recommendation, "I do not know this young pastor, but I know his parents, and he comes from good stock!"

Luther called me one night to talk to me about Red Bridge and the wonderful opportunity it would be for us. As we ended our conversation, he began to pray for my family and me over the phone. My hair stood up on end, and chills ran down my spine. I had never heard of anyone praying over the phone. That phone call cemented my relationship with Luther, and he became one of the closest friends I have ever had in my life. I will forever be grateful for Luther, Wanda, and Melinda, their daughter.

During the month before we preached in view of a call at Red Bridge, Randy made a profession of faith at University Park in San Antonio. He had been talking about it for some time, and I told him that if he wanted to be baptized with his friends there at University Park, he needed to go ahead and make that decision. Looking back, that was probably a shove from me that shouldn't have happened, but he was baptized on the last Sunday we were in San Antonio. Several years later, while we were at First Southern Baptist Church Del City, Oklahoma, he made a profession of faith and then was baptized, this time getting his baptism on the right side of his salvation. He wanted to make right what had been a rushed decision in San Antonio before he had a full understanding of his decision.

On April 28, 1965, I preached at Bethany Baptist Church and met with the Missions Committee after the service. That committee had to approve us before we could preach in view of a call at the Red Bridge Baptist Chapel. We were given the green light to proceed, and on May 2, 1965, I preached in view of a call at Red Bridge.

We were presented to Red Bridge, and the call was 98% in favor of us coming to the church. We were told that was a remarkable vote because, at the time, the divisions within the congregation were such that they couldn't have gotten a unanimous vote about whether it was daylight or dark! We felt an overwhelming call from God that it was His will for us to come to serve at Red Bridge.

It was hard to say good-bye to so many of the wonderful people at University Park. God was blessing the church as they continued to grow and mature in truth and outreach. Even though we knew God

REMEMBER THE ALAMO

had called us to Red Bridge, our journey ahead was still filled with several difficulties, but we stayed the course and headed that way.

Our first home we owned

Terri on the swing

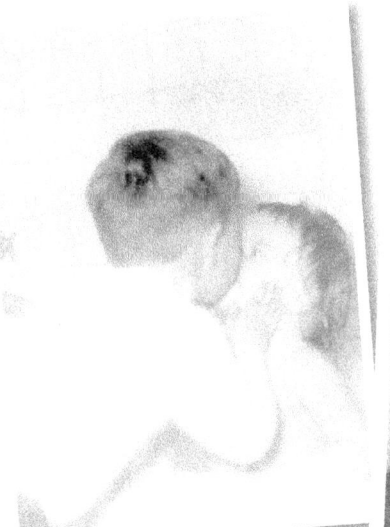
Bailey kissing Terri

Terri, Bailey & Randy

WHO BUT GOD! RIDING THE WHIRLWIND
JIMMY AND CAROL ANN DRAPER

The family in front of Red Bridge parsonage

HOME IN MID-AMERICA

RED BRIDGE BAPTIST CHAPEL

On our way to Kansas City, we had decided our first stop would be in Warren, Arkansas, where my dad was pastor of First Baptist Church. The next morning our boys were playing outside with some other boys when Carol Ann heard a loud scream coming from the church buildings next door. The scream got closer and closer as Bailey came rushing through the back door with blood gushing from his eyes, nose, and all over his face.

She quickly got him to the bathroom and washed him off and saw he had a small cut in the middle of his forehead. The cut was small, but definitely a fast bleeder. The faster he had run, the worse it had bled across his entire face. In the middle of all the excitement, he managed to tell Carol Ann he had been riding a bicycle and hit his head when he fell.

WHO BUT GOD! RIDING THE WHIRLWIND
JIMMY AND CAROL ANN DRAPER

At first glance, Carol Ann didn't think it was too serious, but as soon as I saw it, I knew we needed a doctor to take a look at it. The ER doc agreed and told us the cut would require two stitches to close it fully. Unfortunately, they didn't go in easily. The doctor got the first one in, but it was bleeding so fast, he had a difficult time getting it stopped long enough to put in the second stitch. It was a stressful day for all of us, but especially Bailey and Carol Ann.

The next day Terri was riding the same bike and somehow got her leg caught between the frame and the wheel. When she couldn't get her leg free, two of the town's high school football players heard her crying and managed to bend the frame and free her leg. When we saw the gash she had in her leg from the bike, we headed back to the emergency room for the second day in a row. We were beginning to think someone didn't want us to get to Kansas City, but we weren't going to let a few bumps in the road shake our confidence that God had sent us to Red Bridge. We were committed to answering the call regardless of the obstacles along the way.

Throughout our lives together, Carol Ann and I have seen that life does come at us fast, and things do happen to complicate the journey, but nothing comes as a surprise to God. He is sufficient for every step of the journey! John 16:33 says, "You will have suffering in this world. Be courageous! I have conquered the world." God knew where we were, where we were going, the ministry we would have at Red Bridge, and everything that would take place in that process.

The night Red Bridge voted by secret ballot on our call the vote was 98% to ask us to come to Kansas City, but the weekend was still a very unusual experience for us. The church had arranged for us to stay in a motel on the city's eastern side. We took The Paseo, an historic street through the city to the mission. Even though it was early May, it had had been a very cold week, and the route was unusually bleak. In the ten miles between the motel and the church, we didn't see a single patch of grass or a leaf on a tree. Coming from Texas, we were used to spring being in full swing by that time of the year.

Once we got to the church, the people were gracious but cautious and guarded. They were polite, but nothing like the friendliness of people in Texas. We learned that Missouri really is the 'Show Me' state based on their tentative reception of us. There was no Southern hospitality to be found; no one waving at you as they drove by; no one going out of their way to be extra friendly. It was like moving to a foreign country with a different language and customs and decidedly different from where we came from. Truth be told, there was nothing there that attracted us to the mission or to the city, except for the overwhelming sense that this was God's will for our lives.

It didn't take us long to figure out the devil did not want a church on this corner of Red Bridge and Grandview Roads. The church had been without a pastor for about six months, and it was a challenging transition for all of us. Knowing they didn't love us from the start was difficult after having just left such a loving fellowship in San Antonio. However, we soon learned it wasn't just us and to not take their lukewarm welcome personally. As a group, they had little love for each other and were divided into factions within the fellowship. So we clung to what we did know— that God had sent us there and that the church had called us. And then we set out to do the job the Lord sent us to do—to serve and minister in the love of our Lord Jesus Christ.

WHO BUT GOD! RIDING THE WHIRLWIND
JIMMY AND CAROL ANN DRAPER

It was a lonely, sad summer for all of us that first year. No one called just to check on us or stopped by just for a visit. We were used to seeing people and being with people and sharing good times with them. Carol Ann remembers telling me that she felt sorry for me because she was the only friend I had in the beginning, but it was really a new way of living for all of us.

In spite of all this, and with kids ages 4, 5 and 7-years-olds, we were happy to be there because of our belief that God had sent us to serve Him there. God was true to His own nature and began to make greatly needed changes in the people and in us at Red Bridge as we worked to build relationships with the people.

Our first winter there, we realized we all needed winter clothes—real winter clothes. We never had need of them before, but as always, God provided them for us. By the time winter arrived, we were all prepared and excited to see the cold weather we never saw in San Antonio. We also learned better about what to do when it snowed. Our family had a great day playing in the first snowfall, and we even wondered why all our neighbors were shoveling snow from their sidewalks and driveways instead of playing in it. We had planned to do the shoveling the next day after the fun, but that was before we found out that snow not cleared turned into ice overnight. We didn't let that happen again!

We began our ministry there on May 30, 1965, and it marked the beginning of some wonderful changes for all of us involved in the church. The people who had initially been hesitant to receive us became some of the most responsive and open friends we had ever known. It was a glorious transformation. So much so, that Carol Ann remarked years later that if she could have stayed in one place throughout our ministry, it would have been Kansas City. We didn't stay forever, but we had five years of remarkable ministry there. It was Camelot for us at that time!

Kansas City, Missouri, incorporated as a town on June 1, 1850, and as a city on March 28, 1853. It was the largest city in the state of Missouri at the time and was located at the merger of the Kansas and Missouri Rivers. These waterways provided a navigable port for river travel all the way to the Mississippi River.

The city had been torn with hostility prior to the Civil War. Kansas had sided with the Union as a free state, and Missouri joined the confederacy because of the many slave owners. Chaos and violence dominated the war years as the city was devastated by both North and South troops.

Quantrill's Raiders frequented the area and fought Jayhawkers in Kansas and Federal troops in both Kansas and Missouri. Quantrill regularly stayed at the farm of David Tate on Red Bridge Road, just a couple of miles from where we lived. It took decades for the area to recover from the destruction of the Civil War, and the hostility neighbors and families felt for one another. This long-lasting atmosphere of suspicion-over-trust largely explains why Missouri became known as the 'Show Me' state.

Red Bridge Baptist Chapel was located in the Hickman Mills Community. This area was virtually destroyed on May 20, 1957, by a tornado that killed 44 and destroyed hundreds of homes and buildings. Known as the Ruskin Heights tornado, it stayed on the ground for 71 miles from near Williamsburg, Kansas well into Missouri. It was an F5 tornado and carved a path 1/10-mile wide to nearly a mile wide at a speed of 42 miles per hour and remained on the ground at that speed for 71 miles. Hailstones as large as 7" in diameter struck other parts of Kansas that day. There were 35 tornadoes reported that day in Colorado, Kansas, Nebraska, Oklahoma, and Missouri.

The first month we were in Kansas City, the days were beautiful, but the nights were very stormy. One night Carol Ann was awakened by rain and strong winds. When she got up and looked out into our backyard and into the woods just beyond, she saw the trees were bending to the strong winds. Seconds later, she heard what clearly sounded like an approaching train—the very sound we had been told a tornado makes as it nears.

She came to wake me just as she heard the horn of a passing train on the tracks just beyond the wooded area behind our home. Up to that point, she had never known there were railroad tracks back there. She had a good laugh, climbed back in bed, and thanked God that He is with us in the midst of our storms. We are so glad that we are never alone, and that God never slumbers or sleeps!

On another occasion, the boys were sent home from school because the authorities considered the weather conditions to be conducive to a tornado. But at our house, the sun was shining, and I thought it would be a good time to take the boys to get a haircut. We loaded up the car and hadn't even turned on Red Bridge Road when I looked across the western horizon, probably five miles in the distance, and saw a shelf cloud with a tornado clearly visible dropping to the ground. We turned around quickly, and nobody got a haircut that day.

During our years at Red Bridge, we spent many hours in our basement listening to the wail of tornado sirens and praying. We quickly learned why our area was part of the infamous 'tornado alley." We always managed to get to our basement before conditions became threatening and were blessed to never have a tornado hit our area during our time in Red Bridge.

After we arrived at Red Bridge, I met with several of our leaders and the missions committee every month at Bethany Baptist Church. My responsibilities were to not only lead Red Bridge but to keep the folks on the missions committee at Bethany Baptist happy as well. At one of our monthly meetings with the missions committee and key leaders from Red Bridge, I pointed out some problems regarding the way the builder had constructed the church. I made special mention that a ¼ inch residential water line had been installed instead of a 1 inch commercial one. The problem this presented was that it did not allow enough water pressure to fill the baptistry under normal circumstances, but when a toilet was flushed, the water flow was reduced to a drip.

I told the mission committee that we weren't asking for any money to put in a larger line as we had already done it and paid for it. I was merely telling them what we had done and suggesting we should probably be a bit more careful on future projects and perhaps consider a new builder. What I didn't know at the time was that the builder also happened to be the brother-in-law of a member of the committee.

It wasn't long before that man and his brother-in-law confronted Luther Dyer about me and tried to create some serious opposition against me being at Red Bridge. Luther stood strong against them and stood by me. It was a valuable lesson for me at the time. We weathered the storm, even though those two men continued to be aggressively hostile toward me from that point on.

It was about three months after we arrived at Red Bridge when Luther announced that he would be resigning as pastor of Bethany and become the State Evangelism Director for the Missouri Baptist Convention. I told him that Red Bridge had to become independent from Bethany Baptist Church and constitute into a church before he left because I could not stay there and face those two angry men at Bethany if he was not pastor.

During those months, I reached out to my dear friend, Jack Taylor. We had served in the Northwest portion of San Antonio for four years and had spent a lot of time together. We traded letters and eventually tape recordings during this time and for years afterward.

We constituted as a church in early October before Luther moved to Jefferson City, Missouri, to assume his new position. Becoming a self-sustaining church was the right decision to make, and Red Bridge took off in growth and ministry. We led the state in baptisms three of the five years we served there. We had a part-time secretary, Carol Duncan, a bi-vocational Minister of Education, Bill Roller, and a part-time Minister of Music, Dave Maxey. All three were great friends and co-workers who encouraged us in so many ways in those early days of our ministry at Red Bridge.

The months from May to October were filled with many challenges. We faced a barrage of serious but frivolous criticisms. They would have been discouraging if they had not been so ridiculous. Yet they continued to come up until the day we constituted into a church. On the Sunday night service on October 3, 1965, after we constituted into a church that afternoon, God moved in with great power.

HOME IN MID-AMERICA

One of the ladies, Carol Godfrey, came forward at the invitation and asked to speak to the congregation. She said, "God has been so good to us to bring our pastor and family to us. We have all said things and repeated things that were not helpful in these past five months, and it is time for us to thank God for our pastor and family and move on together."

When she finished, the auditorium emptied into the altar, and the people wrapped their arms around us and brought us into their hearts. That marked a turning point in the new church and propelled us into a remarkable period of growth. By the time we left for Del City, Oklahoma, five years later, we had grown to multiple services with an average attendance of 600 each Sunday morning.

We had some wonderful, godly leaders in Red Bridge. Shortly after we began there, Frank and Shirley Favazza joined the church. He was a strong and highly regarded builder in the area and became our first chairman of the deacons. Twenty-six years later, when I became president of the Sunday School Board of the Southern Baptist Convention, it was Shirley Favazza who came to be my executive assistant in Nashville. She had just retired from being the Executive Assistant for the Midwest Division of Chrysler Corporation. It was perfect timing for them as Frank had retired from the building business at the same time.

We had many great lay folks in the church. To our surprise, one of my Baylor friends, Jim Williams, joined Red Bridge soon after we arrived. He had flown dangerous missions in Viet Nam and was a TWA pilot at that time. His wife Carol was one of Carol Ann's special friends. Harold and Dana Pope joined, and Dana was our church pianist. Both of them had grown up with me in Jacksonville, Texas, beginning in elementary school. We loved those two families because of the many years we had known them. We spent lots of meals together with them, and when Terri spent her first night away from home with a friend, it was at the Pope's home.

One special couple to us at Red Bridge was Earl and Lavon Hardy. They had been married for many years but had no children. He was a mechanic for a Cadillac dealer in Overland Park, Kansas. They adopted our family, and we enjoyed having them as surrogate grandparents to our children. About halfway through our ministry at Red Bridge, Earl gave us a car he had driven for years and had kept in perfect driving condition. It was a Buick, and though it was old, it worked wonderfully for our family!

Strong leaders like J.W. Douglas, who worked for the United States Department of Agriculture office in Kansas City, Fred Cochran, a vice president for Kansas City Power and Light Company, Roger Cozort, an executive with the telephone company, Bob Meloy, manager of Butler Buildings in south Kansas City, Ben Simpson, coach at Grandview High School, Ralph Denny, a young business executive, Ray Boden, who worked for a major company that had moved them in from Chicago, Harold Arnsmeyer, a retired business leader, and many others were cherished friends at Red Bridge. Other families like the Cooks, Chandlers, Browns, and Coxes were special partners in ministry. It was a church of young executives and hardworking laborers with young children. There were even a few 'old-timers' mixed in with the congregation, and the atmosphere was electric week after week!

HOME IN MID-AMERICA

Once Luther had settled in as the Evangelism Director for the Missouri Baptist Convention, he invited me to preach at my first state-wide denominational conference at the annual Missouri Baptist Evangelism Conference. This was the beginning of many, many speaking engagements at state convention conferences.

About a year after moving to Kansas City, Carol Ann and the kids made a trip back to Texas to see her parents and visit old friends. They also experienced a miracle on this trip. They had flown to Houston first to see her parents and then borrowed her dad's car to take the kids to San Antonio to see friends. When they got to San Antonio, Carol Ann told the children to be very quiet because she was about to enter a new freeway that had not been there when we lived in San Antonio. As she entered the freeway, she came on even with the cab of an 18-wheeler.

She noticed his blinker was indicating he wanted to move into her lane. She could also tell he couldn't see her beneath his cab. That would have been trouble enough, but there was a concrete barrier on her right and no place for her to go to get out of his way. He started moving into her lane so fast she couldn't slow down enough to avoid a crash, so she closed her eyes and prayed, "Lord, Help!" When she opened her eyes, the truck was in front of her, and there had been no accident. The good news was that the Lord had prevented the collision, but the bad news was that she missed seeing how God handled that miracle. Either way, it was great to be reminded that God is with us each step of our earthly journey!

In the early Spring of 1967, I invited Jack Taylor to come for a revival at Red Bridge. His friendship had sustained us in those early months and for years afterward. On the Thursday night of that week, as Carol Ann and the kids were getting ready to come to church, Terri told Carol Ann that she wanted to be saved. Carol Ann shared with her the plan of salvation, and she fully recognized that Jesus had died for her on the cross for our salvation. After some more questions and answers between the two of them, Terri knelt in our bathroom and asked Jesus to save her. She had just turned six years old, and that night in the revival service made her decision public.

At that time, Terri was deathly afraid to have her head put under water, so we knew that would be a challenge for her and a real test of the genuineness of her decision. Several weeks later, she marched into the baptistry and had no fear. We knew right then that was a sign that she had, indeed, been saved.

One night after Terri was saved and before Bailey's decision, Grandmother came down the hall and heard Randy and Bailey really arguing about something. When she stopped and asked them, "Is that any way for two Christian boys to behave?" Bailey quickly responded, "Grandmother, you know I'm not saved!" And, as a special service to his little brother, Randy made sure Bailey knew he could not partake of the Lord's Supper since he had not been saved!

In October of 1967, Bailey made his profession of faith on a Sunday night. When I extended the invitation, he bolted out of the pew and rushed to the front to tell me he wanted to be saved. In 1983, at the age of 22 and after struggling for several years with doubt, he made another decision during the Bailey Smith Revival. He said he just wanted to make sure of his salvation, so we knelt together, and he prayed and asked the Lord to save him. His first profession of faith had been 15 years earlier, but now he finally had the peace he had been seeking.

My mother had surgery in mid-January 1966, for a tumor on one of her ovaries. The tumor had been biopsied and found to be benign, so surgery was expected to be simple and noneventful. Needless to say, it was an unwelcome surprise when the doctors discovered a malignant tumor behind the original one. We had planned on making our return home from the Texas Evangelism Conference to Kansas City to include being in Little Rock during mom's surgery. We were so grateful to have been there for both of them. Dad was so emotional about the report that he had me make the calls to family in Albuquerque to relay the news as he did not feel like he had composure enough to talk about it. Mother stayed in the hospital a few more days before we learned the good news: she would not have to have chemo or radiation as the ovary had completely contained the cancer, and there was no need for additional treatment.

Several weeks later, Carol Ann and Terri went down to Warren to help with mother's recuperation. To get there, they had to ride a train to St. Louis and transfer to another train going to Little Rock. Dad would be able to meet them there and bring them on to Warren. The trip itself proved to be exciting for Carol Ann and Terri. The day I took them to the train station, it was snowing heavily. Even though the ride to the train station was only 10 miles away, it wasn't an easy drive. It had already snowed 6," and the snowdrifts were much deeper than that.

The snow delayed the train leaving Kansas City, which, in turn, caused them to miss their train to Little Rock and left them facing an

8-hour wait for the next train. To add to their concerns, Carol Ann had only 35 cents in cash with her! They drank lots of water, walked around and around the train station, and played lots and lots of word games until the next train arrived.

When they finally made it to Little Rock, my dad was there to pick them up and get them to Warren to help mom. All the delays and efforts were worth it in the end because they helped mom and dad so much during her recuperation. Carol Ann told Terri repeatedly what a good helper she was and how much she appreciated her help. Terri replied, "When I get home and am not so good, it will be because of my brothers! So spank them, not me!" Spoken like a true little sister!

Just two months later, on March 22, 1966, another event occurred that changed my life and ministry throughout the decades to follow. My mother called that afternoon to tell me that my dad had collapsed while playing nine holes of golf and died immediately. She called me expecting that I would tell Carol Ann in person, but I was so stunned, I called Carol Ann immediately and told her over the phone. Dad was only 52 years old and was in a significant place of influence among Arkansas Baptists. He was pastoring the church in the town he grew up in and actually living in the very house that he lived in as a boy.

My dad had just completed his annual physical and was told to get more exercise. He was a member of the Lion's Club, so the men had surprised him by giving him a membership in the little country club in Warren. The policy was that one could not play there regularly without being a member. My dad had already had his morning walk, but the men at the Lion's Club insisted that he play nine holes of golf that afternoon.

HOME IN MID-AMERICA

First Baptist Church Warren was in a week-long revival, but after lunch, my dad and the visiting preacher agreed to play a quick nine holes of golf. On the eighth hole, he collapsed and was dead by the time emergency responders arrived. The church suggested they should cancel the remainder of the revival, but our family wanted to continue the revival. We believed that is what dad would have wanted. So, the revival went through Sunday morning, and I was asked to close out his ministry there by preaching on Sunday evening.

Upon hearing the news from mother, Carol Ann and I and the children drove through the late night and into the early morning hours to arrive in Warren around 3:30 a.m. My brothers, George and Charlie, came out and buried their heads on my shoulders as we wept together. The service was conducted on Friday morning there in the sanctuary of First Baptist Church in Warren and was broadcast over the small radio station in the town. George and Charlie joined me in leading the funeral service.

We attended revival services each evening and remarked how much more meaningful the songs were in light of our dad's death. Mother was a rock for us all and remained the strongest member of our family during that transition following my dad's death.

When people ask me what is the most important thing that ever happened for my ministry, I always say it was the death of my dad. The reason is because my dad's death represented my first experience with the death of a close loved one. I had always sympathized with those who grieved in such a moment but did not understand how they felt. Now I could empathize with those who grieved because I had experienced it myself.

One of the interesting things we later found about Carol Ann and Terri's visit earlier in February was the unusual things dad had done. Traditionally, he never bought birthday gifts earlier than at the time of someone's birthday, and he just never made it a practice to file his income tax before the last minute. But during their visit, he bought Terri's birthday gifts almost two months before her birthday in mid-April, and he had borrowed money from the bank for his income tax and put it on a note with an insurance policy covering the loan. Is it possible he may have had a premonition about his approaching death? We will never know, but his actions were most unusual for him.

Because my dad had preached a revival at Red Bridge the fall before his death, his death impacted Red Bridge as well. As a church, our members instructed our church treasurer to send us a check for $100 to help with expenses before we even got back home.

In May 1966, mother came to Kansas City to make her home with us. She lived with us for the next 32 years. It was a wonderful experience for our children to live in the same house with their grandmother, and it was a blessing for Carol Ann because she had never known her grandparents. She and mother had a remarkable bond. I'm certain that if Carol Ann and I had ever had a serious argument, mother would have always sided with Carol Ann. Having mom there also allowed Carol Ann to work closer with me on the church's ministry because we knew mom was available to take care of the children.

Carol Ann was gracious and patient during the transition of mother coming to live with us. After all, she didn't just have a new house guest; it was her mother-in-law moving in. Mom's arrival affected a million little things for Carol Ann, including everything from how to fold the towels and sheets to how to put things back in place in the kitchen after meals. Mom even watched how Carol Ann put her make-up on! It was a big change for everyone, but especially Carol Ann and mom. We all got through the adjustment period and came to see it as one of the greatest blessings of our lives. In the end, everyone came to call her 'Grandmother,' and she was loved by all.

Shortly after Grandmother came to live with us, she flew to Albuquerque to visit her brothers and sisters. One night while she was gone, we got a call from one of our single young ladies explaining that she and her roommate had shared the Lord with a traveling magazine salesman. She thought he was just passing through and told him if he ever needed anything else, to just call Bro. Jimmy.

Minutes later, the salesman, Bernie Jones, called from the bus station downtown to see if he could spend the night at our house. Since my brother, Charlie, lived with us at that time, I sent him to get Bernie for what we thought would be one night. He ended up staying with us for six weeks while he enjoyed grandmother's bedroom and television and other elements in our household. At the end of his stay, he conned one of our members out of $500 and left town as fast as he could. We never heard from him again; only God knows where he is today.

The first 18 months we were at Red Bridge were extremely demanding, to say the least. In just a year and a half, Luther Dyer had left Bethany Baptist Church, my dad had died in March of 1966, my mother came to live with us the following May, and we had endured many struggles in our efforts to build new relationships within the church. We were drained and dry as we approached 1967.

As a remedy for our weary hearts and minds, we decided we would go back again to Texas to attend the State Evangelism Conference in January.

Now that my mother was living with us, we could leave the children with her and make the trip to Texas without much trouble. We were excited to go because we were going to ride the train from Kansas City to Texarkana, Texas. Our dear friends, George and Lynda Harris were living in Mount Pleasant, Texas, and had invited us to ride the train to Texarkana and then go on to the conference in Dallas/Fort Worth. It was with a lot of excitement that we planned to do just that. Texarkana was only about an hour north of Mount Pleasant, so we agreed to do that. We were so excited many people at the train station thought we were newlyweds!

The conference week was a pivotal moment for us as it was our introduction to the remarkable African-American preacher, Shadrack Meshack Lockridge. He never used a note and preached the stars down for us. His famous sermon, "Jesus is Lord," was his first message at the conference. He became a fast friend and preached for us at First Southern Baptist Church in Del City, Oklahoma, on our third anniversary as pastor there, and also on the third anniversary of our ministry at First Baptist Church Euless.

Our second February in Kansas City was very cold. Carol Ann and I were briefly out of town, and Grandmother stayed with the kids. After the kids had gone to school that morning, Grandmother had written some Valentine cards and wanted to put them in the mailbox on our front porch. Remember, this was back when mail was delivered to the front porch!

HOME IN MID-AMERICA

When she opened the door and stepped onto the front porch to place them in the mailbox, the door closed behind her, locking her outside in the cold in nothing more than her robe and gown and crocheted house shoes. She always had her cane with her, so she walked up the street two doors to our neighbors, a retired Lutheran preacher and his wife. They welcomed her in their home until we came home.

To our surprise, when we got home, we saw her purse and shoes, but Grandmother was nowhere to be found. Our neighbors soon called to tell us Grandmother was with them and what had happened. We all had a good laugh and made a cherished memory and were grateful Grandmother was nothing more than just a little embarrassed.

Before long, our household went from two adults and three children to six adults and three children. My brother Charlie had a very complicated knee surgery while at Southwestern Seminary that created so many challenges he had to drop out of school that semester. Our house was the natural place for him to convalesce. The summer before we had two teenagers come from San Antonio to spend the summer with us and to intern for the church. Franklin Krause and Doug Arredondo were special to us even though our home was bulging with new people. They were now back in San Antonio, but we had learned how to use our basement bunk beds. We had room for Charlie.

In spite of all the added chores now on her plate, Carol Ann became a remarkable host for all of our new family. She graciously fought through the obstacles that Satan threw her way as her faith grew even stronger. She came to know more than ever that God was with her and sustained her every step of the way.

During these years, I traveled often to speak across the state of Missouri. On one of those trips I traveled from Kansas City to St. Louis, a short flight of about 45 minutes. The day I was to fly to St. Louis the weather turned into a snow and ice. Travel on the roads was treacherous and dangerous. As the snow intensified, I called the airline about 8:30 a.m. to check on the status of my flight. I was told that the flight had been delayed from its 10:30 a.m. scheduled departure so I stayed at the office working.

About 9:45 a.m. I called the airline again but this time I was told the flight was leaving on time! I explained that I had been told it was delayed, but that I would leave immediately to try and get there in time. Bob Brown drove me the fifteen miles to the airport in downtown Kansas City, just north of the Missouri River. When we got to the airport, I rushed in, found out the gate and ran to the gate.

When I got to the gate the waiting room was completely empty, but the flight number was still posted. The exit to the tarmac was a double swinging door so I rushed outside, looked both ways, but there was no plane to be seen. I was puzzled and looked for someone from the airline to ask about the flight.

A man approached me who had been loading baggage on the flight next door. I asked him about the flight, and he pointed to a city bus just about 40 feet away from where I was standing. It was filled with passengers and had 'Flight #127 St. Louis' on the window by the door.

At that time, Kansas City was building a new airport about 15 miles north of the old airport. The terminals were not yet complete, but the runways were. Because of the heavy populated area around the old airport and the inclement weather, the airlines were bussing people to the new location for take-off in a less populated area.

I raced towards the bus and was able to make it. But as I rode the bus, I wondered how I could have missed seeing the bus in the first place. It was huge, filled with people, and had the flight number posted on the window. How could I have not seen it? Then it dawned on me—I did not see the bus because I was not looking for a bus; I was looking for an airplane! God impressed me right then that people usually see what they are looking for. Even the most obvious things may not register if you are not looking for them.

I remembered the nursery rhyme, "Pussy cat, pussy cat, where have you been? 'I have been to London to see the Queen.' Pussy cat, pussy cat, what saw you there? 'A frightened little mouse under a chair.'" The mouse saw what it was looking for! In life we all need to realize how important it is for us to focus on the right things because we will most likely see what we are looking for!

The trip was uneventful, but the challenges getting back home were challenging, also. To get to the airport in Kansas City at that time required a toll to cross the bridge on the Missouri River. It had to be paid both going and coming. Carol Ann had brought mother and the children with her to pick me up at the airport. When she got to the airport, she ended up at the wrong gate and could not find me. I had actually come in at the other end of the airport.

She was very anxious to find me because she did not have the money she needed to pay the return toll. What would she do if I didn't arrive? How would she get across the bridge to go back home? Frantically, she searched to find me, deeply worried she wouldn't be able to get home. In time, we did make connections and fortunately, I had enough change to pay the toll.

While we were at Red Bridge, I returned to my practice of sponsoring prisoners just out of prison. The one we helped was from the prison in Southern Illinois. I had preached a revival in Anna, Illinois, where my long-time friend Earl Ashley was pastor. He had followed me as pastor of Steep Hollow Baptist Church. He was also the chaplain for the prison in that area. I went with him to the prison one afternoon during the revival week and was introduced to Ray Summers, a tall, strapping 6'5" giant of a man. Ray had a big smile and absolutely won my heart immediately.

Before long, I heard myself say, "I'd like to help you get out of prison and come to Kansas City." I could not believe I heard myself say that, but shortly thereafter, Ray got off an airplane in Kansas City and started living in a small house on the Red Bridge church property. In time, he was saved and baptized and became active in our church.

During Ray's time at the church, I was called by one of the wives in our church to come to their house. She was a teller at a local bank's drive-thru window, and her husband was insanely jealous to the point of accusing her of having an affair with the janitor at the bank. Because she had to be in her teller booth by 7:30 each morning, she always left by 7:00 to drive the few miles to the bank and prepare for the day. Her husband found her early hours suspicious.

I listened carefully to her and her husband without comment. When they had both finished, I told her husband the obvious truth: there was no way she had the time to get to the bank, have an affair, put the money together and be in her teller booth all by 7:30 a.m.

HOME IN MID-AMERICA

This line of reasoning enraged him, and he ordered me to leave. I couldn't do that in good conscience just then because I feared for his wife's safety in his current state. When he finally settled down, I agreed to leave.

A day or so later, I received a long-distance call from an anonymous individual who threatened my life and my family. Our home in Kansas City was on a slope that allowed us to park underneath the living area in the basement in the back. Behind our house was nothing but woods for over a quarter of a mile. I notified the police and was told not to leave our garage doors open at any time and to take the children to and from school. It turned out that the husband had an identical twin brother in Springfield, Missouri, and the police believed it was his brother who had called.

In telling Ray about our situation, he said, "Bro. Jimmy, I have committed just about every crime one can commit. I can take care of this if you will let me!" Of course, I refused to let him seek vigilante justice and declined his offer, but for several months he would not let me get in my car to leave the church without checking to see if any bombs were attached to it. Those were anxious days, but I'll always remember Ray's offer of protection for our family.

Months later, Ray showed up at our house around midnight, pounding on the door. When I saw it was Ray and let him in, he gave me a giant bear hug and exclaimed, "He died for me! He died for me!" Ray shared in vivid detail that he had been driving down the street when he saw the Lord on the cross and realized His sacrifice was for him. That was the night when Ray became a child of the King!

WHO BUT GOD! RIDING THE WHIRLWIND
JIMMY AND CAROL ANN DRAPER

About a year after he was released, Ray was accidentally shot in a gun accident at the house of one of our members. When I got the news, I raced to the home and found him unconscious. I did everything I could to revive him until the ambulance arrived. Ray never regained consciousness, but I found myself asking God to please spare his life, even offering to lose my own life if he would be spared. I stood by his bed for hours and did everything humanly possible I could have done. In the end, I could not help him or restore him, and Ray died.

The Lord used this experience to reveal His heart to me as he said, "You could not save Ray, but the lost around you do not have to die and go to hell. They can be saved." My time with Ray rekindled in my heart the absolutely clear picture of what 'lostness' means and the amazing grace God offers to all who will receive Christ. Ray's death marked another milestone and step forward in my understanding of what God had called me to do.

By this time, our family truly needed some time away from the constant demands of pastoring a church. We headed out for a quick vacation to Lake Jackson to visit Carol Ann's parents. While there, we had made plans for all five of us to go deep-sea fishing. I imagined a great time catching marlin and other exotic fish.

The charter company instructed us to take one Dramamine pill the night before at 10:00 p.m. to ward off seasickness and another one when we reported to the dock at 3:30 a.m. Carol Ann and Bailey did as they had been told, and we all made it to the dock in the early morning. We had never been on a boat as a family, so we were excited about our real deep-sea adventure together, and I was grateful I had saved the $100 to pay for the fishing trip.

HOME IN MID-AMERICA

Before the boat ever left the dock, Carol Ann had already fallen asleep on the deck. I got her below deck, where she slept for the entire trip. And even though Bailey has always been our best fisherman, he also fell asleep before we left the dock. As it turned out, the Dramamine had taken care of seasickness by putting them to sleep, so that left Randy, Terri, and me to be the only ones to fish that day.

We rode for several hours until we were 75 miles offshore. Our guide was taking us red snapper fishing, and that required getting to deeper waters. It was on this trip I learned that since red snapper took the bait so far down, the change in depth actually killed them as they were reeled in. This made it feel like we were reeling in a bucket of concrete as they got closer to the surface. Our efforts were worth it, though, as we ended the day with 13 good sized red snappers to our credit.

We got home from that vacation on a Saturday and had lots to do to be ready for Sunday and for Vacation Bible School coming up in a week. Carol Ann had been asked to be the VBS leader for the third graders. She was told that all the workers were already enlisted, so she agreed even though we would be gone the week before. She would still have one more week to get ready upon our return.

Our 'best-laid plans' didn't hold up too long as the week unfolded. On Monday, I had a softball game, and Randy had a baseball game, so Bailey came with me to play with some of the players' kids, and Carol Ann and Terri went to Randy's game. We thought we had our bases covered—literally—until a foul ball came into play. In the first inning of our men's game, a pitch was fouled off and over the backstop and across the asphalt road behind the backstop. What 7-year-old could resist chasing after the foul ball? Certainly not Bailey! He took off as the fastest one in the bunch and reached the road the same time as a small, British Triumph convertible. The car hit Bailey, knocked him in the air, passed under him, and left him in a heap beside the road.

I think I set a world record racing from shortstop to the spot where Bailey lay. When the car passed under him, the windshield had just barely grazed his head. It left a spot in his hair about the size of a dime that was completely shaved off as if a razor had removed it. Had it been as little as a quarter of an inch lower Bailey would likely have been killed. As it was, he had a badly broken leg where the car hit him between the knee and the ankle, but no other injuries. It really was as though an angel had caught him in midair and gently laid him down by the road.

At the same time, it was the fourth inning at Randy's game. Franklin, one of the two young men from San Antonio who had spent that summer with us, went to find Carol Ann & Terri and told them Bailey had been hit by a car and that he would take them to the hospital. They left immediately to meet us at Baptist Hospital.

The scariest thing about the whole thing for me was the ride to Baptist Hospital. The ambulance raced through traffic at top speeds because they didn't yet know the extent of Bailey's injuries. When we got there, Bailey was rushed into the emergency area. As the doctor and I were talking about what needed to be done, he asked me about the knee-length socks Bailey was wearing. When I told him, "Doctor, just cut it off," Bailey loudly objected because he thought we were talking about his leg!

Bailey was rushed to surgery before Carol Ann, Terri and Franklin arrived and didn't wake up until 2 a.m. When he did wake up, Carol Ann asked him if he was afraid. She was surprised when he said he wasn't. "Why weren't you afraid?" she asked. His answer was priceless. "Remember that verse we learned last week," he asked. "It was Psalms 56:3, 'What time I am afraid I will trust in you.'" We realized then and there just how precious the word of God is that even a 7-year-old child could find comfort at a time of crisis in it.

It reminded us again how important it is to saturate the hearts and minds of our children in every possible way as they grow up. That is why we always put Scriptures on mirrors, on doors, and in the kitchen and talked about how they apply to our lives. It helped us to always remember that God's Word is true and sufficient for all our needs.

Bailey and Carol Ann spent four nights in the hospital. At night she slept under his bed with only a pillow. The last night she told Bailey she was going home since he had slept so soundly the previous night. He didn't respond immediately, but then he asked her, "When you were seven years old, if you had been in the hospital, would you have wanted your mom to stay with you?" Carol Ann couldn't resist the innocence of his question and assured him she would stay the night with him.

Bailey was released on Friday with his leg in a full-length cast, and VBS was set to begin on Monday. Carol Ann managed to teach her young married ladies in Sunday School and cried to the Lord for help with her upcoming time with the third graders. Back then, Bible school lasted two full weeks, so it took a lot of effort. The Lord proved to be faithful again as that week of Vacation Bible School was the best she had ever experienced. Her third graders seemed to be spellbound when she shared the Bible lesson each day. It may have been because of her sweet Southern accent that one could rarely hear in Kansas City, but whatever the reason, she was quick to give God all the glory for seeing her through those two weeks.

We had a strong Evangelical Ministers Fellowship in Kansas City. It was led by the Youth for Christ leader, Al Metsker. He was the founder of Kansas City chapter of Youth for Christ, one of the first YFC ministries in the nation.

In 1967, we had one of the biggest events ever for our church and for Kansas City. The Evangelical Ministers Fellowship had received a positive response to an invitation from Billy Graham to come to Kansas City. The associate director of Kansas City Youth for Christ, Jack Cousins, took a leave of absence from YFC to become the director for the year-long preparation for the crusade.

The office for the crusade was set up between downtown and our home. Needing someone who could relate easily with the pastors and church staff and leaders in Kansas City, Jack asked Carol Ann to join him and be his special assistant. She had not worked since I was in seminary, but she jumped in and helped take care of the relationships and details for the crusade. With mother able to take care of the children, it was a good time for her to have this special opportunity.

About six months before the crusade, the Prayer Chairman on the Executive Committee for the crusade moved out of Kansas City, and a replacement needed to be named. Because he had been a Southern Baptist, they looked for another Southern Baptist to fill his slot and asked me to do that. I was excited to be part of the Executive Committee for the crusade.

One of the tasks for the Prayer Chairman was to mobilize women to meet mid-morning for one month prior to the crusade

HOME IN MID-AMERICA

for a time of prayer. My job was to plan for the prayer groups and organize the places for them to meet. I enlisted the help of my friend Fran Jeffrey, wife of James Jeffrey, who was president of the national Fellowship of Christian Athletes. Fran did a terrific job setting up the prayer groups across the city. The month before the crusade, I recorded a daily 15-minute radio broadcast for the groups giving special prayer requests as they were needed. The broadcast featured songs by George Beverly Shea, Scripture and vital information about the coming crusade. It was wonderful knowing tens of thousands of women were praying specifically for the needs of the crusade.

One of my new friends in Kansas City was Eric Thurman, afternoon DJ and talk show host on KCCV (Kansas City's Christian Voice), a Dick Bott radio station. Eric met me early each morning to help with the recordings, and afterward, he would hand carry the tapes to KCMO, the most powerful radio station in the Kansas City area. The Graham organization had purchased time during the most prime spot, right after the very popular broadcast of 'Dear Abby.' Our broadcast was heard far and wide across the Midwest and gave pertinent information to everyone within listening distance about the Crusade. When the crusade began, we knew preparation had been made for every detail, including being thoroughly undergirded with prayer.

Our church took three busloads of people every night of the crusade and saw many of those who went become believers. It was one of the great boosts for our ministry there at Red Bridge. Because I was the Prayer Chairman for the crusade, I was asked to lead the prayer for the offering one night. It was not unusual for those who prayed to take advantage of the moment and preach a short sermon in their prayers, but I was determined not to do that. Instead, when I prayed, I took about 30 seconds to thank God for the faithfulness of those who attended to give generously. When I sat down, Billy Graham patted me on the knee and said, "Thank you!" I knew exactly what he was saying and greatly appreciated his comment.

That evening I sat next to Ethel Waters, the well-known gospel singer, who made "His Eye is on the Sparrow" a national favorite. As we sat together, I remarked what a wonderful sight it was to see the crowds that filled the stadium. Ethel didn't miss a beat and replied, "Honey, God don't make no flops!" And she was right. God did some remarkable things during that crusade!

The crusade Executive Committee had provided a mobile home on the warning track near the center field fence for Billy's use for his final preparation for the service each night. One night I took Bailey out there to introduce him to Billy. Naturally, Bailey wanted him to sign his cast, and Billy graciously agreed. Bailey kept the piece of the cast with Billy's signature on it for years.

Every week, we saw people making professions of faith at Red Bridge, and the attendance kept rising. It was an exciting time as folks came to see who would get saved next. One week, Bob Brown and I went to the home of Jerry and Kathleen Nash. They had several young children who came with Jerry and Kathleen each week to church. That night as we shared with Kathleen about how to be saved, she prayed to be saved and made her profession of faith the next Sunday. Jerry had not yet made a commitment, but still, he came faithfully to church with her.

At that time, I was preaching a series on the Ten Commandments. I took one of the commandments to deal with each week. The

HOME IN MID-AMERICA

Sunday I preached on 'Remember the Sabbath Day to keep it holy', I truly didn't think the sermon had much evangelistic appeal to it, and it definitely was not one of the best sermons I had ever preached! However, when I gave the invitation, Jerry bolted out of his pew and came to make his profession of faith. He was later baptized, and their family has remained strong in the Lord in the 52 years since.

I always visited most of the day on Saturdays. Carol Ann usually went with me since Grandmother was available to watch the kids, but on this particular day, I visited alone. The last name of my list for the day was a young golf professional who had been attending Red Bridge. He greeted me warmly and allowed me to share the Gospel with him. Within a few minutes, he was ready to kneel and pray to receive Christ. Stories like these could be continued almost endlessly as God continued to move in the midst of Red Bridge during our time there.

One of the 'out of the box' things I did after the Billy Graham Crusade was to turn our parking lot into a drive-in movie theater. Billy Graham's team had developed Worldwide Pictures and had done several outstanding Christian films, so we hung a huge sheet at one end of the parking lot, set up speakers, and showed films one night each week. It went over well, though not great, but it was another way we sought to get the gospel out to the community.

So many special things happened at Red Bridge during those five years. One summer after Carol Ann's parents had come to spend some time with us, Carol Ann and the kids rode back to Lake Jackson with them. We had planned to go visit them at their home soon thereafter, but I could not go at that time, but would follow after the evening service on Sunday. Since our car was larger than theirs, we swapped cars and I would follow the next Sunday evening.

Several hours after they had left, a man knocked on our door. When I opened the door, he was standing there with Carol Ann's purse in his hand. He explained that he had been in a service station and found the purse lying on the ground. Carol Ann's name and address were inside, and since he was coming our way on his way home, he stopped by to return it. I remember being so surprised and shocked that I don't think I even thanked him for his kindness!

Sometime later, Carol Ann called me to tell me that she had left her purse on the top of the car when they stopped for gas and had lost it. She was greatly relieved and as thankful as I was when I told her what had happened. I never got the man's name, but he was an angel in disguise for us.

When I did head to Lake Jackson to join the family, I had an interesting experience traveling through Kansas. It was nearing midnight when I came through Emporia, Kansas. I was stopped several miles out of town by a highway patrolman for speeding, but it ended up being a complicated stop for me. To begin with, I was driving the Floyd's car that was not my own. I had planned to drive it to Lake Jackson. For some unknown reason, I had swapped the papers out of the glove boxes in each car. I'm still not sure why I did that, but I found myself trying to explain to the patrolman why I did not have papers for the car I was driving, which actually wasn't mine.

After I finally convinced him that I had not stolen the car, he had me follow him back into town to put $15 in an envelope to deposit at the courthouse to pay the fine. The problem was that I didn't have $15 in cash. All I had were credit cards. Eventually, he let me find an all-night service station and use my credit card to get the money

HOME IN MID-AMERICA

I needed. Just to be sure I was good for it, the patrolman followed me all the way back to the courthouse just to make sure I made the deposit.

I drove straight through to Lake Jackson, arriving on Monday afternoon after a very long trip. It was a weekend that had many challenges and adventures for me, and I was so glad to get to Lake Jackson!

After we had been at Red Bridge for a couple of years, we expanded our staff when we brought Bob and Janelle Brown on board. Bob was in the kitchen cabinet business and he and Janelle were already members of our church. Bob came on staff fulltime to lead our music and help me with the growing congregation. He was a world-class singer and was greatly used by God to add to the appeal of Red Bridge Baptist Church.

One really funny thing happened right after Bob & Janelle came on staff with us. Our wives went to a camp outside of Kansas City for a women's retreat. They left on Friday and were to return Saturday evening. Bob and I were to conduct a wedding at the church on Saturday afternoon but realized around noontime that Bob did not have a key to his house and needed to change clothes for the wedding. Since my brother Charlie was living in the basement and was about Bob's size, Bob wore Charlie's khaki suit to sing for the wedding. We had planned for him to stand behind the banister in the choir loft so no one would know the pants were about 10" too short. But that was just the beginning of our troubles that day.

The entire wedding ended up being a disaster. It seemed as if everything that could go wrong did go wrong. We found out the couple had not made any arrangements to have anyone play the organ during the ceremony. We called Bob's brother, who lived 30+ minutes away, but who agreed to come immediately to play. When he arrived, he realized he had left in such a rush that he had forgotten to bring any music to play during the wedding. So as the time for the wedding came he began to play everything he could think of to play that he knew. This was probably the first wedding ever to have "Mares eat oats and does eat oats and little lambs eat ivy" played at the ceremony!

Then, the bride had forgotten her veil. Jumping to her aid, the maid of honor made a quick return home to get it, but on the way back, she had a wreck, which made her late getting to the church. So the ceremony had to be delayed and Bob's brother-in-law had to really be creative in playing the songs he could remember. It never occurred to us to get him a hymn book!

Just as we were finally ready to start the processional for the wedding party, the grandfather of the bride came wandering into the church and wobbled down to his place by his wife. At that point, the lady assigned to light the candles, who was dressed in a mini skirt, went to do so with a cigarette lighter. Her skirt didn't hide much when she was just standing, but when she reached up to light the candles, it was inappropriate attire. She was having difficulty lighting the candles, so I sent Bob out to light the candles and send her back to her seat even though it meant everyone seeing his way-too-short pants. At this point, we were already 45 minutes late. When Bob started to sing, "Because," the crowd nearly went into hysterics laughing because the song begins, "Everything went wrong, all the whole day long…." It was definitely one of the most memorable weddings I ever performed.

HOME IN MID-AMERICA

At Halloween, our kids were excited to go trick-or-treating around the neighborhood. When we found Terri's costume from the previous year, it was too small, and she started to cry because she had no costume. Carol Ann remembered that Joan, her sister-in-law, had sent some clothes for Terri after her daughter, Carol Denise, outgrew them. Near the top of the box, they found a blue velvet dress with a tattered white collar, and Carol Ann had an idea. "That looks good," she told Terri. "You can go as Phyllis Diller."

All that was left was to fix a Phyllis Diller hairdo! Terri had lots of hair, so Carol Ann had no problem 'ratting' it up into the scarecrow look that Phyllis always had. Soon, we were out with the children scouring the neighborhood. That night there was a fine mist that didn't really get us drenched but did make it extremely hard to comb her hair out afterward. A couple of days later, Terri went to a costume partly again dressed as Phyllis Diller because she loved that costume so much!

Bailey has always been a fisherman. Even as a little boy, he could fish for hours and not grow weary of it. A few miles from where we lived was a lake called Sunny Shores. It was stocked with fish, and parents were encouraged to bring their children to come and fish. We loved going there and, over time, got to know the proprietors well. We were so comfortable with the people there, we would take Bailey with his fishing pole, bait, and a sack lunch and let him stay there alone from mid-morning into the afternoon. We certainly could never do something like that now, but it was a great memory for him.

One of the highlights for our young church was to take the youth choir on a singing tour that took us all the way back to San Antonio.

Bob Brown and I went with the choir, and one of our college students, Lloyd Arnsmeyer joined Carol Ann and Linda Chandler as counselors Bob had all of them sing in the choir.

It was a wonderful trip, but toward the end, we learned some tragic news. One of our teenage boys, George Godfrey, who did not make the trip, had drowned in a lake east of Kansas City. It was difficult to tell the choir about George after we had finished our last concert at Calvary Baptist Church in Tyler, Texas, where Bro. Johnny and Marti Beard were serving. Understandably, the news cast a somber mood on everyone and made for a sad trip home.

It was during this time that we added another staff member at Red Bridge. Irving and Jo Cook were serving in the St. Louis area, and we needed to add a full-time Minister of Education to our staff. After many phone calls and getting thorough information about their ministry, we brought them to Kansas City to meet with our staff and personnel committee. The Cooks were warmly received and soon moved with their five children to Red Bridge to join our young church team.

The Cooks bought a home about two blocks from the church. This proved to be very important because as our church grew we eventually ran out of space. So, our young adult Sunday School class met at the Cook's home every Sunday morning before coming to our auditorium for worship service. Their daughter, Joy, quickly became one of Terri's best friends. Because our two homes were close together, the girls spent many hours at each other's homes, and their family soon became cherished partners in ministry and lifelong friends.

HOME IN MID-AMERICA

After the April 4, 1968, assassination of Martin Luther King, riots broke out several days later as the city boiled over when the school board refused to close schools in observance of MLK's funeral. The protestors began at City Hall and made their way south along the Paseo. When the protests became violent, the Missouri National Guard was called in. They brought in tanks and heavily armed troops and bivouacked in Minor Park, which was only a short distance from our home.

During the riots, five people were killed, 20 wounded, and over 100 arrested. Although the tensions were high, the unrest was contained. This was due largely to an incredible joint effort of pastors from both the Caucasian and the African American churches. It took several weeks of working together, but tensions eventually calmed down, and normal daily life returned.

In the spring of 1968, we held a revival led by Mike Brumley, a former major league baseball player. He had been signed with the Brooklyn Dodgers and played in their minor league system before coming to the majors leagues. He earned the nickname 'Iron Mike' for having caught every game of his rookie year in 1964. After playing in New York, Mike was traded to the Washington Senators and began preaching even while signed with the Senators. We had a great revival and formed a fast friendship.

Through Mike, I met another major league baseball player, Don Demeter. Don played in the major leagues from 1956-1967. Don was signed by the Brooklyn Dodgers in 1956 and later moved with the team to Los Angeles. During his years with them, he set a major league record for 266 innings of error-free games in the outfield. He also had a near-perfect .980 fielding percentage in his career and hit 163 home runs before retiring in 1968.

We closed out 1968 and welcomed 1969 with Mike and Carol Brumley and Don and Betty Demeter in Oklahoma City. On New Year's Eve, we celebrated at the Demeter's. Joining our three families for that evening was Jerry and Shelly Reimer. Jerry was a full-time evangelist and a member at First Southern Baptist Church in Del City, along with the Demeters and Brumleys. It was one of the most enjoyable evenings ever with these precious friends.

Jerry had come up with a hilarious game that we played for several hours. He would read an unusual, and usually unknown, word and give us four choices for the dictionary definition. If we picked out the correct one, we would get points, but if not, we lost points. We got delirious as we played it and welcomed in the new year.

The next night Mike and I went to the Oklahoma City Invitational basketball tournament. It was one of the most popular tournaments in the country at the time. I will never forget that night and how cold it was outside and inside. It was terribly cold outside and not much better inside because the arena where the tournament was held was also the arena where the hockey team played. Just beneath the basketball court was a layer of plywood over the ice that extended to the sidelines where we sat.

Despite the cold, the game was incredible. It was a key game in the tournament that pitted St. John's University against Louisiana State University. St. John's had a set of 6'10" twins who were very intimidating, but LSU had Pete Maravich. Watching 'Pistol Pete' play that night was unforgettable. He scored nearly every time he shot; his game was basketball wizardry at its very best. We weren't surprised

HOME IN MID-AMERICA

in the years afterward to watch his career in the NBA take off and for his legacy to be known as one of the most exciting basketball players ever.

In early spring, 1969, I preached a revival at First Baptist Church of Chillicothe, Missouri. During the revival, an early spring snowstorm hit the Midwest with snow so severe the schools were canceled for the first time in decades. The pastor was greatly concerned the weather would prevent people from coming to the revival, but I thought it was a blessing in disguise.

Though getting around that day was not easy, we kept at it, trudging through the snow to make visits. By the time the afternoon was over, we had seen 12 people make professions of faith. That evening, as the temperatures dipped and the icy and snowy conditions prevailed, we only had about 50 people in attendance, but had eight or nine public professions of faith. We asked ourselves, 'Who but God?' It was a wonderful reminder that we can trust the circumstances to God.

We had so many special friends while at Red Bridge. In addition to Jeff and Fran Jefferies, we had a special friendship with Norm Sanders. He was a young African-American minister we had met during the Billy Graham Crusade. He would often attend Red Bridge and always come to our home for lunch. His friendship was one of the best relationships we had while in Red Bridge. When we left for Oklahoma, he wrote a special note with a poem that spoke of how only God can tell us when to go and come. It came at just the right time as we grieved leaving Red Bridge. Norm married the daughter of an African-American evangelist who served with the Billy Graham Association and was on staff of the Billy Graham Evangelistic Association for years.

WHO BUT GOD! RIDING THE WHIRLWIND
JIMMY AND CAROL ANN DRAPER

I have mentioned several times about the fun times our family had over the years. When we would leave Kansas City heading to Lake Jackson or anywhere else, we would stop along the way to get a soft drink from time to time. The routine was always the same: I would ask what everyone wanted, but then I would order all cokes. When I got back to the car, I would ask who wanted the different drinks and give each one of them a coke—regardless of what they had requested. For a long time, they didn't know the difference, but they finally caught on to me, and I had to stop the charade!

Carol Ann was always incredible at keeping my clothes cleaned and ironed. While we were in Kansas City, the rage in dress shirts was a no-iron, no-wrinkle shirt made out of 'dectaline' material. All she had to do was wash them and have them drip dry, and they were ready to go again. One Saturday evening, after she had prepared the shirts, I took them out of the closet and hung them behind the door in the bathroom. Then I called Carol Ann and told her that I didn't have any dress shirts to wear for church the next morning. She came into the bedroom and said, "Get down on your knees and beg forgiveness. I have already fixed the shirts, and they are here in the closet." With that, she opened the closet door, but there were no shirts to be found. It took her a few minutes before she realized what I had done, but we had a good laugh about the disappearing shirts.

In Spring 1969, Homer Martinez came to preach a revival for us at Red Bridge. Homer shared with some of the folks that he was taking a trip to Israel at the beginning of the next year. Unbeknownst to Carol Ann or me, the church members began to talk among themselves and arranged for us to make that trip with Homer. It took several months for them to make this dream trip happen, but they rallied as a church to give us this precious gift.

It was during a Wednesday evening service in July when our members presented the gift. They had placed a miniature TWA plane next to a world globe and open Bible on the communion table and a sign which read "Christmas in July". When the service began, they presented us with the gift of going to the Holy Land with Homer and his wife, Carmen. It was a wonderful dream come true!

By early December, our two great friends from Oklahoma City, Don Demeter and Mike Brumley, called to tell me that John Bisagno had resigned as pastor of First Southern Baptist Church of Del City, Oklahoma, and would soon be moving to serve at First Baptist Church in Houston. Both were still playing baseball at the time and wanted me to pray about coming to be their pastor, something that had never occurred to me.

They checked in again as it got closer to Christmas and to see if I had been praying about making the move. In response, I asked them, "Did either of you ever sign a contract before you received it?" We had a good laugh, but that was the end of our discussions.

In the meantime, John Bisagno had given the church two months' notice before his actual move and had asked the church to appoint a pulpit committee to begin the search for a new pastor. The church agreed, and the committee began to meet. John had recommended three names to the committee, including mine. I had met John many times in evangelistic meetings in Missouri during our time at Red Bridge. Truth be told, I was too excited about the Holy Land trip to think much further about the calls from Don and Mike.

The trip was one of those unforgettable times for us. I was so much better able to understand Scripture as we visited the actual sites of Jesus' earthly ministry. I honestly think I learned more about the Bible from traveling there than I had learned before. In the week following our return, the Billy Graham Association released their film about Israel called "His Land." We went to the premier and wept through most of it as we relived the cherished moments of our visit to Israel.

A week later, Carol Ann and I went to the State Evangelism Conference at First Baptist Church in St. John, Missouri. We sat just behind our friend Dick Cole who turned around to talk with us. When he asked Carol Ann, "Well, are you packing yet?" she didn't know what he was talking about and reminded him that we had barely gotten unpacked from our trip. Dick didn't waste any time pointing toward me and said, "Jimmy's going to be the next pastor at First Southern Baptist Del City."

A week later on Saturday night, our church basketball team had played a basketball game in our church league. I must have caught something while playing because I woke up in the middle of the night terribly sick. I also had the distinct thought, "The pulpit committee from Del City is going to be here today." By daylight, I was dehydrated and had lost eight pounds and had deep, dark places under my eyes. I inadvertently made my appearance look even worse than it already was for Sunday services by wearing a black dress shirt and an army green suit and tie to preach that morning.

Between services as I was making my way to greet our visitors, I ran smack into Don Demeter. I was shocked but also remembered the premonition I had about the pulpit committee being present that day. Don was an alternate on that committee and came when one of the committee members could not make the trip.

Of the three names John Bisagno had given the committee, Dick Cole's name was also one of them. He was pastor at First Baptist Church in Raytown, Missouri, one of the largest churches in the state, in the east central part of Kansas City. The pulpit committee had come to Kansas City to hear both of us since we were so close together.

Shortly after lunch that day, our phone rang; the pulpit committee wanted to come by the house for a visit. We had a good visit for over an hour, and the connection was immediate with the committee. When I objected that I was not qualified to pastor First Southern Baptist Church, one of the deacons on the committee, Cecil Tilley, said, "Brother Jim, if our next pastor is now on a Choctaw Indian Reservation, we don't care, we just want God's man. And if you are God's man and you don't come, you will be miserable!"

Before they left, they asked me to pray for them. When I finished my prayer, each of them was weeping. It was a sure sign something was in the making. I thought they were going to hear Dick Cole that night. However, about 30 minutes after they left, the chairman of the committee, Jess Easton, called and said that they did not want to hear Dick that night and were going home to pray over our visit and would be in touch with us later.

I spent the next few days with Luther Dyer preaching at regional evangelism conferences across Missouri. On Thursday of that week, we arrived at the First Baptist Church of Sikeston, Missouri. The pastor told me that I had received a call from Oklahoma and needed to return it. It was Jess Easton, chairman of the Pastor Search

WHO BUT GOD! RIDING THE WHIRLWIND
JIMMY AND CAROL ANN DRAPER

Committee at First Southern, and he wanted to know if Carol Ann and I would come to Del City to have further discussion about coming as pastor of First Southern.

We flew to Oklahoma City the next week for the meeting, and the pulpit committee member who had been unable to come hear me preach met with us that afternoon. The committee wanted him to have some time with us while we were there. We had a fast but incredible time with the committee, and plans were made for us to come preach in view of a call a few weeks later on February 22, 1970.

We brought the whole family that weekend. The church gave us a unanimous vote, complete with a standing ovation when the vote was announced. Less than a month later, on March 15, 1970, we began our ministry at First Southern Baptist Church in Del City, Oklahoma, exactly six weeks after the Bisagnos had moved to Houston! Who but God could have orchestrated such a whirlwind of decisions and activities in such a short period of time?

In 1969 we had begun construction on a new auditorium for Red Bridge. At the time we left to go to Del City, the building was taking shape, but was not completed. We were blessed to be able to return for the building dedication.

We had served five years at Red Bridge. We came alongside wonderful, friendly, and loving people and God did His work among us. We made many new friends who have remained friends over many years; others now await us in heaven as we await our own coronation into the Lord's presence. We remain cognizant that we are all terminal and that none of us will miss our appointment with death. We each have a limited time to live for the Lord, and that time is quickly gone.

HOME IN MID-AMERICA

As we write these pages, Carol Ann and I have been married nearly 64 years, and our entire life seems like it has happened so quickly. What a privilege we all have to live in such a way that God is honored and glorified. We do what the Apostle Paul directed in 2 Corinthians 4:18, "We do not focus on what is seen, but what is unseen. For what is seen in temporary, but what is unseen is eternal!"

We learned so much about ourselves and God's provision and faithfulness at Red Bridge. Those were the Camelot years for us, and the opportunities God opened during those years were staggering as we look back at them. God prepared us for the rest of our lives through those wonderful experiences at Red Bridge!

MY FAVORITE

Terri, Bailey, Carol Ann, Randy & Jimmy
1967

WHO BUT GOD! RIDING THE WHIRLWIND
JIMMY AND CAROL ANN DRAPER

Jimmy, Carol Ann and Jimmy's brother Charlie

Randy & Terri

Jimmy & Terri 1969

Terri & Bailey

Terri & Carol Ann

Kids at Halloween

HOME IN MID-AMERICA

George & Lynda Harris Carol Ann & Jimmy

Jimmy, Randy & Bailey
July 1969

Jimmy & Carol Ann

WHO BUT GOD! RIDING THE WHIRLWIND
JIMMY AND CAROL ANN DRAPER

First Southern Baptist Church

WHERE THE WIND COMES SWEEPING DOWN THE PLAINS

FIRST SOUTHERN BAPTIST CHURCH
DEL CITY, OKLAHOMA

D el City is located in the 'Frontier Country' region of Central Oklahoma. It is a region dominated by cross timbers, which means it is an area of both prairies and patches of forest on the eastern extent of the Great Plains. It is also at the heart of another 'Tornado Alley' and is one of the most tornado-prone areas in the United States. The city borders Oklahoma City, Midwest City, and Tinker Air Force Base.

Tinker Air Force Base opened in 1941 during the Second World War as a maintenance base for military equipment. It remains the largest single-site employer in Oklahoma, with 7,500 civilian and military personnel. It is the home of the 75th Maintenance Group, which has five sub-divisions of workers.

WHO BUT GOD! RIDING THE WHIRLWIND
JIMMY AND CAROL ANN DRAPER

First Southern Baptist Church was founded in 1951 and had several excellent pastors in the 14 years before John Bisagno arrived in 1965. Our arrival in 1970 made us the fifth pastor for the church. Under John Bisagno, the church had become one of the most effective churches in the nation in winning people to Christ and baptizing them. John had led the people to be upbeat, to follow their pastor and staff, and to not be afraid of making needed changes. When we arrived, the church was already engaged and moving forward aggressively.

We moved into a very small house for the first few months while the parsonage was being remodeled. All our garment boxes and lots of others were in that small house and garage. To walk through our house was like walking through a maze of boxes. On our first Easter there, we woke up to 3" of snow on the ground. It was our first white Easter ever!

After several months in Del City, Irving and Jo Cook came through and wanted to take Terri home with them for a few days. I was in an all-day staff meeting, and Carol Ann called to ask me about us letting her do that. My secretary had stepped out of the office, and my associate pastor, Jake Self, was returning to our staff meeting when the phone rang. He told Carol Ann that I had left instructions for no one to interrupt, and he would give me the message but could not get me on the phone right then.

Carol Ann talked it over with Cookie and Jo and decided to let Terri go on with them. When she told my mother about it, mom was very upset. She said, "It just isn't right. I can't talk to my Jimmie (meaning my dad), but you should be able to talk with your Jimmy anytime you want to do so." Soon thereafter, I had a direct, unlisted

WHERE THE WIND COMES SWEEPING DOWN THE PLAINS

phone installed in my office and have done so ever since! I never wanted to be where Carol Ann was unable to reach me again!

We moved into the parsonage at the beginning of the summer when the remodeling was complete. The garage had been made into two bedrooms for Randy and Bailey. Mother and Terri each had their own room in addition to ours. It was a great place to live and less than a mile from the church. Del City High School property was behind our house and the football field was directly behind our house. We held the Starlite Crusade every July in that stadium.

That summer was fun with many friends from Kansas City coming to see us and new friends stopping by, but it really was a whirlwind summer. Thankfully, our children made friends quickly. One of Terri's new friends was Brenda, whose parents were deaf. That prompted Terri to learn sign language so she could better communicate with them. It wasn't long before she became very good at it.

Bailey was elected the seventh grade 'favorite' in his school and was required to attend the dance where the favorites from each grade were presented. He didn't want to go and didn't want to dance. Carol Ann tried to teach him to dance, but she didn't know how to dance either. Bailey agreed to go to the dance all dressed up but was quite happy when he found out his counterpart, the seventh-grade girl 'favorite,' didn't want to dance! The went through with the presentation but didn't make it to the dancefloor.

Looking back at my years at First Southern, I can easily say I learned more from them than they did from me. I had never even dreamed of doing some of the things they were already doing. At times I felt like I was holding a tiger by the tail. Activities swirled everywhere like a three-ring circus. It was just hard to keep up with the whirlwind of activities and the speed it was all happening.

From the first day I stepped on the campus of First Southern, I was the pastor. Several weeks after I got there, I met with the Personnel Committee. The chairman of the committee was Dr. Ed Blick, chairman of the Aerospace, Science, and Mathematics Department at the University of Oklahoma. The Tinker Air Force base hospital commander was also on that committee as was a locally well-known doctor. After an opening prayer, Ed looked at me and said, "Now pastor, we are your personnel committee. Tell us what to do, and we'll do it!" This was the kind of amazing church we inherited from John Bisagno!

I believe that First Southern Baptist Church was the greatest church I have ever seen in my life. We had a praise team and band like many contemporary churches do today, only we had it in 1970. The praise team was named 'The Revolution.' They were outstanding and provided the music for our early worship service on Sunday mornings. They were so good they traveled with Governor David Hall when he had Town Hall meetings across the state. It was their job to warm up the crowd before the governor took the stage.

First Southern was a remarkable church because of the incredible flexibility and generosity of the people. On our first anniversary, I invited Larry Walker to come and preach revival services with us. On the first Sunday morning of the revival, the chairman of the personnel committee, Bob Stephens, sat nearby with a large gift-wrapped box for us. Even though Larry had no idea what was inside, he jokingly leaned over and said, "It's a car!"

WHERE THE WIND COMES SWEEPING DOWN THE PLAINS

Bob presented the box to me and when I opened the box, it truly was a car—a child's toy car. As I pulled the toy car out of the box, Bob presented me with the keys to a new car that was parked just outside the auditorium. That was when I learned the church made it a habit to provide a new leased car to the pastor each year at his anniversary! What a wonderful gift!

The hippie movement, and the subsequent Jesus Movement that grew out of it, was going full steam at that time. While many churches in the very conservative Oklahoma City area were preaching against long hair and mini-skirts, First Southern welcomed everyone—including all the hippies that constantly came through Oklahoma City. Our members realized the problem many churches had was focusing too much on how the hippies looked instead of what was in their hearts.

I preached many times with barefoot hippies in cut-off blue jeans sitting in the altar. After one such Sunday, two young women stayed to talk with me. I sat on the steps of our platform as they sat on the floor, and both of them prayed to receive Christ. They came back for the evening service, and in what our members considered to be 'clothed and in their right minds.' I had never mentioned their clothes in our conversation, but the Lord convicted them once they were saved.

One year we baptized 743 people because the church was willing to change and do whatever it took to get the gospel to those around us. When we built our new auditorium, we built one that was big enough to baptize six people at a time! We continued to host the special events and attractions designed to reach the lost that were already in place when we arrived. John Bisagno had begun the Starlite Crusade in the Del City High School football stadium every July and did so during his years as pastor. He preached every Starlite as I did when I became pastor. He believed in taking times during the year that were usually low in attendance and making them into big events. It was a two-week event that fell over the 4th of July and our anniversary. We continued the tradition for four more years and celebrated our wedding anniversary every year at Starlite!

In many ways, the Starlite Crusade became bigger than life. People came from all over Oklahoma and well beyond. It was not only a community event, but one that reached people hundreds of miles away. Many even planned their vacations just to spend a few days at Starlite. The stadium held around 5,000 people, and we filled it each night with overflow guests sitting on the track and in lawn chairs.

In the second year I preached at Starlite, our anniversary fell on Saturday evening. About noon that day, I asked Carol Ann if she would share her testimony during the service. She did a fantastic job but took a bit more time than I had planned. She did so well though, I decided not to preach and instead issued the invitation to come forward. We both had the privilege to watch as many responded that night.

The next morning, I preached the sermon I had planned to preach on Saturday evening, and there were 63 who responded to the invitation. It was evident that God's plan all along was for Carol Ann to give her testimony on Saturday and me to preach that sermon on Sunday. We believed it to be confirmation that God was faithful to show us He was still sovereign and would lead us as He pleased.

WHERE THE WIND COMES SWEEPING DOWN THE PLAINS

We enjoyed some great, well-known Christian individuals and groups during our years hosting the Starlite. Traditionally, the Continental Singers opened the first few nights, followed by the Imperial Quartet on later nights. Each year we had several Christian celebrities speak as well as Governor Hall.

We moved into a new home just before the Starlite Crusade one year. Carol Ann was gone for the opening weekend of the crusade, so I invited eight of the Continental Singers to stay at our new house. It turned out to be a week of several unexpected events. First, it rained torrentially, and every window in the house leaked! We had towels in every window. Second, I had just started construction of a small metal storage building in the backyard, and the rain and wind completely destroyed it, leaving pieces all over the neighborhood the next day. Third, the weather prevented us from holding the crusade outside, so it was moved to our new auditorium for that one night. We were able to rebuild the stadium platform and continue the services there.

On the Tuesday morning that the Continental Singers were leaving for their next concert, and I went to see the bus off. One of the group's most outstanding singers was Joy Steele. She was from Hamilton, Montana, and was raised in a Lutheran Church. She lit up the platform when she sang, and our congregation responded enthusiastically. As she was getting on the bus, I had one of those out-of-the-body experiences I just can't explain. I heard myself tell her, "Joy, if you ever want to come back, let us know, and we'll send you a plane ticket to come back to see us."

We did not hear from her for several months, but in November, she called and said she wanted to come right after Christmas. I sent her a pre-paid ticket, and she arrived at our house around New

Year's. Grandmother had twin beds in her bedroom, so Joy stayed with her for about three weeks. During that time, Joy hung out with our family and was at the church a lot. She was engaged to a young man in Ohio but was not comfortable with the engagement. She had planned to meet him in Dayton, Ohio, later in January. In the meantime, she realized that she had never been saved as we began to share the gospel with her. For the first time in her life, she understood the meaning of the gospel, and on the day before she was to fly to Ohio, she was saved.

At the same time, the Oklahoma Baptist Evangelism Conference was taking place in our church. The state evangelism director was C.B. 'Bill' Hogue. The conference was always held at First Southern. He always gave us 15 minutes on the program of the opening night of the conference each year, so I called him and asked if I could baptize Joy at the conference that night. He readily agreed, and Joy was the first person to be baptized at our State Evangelism Conference.

The next day I was scheduled to go to Dayton, Ohio, to preach at the Ohio Baptist Evangelism Conference. Joy rode with me to Dayton to meet her fiancée and only took an empty suitcase. She broke up with her fiancée and returned with me after I spoke at the Ohio Conference. For the next seven months, she lived with us and stayed in Grandmother's room.

During that time, a handsome young banker joined our church. He was a recent graduate of Oklahoma State University and had his sights set on a banking career. His name was Charles McLain, but everyone called him 'Smokey.' When he met Joy, they both had an immediate attraction and began to date. Their relationship moved

WHERE THE WIND COMES SWEEPING DOWN THE PLAINS

along quickly, and I had the privilege to perform their wedding ceremony that July.

Since then, they have been some of our dearest friends. Not long after they were married, Smokey realized God was calling him into ministry, and he made his decision public. He received his seminary training at Southwestern Baptist Theological Seminary in Fort Worth, and served many years as pastor, and was an Associational Director of Missions in Omaha, Nebraska, for many years. From there he went to Festus, Missouri, to be pastor. Most recently, he has been in transition into retirement from serving as pastor at First Baptist Church of Festus/Crystal City, Missouri. He is an excellent preacher and has always allowed me the privilege of preaching for him in churches he has served.

Who but God could have put such a sequence together that summer that began at Starlite and ended with Joy getting married to Smokey the next year? Surely His ways are beyond our understanding, but we can always trust Him!

At our new home, I had a basketball goal placed at the end of the driveway. The goal was mounted on a tall 4" x 4" pole. One afternoon when I came home, the pole was broken off about 18" above the ground and was leaning toward the house. I wondered how that could possibly have happened. I discovered that mother had backed the car out even though she had not driven in quite some time. When she hit the pole, she decided it was best just to pull back into the garage. I had to ask her, "Mother, what were you thinking? You haven't driven in years." Undaunted, she replied, "Well, I could if I wanted to!" Her positive 'I can do it' attitude came out all throughout her life, and we loved it.

WHO BUT GOD! RIDING THE WHIRLWIND
JIMMY AND CAROL ANN DRAPER

One day a long-haired stranger came to our door when Carol Ann was there, but I was not. He introduced himself as Darrell Davis and said, "I have something for you." With that, he began to unload a round, antique kitchen table his recently deceased mother had designated for us upon her death. His mother was my Aunt Sugar, the daughter of the lady who had raised my dad in her home. My daddy's mother died while he was just an infant, and he was sent to live with Grandmother Macomber. In one of my mother's visits to Aunt Sugar, she had remarked that Carol Ann would love that table whenever Aunt Sugar was ready to get rid of it.

She told mother that if I would officiate at her funeral, the table would be ours. I held up my part of the bargain and flew in a small private plane with mother to Malvern, Arkansas, to preach Aunt Sugar's funeral several years later. Darrell was fulfilling her promise to mother, and just to be sure, Aunt Sugar had pasted a note under the table instructing it was to be given to Carol Ann.

During our years in Del City, I wrote my first book. Jack Taylor was instrumental in getting it published. His book, 'The Key to Triumphant Living,' had been the best-selling book Broadman Press had ever had up to that time, so he had strong connections. He made the call to Broadman Press, and my book, 'The Church Christ Approves,' was soon published. It was a thrill to see that book become a reality.

On our fourteenth wedding anniversary, I surprised Carol Ann with a bicycle-built-for- two. We enjoyed it both times we actually rode it! The kids thoroughly enjoyed it, but we never got around to riding it regularly. The bike was a real disappointment for Carol Ann because she was expecting a king-sized bed, not a bicycle!

WHERE THE WIND COMES SWEEPING DOWN THE PLAINS

During our years in Del City, our home became known as the 'Draper Motel.' Our home had always been open to others, but it kicked into high gear one summer, with 14 people staying with us for three months.

One Sunday after several hippies were saved, one of the couples was expecting their first child. We couldn't turn them away, so we just brought them home with us for several weeks until after the baby was born. One day they just picked up and left, but it was our prayer that our home had been used by God to cement their commitment to Christ.

We also had two other revival crusades during the year in addition to Vacation Bible School and Youth Camp. There was rarely a time when we were not baptizing or seeing converts in our services. The night we had the business meeting as a church to vote on building a new sanctuary, we did not have time for a sermon. I just extended an appeal for folks to be saved after the business meeting, and we had six professions of faith! Unusual things like that happened all the time at First Southern.

Our music minister, Aubrie McSwain, had come to Del City from the Northside Baptist Church in Weatherford, Texas. Without a doubt, Aubrie was one of the best, if not the best, platform musician I have ever known. He grew up in Center, Texas, and excelled at playing the cornet (trumpet). Early in his adult years, he had sung in quartettes that backed up Elvis Pressley, and he had been an extra in movies while he was in California. He could generate excitement in a congregation quicker than anyone I had ever seen. His expertise with the choir and with our singing groups was excellent. It was his efforts that created and developed the Revolution into an excellent singing team and band.

Aubrie was excellent at all kinds of music. Not only did we have the best contemporary music to be found, but we also did classical Christian music. We did all the Christian youth musicals, like 'Celebrate Life,' 'Natural High,' 'Good News,' and many others. We did the 'Seven Last Words' focusing on the seven last words of Christ and featuring me dressed in first-century attire and preaching the message of each word presented. We did one word from the cross each night for 7 evenings with full choir and orchestra. We also sang the great hymns of the faith alongside the more contemporary and classical.

For Easter one year, we moved our service to the Del City High School basketball facility because it was larger than our auditorium at the time. Paul Harvey was a nationwide radio host of a very popular syndicated program in those years. He was also the top news commentator in the country at that time. His programs were always well researched and usually dealt with events no one else knew about. It was an exciting time when he did a full broadcast about his visit to First Southern the next week.

Paul Taylor came to be our youth minister for several years. While he was with us, a report came to me that one of our deacons had been very verbal in criticizing Paul in the halls of the youth area on a Sunday morning. When I heard about it, I called Paul and the deacon and asked them to meet with me at the church before our services that evening. When we got together, I told the deacon what I had heard, and he admitted saying some things. I told him that he had just violated his oath as a deacon not to be a destroyer of the unity of the church, but to be a unifier.

WHERE THE WIND COMES SWEEPING DOWN THE PLAINS

As soon as I finished telling him that, he broke out in tears and confessed what he had done and asked Paul for forgiveness. We prayed together, and he earnestly prayed for God to forgive him. This was a classic example of the kind of people we served with at First Southern—not perfect people, but people sensitive to the convicting power of the Holy Spirit and quick to repent when mistakes were made.

I worked hard to model that behavior as well because I remembered the meeting I had with the deacons when we came in view of a call at First Southern. Deacon Cecil Tilley said, "Brother Jimmy, you may not always be right, but you will always be our pastor. We just ask that you not make the same mistake twice!" Several times I had to apologize to the deacons and remind them, "We won't do that again!"

When Paul resigned to become a pastor, Bennie Powell became our minister of youth. In keeping with the nature of First Southern, one particular event was very typical. One Sunday morning, Benny was baptizing in the early service, and when he stepped into the water, he loudly said, "Oh, this water is cold!" The congregation broke into laughter, but what happened next was stunning.

Bennie was to baptize an older lady. When he got ready to lay her back to baptize her, she panicked and threw her arms around Bennie's neck. Bennie looked around for a moment as if to ask, "what do I do now?" and then took a deep breath as both of them went under the water. The congregation broke into clapping, cheers, amens, and a lot of laughter. It was just genuine believers celebrating things that were funny, but deeply spiritual in meaning. They were not uptight about anything and realized that some things need special celebrations! What might bring frowns and criticism in most churches, were celebrated because of the sincere, innocent spirit of the people. Not much ever seemed out of place at First Southern.

Herschel Creasman came to serve as minister of education. Herschel, his wife, Joanne, and children lived with us the first three months they were on staff. They would stay with us during the week, and when the many visitors would come on the weekends to visit with us, they would all pack their clothes in paper sacks and move out to stay with someone else for the weekend. He later came to First Baptist Church Dallas to serve with me there.

One of the best staff members I ever served with was Jake Self. He grew up in the oil fields of Oklahoma and was an outgoing country boy. As my associate pastor, Bro. Jake visited the hospitals and made sure to always tell the patients, "I am visiting for Bro. Jimmy." He was so convincing that he was truly representing me, people would often thank me for my hospital visit even though I had never visited them.

Bro. Jake was a quiet country philosopher. When one of the Independent Baptist Churches in Midwest City, Oklahoma, took out a full-page ad in the local newspaper to condemn First Southern for covering up the cross in the baptistry to create a set for a youth musical, it upset me greatly. Bro. Jake put it in perspective when he said, "Brother Jimmy, the higher up the flagpole you get, the lonelier and windier it gets!" I got the message. The more exposure one receives, the more criticisms are likely to come.

Bro. Jake was loved by everyone at First Southern. He was on staff when we arrived, and I was very thankful. The F5 tornado that tore through our area in 1999 killed 36 people, including Bro. Jake. We

WHERE THE WIND COMES SWEEPING DOWN THE PLAINS

learned of his death from his son, Phil, a doctor in Alva, Oklahoma. This is Phil's account of the day:

"That midafternoon a large tornado formed near Chickasha, Oklahoma, and began heading towards the Oklahoma City area. The television coverage showing the path it was traveling appeared to be approaching my parent's home.

"I called my mother to make sure she was aware. She did not know about the approaching storm because she had been soaking in the bathtub. I asked her what the weather looked like, and she said it looked pretty rough. Mom said, 'Gary England (the local weatherman) said we should take cover and I wanted to get Jake into the closet....oh.... The TV just went.....(phone disconnects).'

"Mom later related to me that she helped dad into a chair into the closet, and she knelt down over a cedar chest. As she was closing the door, the roof came off the house, and everything came in. She told me, 'I heard Jake call out, "Help me, Help me," and then he was silent. I knew he was gone.' A neighbor's minivan from two doors down had landed on the roofless closet. It settled to within about 3' of the floor and, because dad was in a chair, his upper torso was crushed, but mom was unscathed other than a small bruise on her left arm. It took rescuers over two hours to free my mom. Dad could not be taken from the home until noon the following day. A forklift was brought in and removed the minivan. As he was uncovered, a Bible was discovered resting on his chest."

The fact that a Bible was resting on his chest is a fitting testimony to the great love Bro. Jake had for the Word of God. Once he was saved from a very hard and sinful life, he clung to God's Word fiercely for the rest of his life. It is fitting that the item that was used to identify Jake during the hours before his body could be removed was his Bible, which had his name on it!

Phil's report continued: "When the phone disconnected, the only thing I knew is that they were without phone service or electricity, so I began to head their way. Normally this is about a three-hour drive, but as there had been 51 tornadoes across Oklahoma that day, we kept running into roadblocks of storm damage along the way. Approximately three hours after the storm, my mother was rescued from the debris and was taken to the hospital. She contacted me from there to let me know that she was okay, but dad that had passed away. After seven hours of driving, I met my mom at a friend's apartment. Surprisingly, she was actually in good spirits considering what she had been through.

"The following day, mom shared that her biggest fear would be that something happened to her and left Dad alone. He was 86 years old and, because of some dementia, mom had to help him with the activities of daily living. Mom was nine years his junior and lived independently another nine years. My feeling is that if mom had been killed and dad survived, it would have been a cruel joke. As it happened, my mom's prayer was answered, and dad had a very quick death. She later jokingly said, 'He always wanted to go to heaven in a chariot of fire, but he didn't have to take the whole neighborhood with him!'"

There was never another couple like Jake and Gelela! They touched all of our lives in a special way.

While in Del City, we began to make regular trips in the summertime to Uncle L.M.'s cabin on the Conejos River in southern Colorado. The cabin was simple but adequate. It did not have any

WHERE THE WIND COMES SWEEPING DOWN THE PLAINS

phone service, television sets, or radios. In many ways, it was boring yet liberating. On the way to the cabin one year, we bought 20 pounds of cherries beside the road as we came through Santa Fe, New Mexico, for 50 cents a pound! What a bargain for our family that loved cherries! We managed to eat all 20 pounds that week and fed the pits to the chipmunks.

Bailey passed his time easily fishing in the river. The Colorado Wildlife Program kept it stocked with rainbow trout each week. He never tired of fishing in the river. One day after he had been out in the water with waders for several hours, Carol Ann went out and asked him, "How many have you caught?" He replied, "About three or four." This prompted Carol Ann to ask, "How can you say you are having a good time when you haven't caught many fish?" Without batting an eye, Bailey answered, "The same way you can shop all day and not buy anything and say you had a good time!" Right then, Carol Ann knew that Bailey just liked to fish!

While Bailey was busy fishing in the Conejos, Terri and I went hiking in the mountains. We left early in the morning and did not return until almost dinner time. We had no compass, just the river to guide us. When it was time to head home, we walked toward the river, and headed east until we got to the cabin. It was an incredible day for both of us. High up in the mountains, Terri and I carved our initials in an aspen tree. Believe it or not, we found that tree again in a subsequent visit to that mountain.

During our hike, we passed through pockets of snow that had not completely melted from the previous winter's snowfalls. We had taken some food and supplies but had long since exhausted our meager fare shortly after noon. We kept on and finally turned toward the river, both pretty tired by this time. At one point, Terri was so tired, she just laid on the ground and said, "Just go on without me, I'll just die right here! I am too tired to go on." We rallied and trudged on toward the river and then on to the cabin just before dark. Carol Ann and the boys had begun to worry about us, and we were happy to all be back together again, safe and sound in the cabin and with a great meal waiting for us.

One year at Uncle L.M.'s cabin, Carol Ann brought along a large jigsaw puzzle with 2,000 pieces. Her idea was for us to work on it together and finish it by the end of the week. I got a little too engrossed in putting it together and had it completed in 18 hours!

James Robison was a frequent visiting preacher over the years at First Southern. We also had other evangelists who were members of the church. Mike Brumley was an evangelist even while he was a major league baseball player. He preached during the offseason and went into full-time ministry when he retired from baseball. Richard Hogue and his evangelistic team were members, as were Jerry Reimer and Darcy Hodges. First Southern was a church skilled in welcoming both the lost and the evangelists and a place where both would find genuine Christian faith.

We built our first house about a mile from the church in Del City. Our dear friend, Frank Favazza, drew up the plans for us, and a local builder built it. It was two stories with five bedrooms and a small study. Four bedrooms and two baths were upstairs, and Grandmother's bedroom and bath were downstairs. It was a great experience building that house. We especially loved that the house was situated on one-and-a-half acres. We had an open house for the

WHERE THE WIND COMES SWEEPING DOWN THE PLAINS

deacons, and they presented us with a riding lawnmower. It came in very handy with so much yard to mow.

We lived there just 14 months before God led us to First Baptist Church in Dallas. It was hard to leave First Southern and our new home. We had always pledged to be obedient and knew that when God says, "Go!" we were meant to go. In seeking God's will in the decision to go to Dallas, Carol Ann and I both asked God to give us a Scripture to confirm our decision. I was preaching a revival in Vista, California, during that time and diligently sought the Lord for an answer. All He gave me was Philippians 4:6, which simply told me not to worry about anything but keep everything before the Lord. Carol Ann was at home in Lake Jackson, and when the pastor preached from 1 Chronicles 28:20, she took it as if the Lord had given her that verse for our lives at that time.

Since she has always made it a habit to put her name in the Scripture, the verse in the Living Bible read, "Carol Ann, be strong and courageous and get to work. Don't be frightened by the size of the task, for the Lord my God is with you. He will not forsake you. He will see to it that everything is finished correctly." With that promise in her hand and heart, she knew that we had to go and depend on Him alone for our needs and strength. It was a daunting assignment for us, and we would need His power and strength daily.

I became good friends with the Governor of Oklahoma, David Hall. He was one of the most gifted public servants I have ever known. He had our family to the Governor's mansion for meals, shared his testimony at the Starlite Crusades, and even declared 'Jimmy Draper Day' in Oklahoma just before we moved to Dallas. Sadly, he was caught in a bribery scandal, was forced to resign as governor, and ultimately spent several years in a federal prison. I considered it such a tragedy because the man I had come to know was a charismatic and attractive leader and could well have been elected President of the United States.

One of our stand-out members at First Southern was an African-American single mother named Dot Gray. She had several children, including a son named Erastus, who became best friends with Randy. One Sunday night after the service, Randy and Erastus came to me with a question—they wanted to know if Erastus could come to live with us. I agreed immediately even though I didn't know the circumstances at the time.

We later learned Erastus had been targeted by several white students attempting to bully him in his high school in Oklahoma City. He resisted their aggressive behavior and ended up sitting on them to hold them down until the school authorities could get there. Not having seen any of the struggle, the school officials made the choice to suspend Erastus and his two attackers for three days.

In the meantime, Dot was in the process of buying a house in Del City, but Erastus couldn't attend Del City High School unless he lived in Del City. In order to do that, he had to have a Del City address. That is where we came in. It was a detailed process that involved me having to go and certify that I was assuming legal custody of Erastus. We got the approval, and Erastus stayed with us as a member of our family until their house was completed.

Having Erastus living with us made for some memorable laughs, too. One Sunday night, our youth choir broke out in laughter in the midst of my sermon. I found out later I had made some reference

WHERE THE WIND COMES SWEEPING DOWN THE PLAINS

that seemed strange to Erastus, and he had turned to Randy and said loudly, "We need to talk with our dad about that!"

On another occasion, Carol Ann found Erastus sunbathing in the back yard. His coloring was much lighter than most African-American men, but to be tanning himself seemed strange. When Carol Ann asked him about it, he said that he could not let Bailey get browner than he was!

Probably the most memorable moment of our time with Erastus happened the second time I preached at Falls Creek Baptist Assembly for one of the youth camps. For six weeks each summer, over 5,000 youth and sponsors gathered each week at Falls Creek for a time of preaching, singing, discipleship, and building friendships. I had preached once in 1971 and was scheduled to preach again in 1974. When the time came for me to preach, we had already been in Dallas for nearly ten months.

Carol Ann, Randy, and I went on to Falls Creek for the week while Bailey and Terri Jean had gone on a choir trip with First Baptist Dallas. During our week there, there was a large delegation of youth and sponsors from First Southern, including Erastus. After the opening service on Monday night, Randy complained to me about not introducing him during the service. At the time, I thought it was very unusual for Randy to bring this up, but that was because I didn't know the plan he and Erastus had concocted. I told him I would introduce him the next morning.

When the time came for me to preach, I mentioned my oldest son was there and that Bailey and Terri would join us on Wednesday. When I asked Randy to stand, Erastus stood up! The gasp that went through the crowd was audible. Those two had set me up as a joke and succeeded in a big way! We loved Erastus dearly and were so grateful to be his 'parents' even for a short while.

We made so many great friends in Del City. Bob and Frances Stephens became some of our very best friends. When our kids each got married, they came down for the weddings, and whenever we were near the Oklahoma City area, we always stayed with them. I performed their children's weddings, and when Bob and Frances died, it was my privilege to preach their memorial services.

There were so many more families—truly too many to mention, but there were some special standouts, including the Demeters, Brumleys, Tilleys, Pitmans, Cranfords, Wises, Powells, Stowells, Bakers, Martins, Cobbs, Reimers, Starkeys, and Allens. We had many young people go into ministry from First Southern. Those included Bob Simpson, who went on to become editor of the West Virginia Baptist newspaper; Mike Thompson got his doctorate and taught at Golden Gate Seminary before moving on to hold a special Chair for Religion at Oklahoma State University until his retirement.

Our family always enjoyed kicking back and having fun. That was never more the case than when we went from Del City to San Antonio and led the youth camp for Castle Hills Baptist Church there. Jack Taylor was pastor of Castle Hills First Baptist Church and had been one of my closest friends while we served in San Antonio. At camp, the youth tried every way they could to play pranks on me. It got to be a cat and mouse game for us.

One night I crawled into my sleeping bag to find they had emptied a can of shaving cream into the end of the bag. I never let on that I even noticed. Then they put salt where the sugar should have been at the dinner table, and I acted like I didn't notice. They even

WHERE THE WIND COMES SWEEPING DOWN THE PLAINS

rigged a large container of water up in the rafters and positioned it right over the place I usually stood to speak. They had a fishing line attached to so they could pull the line and dump the water on me. They dumped the water, but it didn't fall on me. They were getting increasingly frustrated that everything they tried to do to me failed.

After the camp, we stayed over for me to preach on Sunday at Castle Hills. The week had been great, and we had connected well with the youth at the camp. I have always had many friends there and have preached over 75 times there over the years. Jack had gotten wind that the youth were going to try one more prank and were coming out after the service on Sunday night to 'Teepee' their home. We were not to be outdone! Jack and I climbed on the roof, armed with hoses connected to water hydrants, and were ready to spray the kids as soon as they showed up. Our wives and the Taylor kids were armed with water balloons and shaving cream. We had the hoses shut down, but the water faucets were on full force, and we were ready for them!

When the kids arrived, we launched an attack on them as they began to toss roll after roll of toilet paper into the trees. Our kids and wives joined in the chaos. It was a blast until one of the kids realized if they cut the water faucets off, we had no ammunition. When the water balloons and shaving cream ran out, we were free game for them. It was a fun night with a lot of laughter for all of us.

One summer Sunday afternoon in 1972, we rented a small theme park on the north side of Oklahoma City. After church, we all went to the park and brought a covered dish meal. After an afternoon of fun enjoying the park and the fellowship, we had our evening meal and then had a worship service. The Revolution sang, Aubrie led us all in singing, and I preached. It was a great time of fellowship, and there were many saved that night at the theme park.

Carol Ann had prayed for months, especially for her friend, Cindy Freese's dad. We had all been witnessing to him, and it was wonderful to see him saved that night. It had been my privilege to lead Cindy's husband, Dwayne, to faith in Christ about a year earlier.

While at Del City, we met our Southern Baptist missionaries, Alex and Charleta Garner. They stayed one year in our mission home in Del City and became fast friends. We had the pleasure of going to South America to visit them in 1973. On the way, we stopped in Rio de Janeiro, Brazil, where Charleta's sister and husband, the Bumpases, lived and served as Southern Baptist Missionaries. We stayed for two days with them before heading on to Buenos Aires. We spent a wonderful ten days in the beautiful country of Argentina traveling into the interior to visit with many missionaries along the way. That was our first journey out of the country to visit missionaries and to minister overseas.

One of the incredible blessings I had at First Southern was Marge Malone as my special assistant. Marge taught me how to properly use the talents of a good assistant. Though she did not belong to First Southern, she was a visitor often in the services. She loved her own church, she loved First Southern, and she loved the pastors she served with.

Our time began to wind down as pastor of First Southern. We didn't know it at the time, but the wheels of Divine Providence were already turning. One afternoon when I came into the office, Marge said, "Dr. Criswell, pastor of First Baptist Church in Dallas, called

WHERE THE WIND COMES SWEEPING DOWN THE PLAINS

and left a message for you to call him." When I saw the number, I knew it was the phone number of First Baptist Church Dallas.

I told Marge to call the number and tell Dr. Criswell's assistant that someone called claiming to be Dr. Criswell, and that she was just checking if it was for real. I told her to enjoy a good laugh if it was just one of my friends pretending to be Dr. Criswell, but if it was for real, to get me on the phone.

The message was legitimate, and his assistant had interrupted a staff meeting for him to take my call. I was soon speaking to someone who sounded like Dr. Criswell even though I still wasn't sure it was really him. He asked me to come to Dallas in the spring for a Median Adult Retreat at the Fairmont Hotel on a Friday and Saturday and then stay over to preach at First Baptist on Sunday. Still skeptical that he was really W.A. Criswell, I told him I would have to pray about it and get back to him. I am told that when he returned to the meeting, he looked perplexed and said, "I just don't understand. Nobody ever believes it is really me!"

We came to Dallas for the retreat and for me to preach on February 22, 1973. We were greatly blessed that weekend. One of the special treats was getting to meet Zig and Jean Ziglar. Zig was one of the most prominent motivational speakers in the nation. We immediately developed a strong friendship. Several months later, Zig called and said he was speaking at a large event at the Music Hall in Oklahoma City to train personnel in the real estate business and wanted to invite us to come. We had dinner with him and attended the event. There was absolutely no one who could do it like Zig! Our friendship remained strong until his death. He was a special friend and even came to LifeWay at his own expense one year to train our leadership team.

We were voted on by First Baptist Dallas in early July. Randy was at Boys State as the president of the student body of Del City High School. He was the only student body president at Del City High School to have been elected as a sophomore to serve during his junior year. When I picked him up from Boys State, I had to tell him that he would not get to be student body president of Del City High School because we were moving to Dallas.

The pace and the logistics of leaving Del City and coming to Dallas were difficult. Because I was not expected to come until after Labor Day in September, there was a time of separation for me with Carol Ann and the children. School was starting in mid-August, and our children needed to be in Dallas for the beginning of school. They went to Dallas three weeks before I arrived, while I stayed in Del City to complete my responsibilities there.

The transition was very difficult for all three of our children. Terri was going into seventh grade and had quickly met five new friends she saw her first day of school, so that was helpful. Bailey's day was a lot different. All day long, he was pressured to use drugs. He walked to Carol Ann's brother, Don Ray's house, and called her to come get him. When they got home, Bailey emphatically announced, "I'm not going to go back to that school." Carol Ann reassured him that by taking such a strong stance, he probably wouldn't be faced with it on a regular basis. Randy was beginning his junior year at Lake Highlands High School in Dallas. When he got into the car, and Carol Ann asked how his first day was, a big tear ran down his cheek as he said, "It was OK, I just don't know anyone."

WHERE THE WIND COMES SWEEPING DOWN THE PLAINS

Later that day, Terri came to Carol Ann and said, "I guess God can't just help everyone. He did not do anything for Randy!" That was a great teaching moment to help her understand that God is always with us and will get us through the really hard times. What Terri couldn't fully understand was that Randy had gone from being president of the student body at Del City High School to being anonymous at a new school. While he had a tough beginning at Lake Highlands, he took it in stride and ultimately made a very positive transition to Dallas. I still marvel at his resilience during those days. Bailey and Terri had started school at Forest Meadows Junior High School and quickly settled into their new surroundings. I'm grateful to God for giving us three of the most remarkable children He has ever sent to this earth!

The time from when we resigned in Del City until I preached my first sermon at First Baptist Church Dallas took almost two months, and it wasn't a good thing at all. In fact, it was more like a two-month-long funeral. The last three weeks of that time, Carol Ann and the children felt isolated in Dallas by themselves, and I was alone in Del City and feeling miserable.

It was hard to leave First Southern. Many people told me not to accept the invitation to Dallas. I even had a dear friend whose dad had been on my ordination council, Doyle Sumrall, fly to Oklahoma City to tell me not to come. He said it would not work out well and urged me not to accept the invitation. I appreciated the concern from Doyle and others, but there was no doubt that God was calling us to assist Dr. Criswell at First Baptist Church in Dallas.

The Wednesday night I resigned at Del City; Carol Ann did not come to church. She said she was a good comer, but not a good goer! I announced our decision to accept the position at First Baptist Church in Dallas and then asked the church to let me leave without talking with anyone. They obliged, and I walked over a mile home. Leaving was a bittersweet time for us and one of the most difficult decisions we ever made.

A new era of our lives was beginning, and changes were coming. The typical church member at Del City was middle-income and middle-class. Some were blue-collar workers; some were business leaders; we even had a fair amount of young counter-cultural people. The average age of our members was only 23. In contrast, the congregation of First Baptist Dallas included many millionaires and hundreds of nationally prominent businessmen. The membership there included all economic and social lines from one extreme to the other, but the influencers were decidedly affluent.

This move was different from the other moves we had made. There was a great sense of sadness and excitement. There was an unmistakable ominous presence this time, which revealed the mixed sense that our desires and God's calling were separated by a great sense of uncertainty and grief. I knew Dr. Criswell's expectations were that I would become pastor at First Baptist Dallas, but I also knew in my heart that would not happen. My overwhelming sense was that I was going to help Dr. Criswell and nothing more.

When we met with the Personnel Committee in Dallas with Dr. Criswell, he told them that in time I would become the pastor. When he said that, I told him, "Pastor, I can't come on that basis. The church has a right to call its own pastor. If I come, it will be to help you." Later on, Del Rogers, a deacon on the committee, told me, "I respected you before that, but I loved you after you said that."

WHERE THE WIND COMES SWEEPING DOWN THE PLAINS

Starlite Crusade 1971

Jimmy & Aubie

The Family

WHO BUT GOD! RIDING THE WHIRLWIND
JIMMY AND CAROL ANN DRAPER

Jim Irwin, the eighth man to walk on the Moon

Easter Sunday

First house we built

WHERE THE WIND COMES SWEEPING DOWN THE PLAINS

A gift from the deacons

Carol Ann & Jimmy

Richard, Don Ray Floyd & Jimmy

WHO BUT GOD! RIDING THE WHIRLWIND
JIMMY AND CAROL ANN DRAPER

First Baptist Church
Dallas, TX

13

NEW ROLE IN BIG "D"

FIRST BAPTIST CHURCH, DALLAS, TEXAS

Dallas is the ninth most populous city in the United States and the fourth-largest metropolitan area. The Caddo Indians were here before the Spanish colonists claimed the territory in the 18th century. The Adams-Onis Treaty of 1819 established the northern boundary, the Red River, for what was called New Spain. In 1821 Mexico declared its independence from Spain and claimed the territory.

Texas won its independence from Mexico in 1836, and in 1841, John Neely Bryan established a permanent settlement named Dallas. The origin of the name is unknown. In 1909 the Praetorian Building opened in Dallas. With 15 stories, it was the tallest building in Texas at that time.

Dallas is also known today as the place where President John F. Kennedy was assassinated. All of us alive that fateful day will never forget where we were when we heard the news on November 22, 1963. It will always be a tragic day in the city's history.

First Baptist Church Dallas was founded July 30, 1868. In the 151 years since the church began, it has only had seven pastors. W.W. Harris was the first pastor and served for 29 years. George Truett served for 47 years, and W.A. Criswell served for 51 years.

Since 1995 the church has had four pastors. Joel Gregory was the first to follow Dr. Criswell and now serves as a preaching professor at Truett Seminary in Waco, Texas. O.S. Hawkins served for a number of years and then became the president and CEO of Guidestone Financial Resources of the Southern Baptist Convention. Mac Brunson came next and served for several years before moving on to First Baptist Church of Jacksonville, Florida. The current pastor is Robert Jeffress; he was a teenager when we were there. He has just completed his thirteenth year as pastor and is one of the most gifted, effective pastors and expository preachers of the Gospel in the nation today.

The church established First Baptist Academy in 1972 as a Pre-Kindergarten through 12th-grade school. Criswell College began in 1970. In 2019 alone, Criswell College distributed 10,000 Bibles to prison inmates. The college has a world-class faculty and outstanding student body.

In 2014, I served as the interim president for Criswell College before the current president, Barry Creamer, was elected as president. Dallas radio station KCBI FM radio began broadcasting in the early 1970s. The identification of the radio station, KCBI, was chosen because it was initially founded to promote the Criswell Bible Institute.

NEW ROLE IN BIG "D"

We made the transition to First Baptist Church of Dallas in September 1973. Though the decision was made in July, Dr. Criswell did not want us to come until after Labor Day that year. I officially started the week after Labor Day and preached my first sermon as associate pastor on September 9, 1973.

On a house-hunting trip to Dallas, we met our real estate agent at 10:00 a.m. and told her we had to be on the road back to Oklahoma City by 1:30. She showed us 12 houses, and we ended up buying the first one. Our first night in our new home, we all slept on the floor because our furniture did not come until the next day. That made it a special memory for all of us. The house had a large den area with a 20' ceiling and the second floor had a balcony that looked down into the den. We put a nerf ball basketball backboard on the balcony railing and the boys and I had a great time playing nerf basketball together.

The house had a modern look outside, but inside it was a perfect fit for our needs. The boys shared a room and, Terri had her own room but with a connecting bath with the boys. Our bedroom was downstairs with a connecting bath between us and Grandmother's bedroom. The bathroom had a walk-in shower which was just what we needed for Grandmother. The den, or great room, was very large with a connecting dining room and large kitchen and breakfast area. It even had an indoor grill for us to use with a vent-a-hood over it. The garage opened off the kitchen and stairs went upstairs for a bonus room above the garage. We put a ping-pong table, an extra bed, and some chairs upstairs. I had a small study off that room.

One evening when Randy came home late from a youth choir practice, he smelled smoke. He came to wake us up, and in no time, the house was filled with smoke. We called 911, and soon a fire truck, ambulance and two police cars arrived with sirens blaring. At 1 a.m., it created quite some excitement for our neighbors. The firemen located the source of the smoke—the furnace. Apparently, the fan had gone out, but the gas fire for the furnace kept burning. The smoke came from the heat in the furnace metal that had fire, but no moving air. We were grateful there was smoke but no fire! The fire chief told us had it not been found, it would have eventually caught the house on fire. Thank God that He was watching over us that night, as always.

We loved that house and enjoyed living there. We had ping pong in the bonus room and basketball in the den. When we weren't occupied with that, the boys and I were wrestling in the den! Carol Ann managed to have a surprise birthday party for me one-year at our house. All the key staff leaders came, including Dr. Criswell!

While serving at First Baptist Church Dallas, Carol Ann began a weekday Bible Study for young women. It was a blessed time for her as she got to know so many new friends.

We were invited to a get-acquainted social for our family nearly every night of the week for nine months! It was a busy time, but we felt loved and welcomed. One event was on a Friday evening for a sit-down dinner in one of the church member's exquisite home. Carol Ann wore her grey jumper and navy-blue blouse with a piece of jewelry made by a sweet friend in Oklahoma. She knew she was underdressed when two men met our car and opened the doors for us and parked our car. It was too late to do anything about it, so we stayed and rang the doorbell.

NEW ROLE IN BIG "D"

Our hostess opened the door in a lovely sequin gown. As we looked just past her, we saw beautiful gowns and formal attire everywhere. We were decidedly underdressed, but I knew Carol Ann had made peace with it when she said, "I had already told the Lord that I didn't know how to be anyone else but me." That evening was a formal sit-down dinner with 42 people. It was beautiful and delicious, and we had a wonderful time. There was even special entertainment after dinner. Carol Ann said that if she had any pride left, it got knocked out of her that evening! Unfortunately, I came down with pneumonia soon after that evening, so our schedule came to a sudden halt. We thanked the Lord for small favors…like pneumonia, at that time!

Things at the church continued to go well. I was preaching on Sunday nights and Sunday mornings when Dr. Criswell was out of town. In the two-plus years we were there, I preached over 150 times.

One of my first decisions when I came to Dallas was to bring Herschel Creasman to serve with me as Minister of Education. We had served together in Del City, and I had great confidence in him. He was one of the best in his position that I had ever seen. He and his wife, Joanne, remained cherished friends until both of them died in the early years of the 21st century. Their son Robin remains a close personal friend with Randy to this day.

Many special things happened while we were in Dallas. The Criswell Bible institute was founded just before we came to Dallas. Dr. Leo Edelman, a legendary leader in the Southern Baptist Convention, had come to be the first president of the Criswell Bible Institute in his retirement. It is interesting that he reported to me when I came to Dallas. What a privilege for me to get to serve with Dr. Edelman during those days.

One of the first things I did was to have the church pay to move Larry and Carmen Walker and family back to Dallas from New York, where they had lived for several years. Larry became our staff evangelist and taught a large Bible study class called 'Thee Class' when he was not on the road preaching. He continued doing that for over 40 years and also played the violin in the church orchestra every week he was home during those years.

In my early sermons in Dallas, I preached verse-by-verse through Hebrews, followed by a series of sermons from Proverbs dealing with various subjects. These series both became books released by Tyndale House Publishers.

Dr. Criswell and I met each month with the deacons, and both of us spoke to the deacon body of several hundred men during my time as his associate. It was also my responsibility to direct all of the staff, some 300 people, during that time. Only near the very end of our time in Dallas did Dr. Criswell meet with the general staff of the church.

My best friend on staff when I came to Dallas was Mel Carter. He and his wife, Margie, became tremendous encouragers for us during our time at First Baptist Dallas. When I came on staff, Dr. Criswell moved Mel from his staff position to become the headmaster of First Baptist Academy. He felt Mel would be a hindrance to me since he had already been at the church for several decades and had held many different positions. As it turned out, and to Dr. Criswell's surprise, Mel became a great friend and confidant during our Dallas years.

NEW ROLE IN BIG "D"

It was also my privilege to affirm and announce Gary Moore as Minister of Music. He had previously served as the Associate Minister of Music and had filled in during the absence of his predecessor, Leroy Till. When Leroy became incapacitated, Gary stepped in and was an incredible musician and minister. Some years later I got a call from Ed Young, pastor of Second Baptist Church in Houston, asking for recommendations for a Minister of Music, I was pleased to recommend Gary to him. Second Baptist did call him, and he has served there for decades since.

One of the stand-out moments in Dallas was the Easter Billy Graham and Cliff Barrows came to lead worship at First Baptist Church. We had the Sunday School hour at the Dallas Convention Center and then the service. It was a spectacular day, and many were saved in that memorable service. I still have a picture with Billy on that special day.

Cliff Barrows later came back and preached a revival for the church. Cliff was an accomplished preacher himself, but usually devoted himself to leading the music for Billy's crusades. After one of the evening services of the revival, we went with Cliff and his wife, Billie, to eat in Gil and Ann Stricklin's home. Gil and Ann had been Baylor classmates of mine and close personal friends. Gil had served for several years with the Billy Graham Association and knew Cliff and Billie well.

We finished our time together late that night, nearly 1 a.m., but when we arrived in our neighborhood, we saw a house a few doors down from ours that was on fire. Smoke billowed from the fire and flames leaped high in the air. Normally, I wouldn't stop at such a scene and get in the way of the first responders, but as we got closer, we saw there were no first responders there. It was burning to the ground, and no one knew.

Concerned about who might be inside the house, we stopped. I jumped out of the car and ran to the front door. I beat on the door and shouted, "Open up! Open up!!" I tried to kick the door down, but there were multiple deadbolts on the door, and I could not break it down. About that time, through the opaque glass in the door, I saw a figure and someone trying to open the door. After several tries, the door opened, and smoke belched out of the doorway. Three young children rushed into my arms.

As soon as I got them out on the grass in front of the house, I asked if anyone else was in the house. The older girl, about 12 years old, said their mother was still in the house. I ran back to the door to find the smoke was swirling and had come down to about knee-high. I began to crawl through the house and met the mother crawling toward me and helped bring her to safety. The Fire Marshall said that if we had not come by at just the time we did, all four of those inside would have died from smoke inhalation. We were grateful that we had been late coming home so we could be there at the right time.

A few months later, I began a book entitled 'Say Neighbor, Your House is on Fire,' which focused on the warnings of the Bible. It dealt with Scriptural warnings such as the unpardonable sin, the sin unto death, Hell, grieving the Holy Spirit, the Second Coming, and many others. When I finished the book, I asked Cliff Barrows to write the forward for it, and he did. He remained a close friend until his death a few years ago.

NEW ROLE IN BIG "D"

Our time at First Baptist Church Dallas was a special time for us. I can never cease to praise God that He allowed me to serve with Dr. Criswell. I met him every day in his office at 4:00. I also received and responded to all his mail. He was a preacher without peer, but, also, an incredibly creative and innovative church strategist. He was the first pastor to establish staff members representing every age in the church ranging from Cradle Roll (when a baby was born) to Senior adults.

Another highlight for me was to host a one-hour talk show on WRR FM radio late each Sunday night. It had a wide audience, and I enjoyed interviewing special guests. It was also a great platform to tell listeners about the church. One night while I was on the air, I received a call from our Chapel Choir during their international tour. They called from Hong Kong that evening to give an update to all the parents at home about how their kids were doing.

First Baptist Church Dallas had many Sunday School classes that were very large and functioned much like separate churches. Each educational division even had their own bank accounts, as did many of these large classes. Shortly after I came to Dallas, Dr. Criswell asked me to teach one of those large Sunday School classes called the Schaeffer Class, and I did so for almost two years.

Dr. Criswell was a remarkable communicator and preacher of the Gospel. He was a gifted scholar and incisive expositor; I never heard him deliver a poor sermon. My years with him were filled with wonderful memories. The church thrived in every way. He preached to a full sanctuary twice on Sunday morning, and in the evenings when I preached, the building was also full. Attendance and finances grew substantially, and the many-faceted ministries of the church expanded. They were good and exciting years.

I began serving as a trustee of Baylor University in 1974 and continued until 1983. In the same year, I was asked to serve as a trustee of the Annuity Board (now Guidestone Financial Resources) of the Southern Baptist Convention and was a trustee until 1983. Howard Payne University bestowed a Doctor of Divinity degree upon me in 1974.

At the Southern Baptist Convention meeting in Miami in 1975, both Dr. Criswell and I were on the program to address the convention. On the way back, he told me that if the church were to vote at that time to call me as pastor, 98% of the people would vote for me. He went on to say that the 2% of the people would be so vocal in opposition that they would never let it happen. For the first time, I realized the extent of the opposition that existed with my presence at the church.

I knew this conflict that was erupting around me was a familiar pattern for the church. Others had been brought in to serve in a similar capacity with the expectation that they would become pastor at some point. Invariably things would not work out, and they would move on. That is the reason I insisted on the church voting for us to come to Dallas, rather than Dr. Criswell just announcing it as was his practice.

What I didn't realize was that Dr. Criswell would always say when a matter was voted on, "All in favor raise your hands. And that's all of us." There was never a chance for anyone to express opposition. The decision was made, and that was it. The vote was not actually a vote of the church, only an approval of a decision already made.

NEW ROLE IN BIG "D"

Mrs. Criswell became very opposed to me in my second year at Dallas and led the faction that wanted me to leave. One significant staff member did her bidding and a prominent deacon joined in. It became so obvious, that at one of our meetings at 4:00 in his office, Dr. Criswell asked me, "Why is Mrs. C so opposed to you?" I asked if he genuinely wanted to know, and he said he did. I told him, "She thinks I am a threat to you!" At that, his face turned red, and he slapped his hand on his desk and said, "That is an insult to me!" Then relaxing and shrugging his shoulders, he said, "But you are right. That is what she thinks." I reassured him that I was not and would never be a threat to him and that I had come to help him as much as I could. I could never have filled W.A. Criswell's shoes!

As the next few months came and went, the opposition became more vocal. Before it became clear that they were after me, they attacked Herschel Creasman. When he told me about it, he said that I was their real target, and not him. Accusations abounded, and it became more of a public issue. The staff member who encouraged the attacks was reported to say on a crowded elevator one Sunday morning, "Well, you know Jimmy and Herschel have embezzled lots of money from the church." All of the attacks were specific and orchestrated to discredit us.

One week the Dallas Morning News ran an article with the headline, 'Criswell Aide May Not Stand in Pulpit Here.' The article speculated that I would be leaving First Baptist Dallas soon. We received over 165 calls that week from deacons, church leaders, and members to encourage us. Carol Ann kept a written record of each call. It became apparent that I would have to resist the opposition or leave the church. I told Carol Ann, "I am going to leave as I would want a staff member to leave if I were the pastor. I will not do anything to hurt this church or burn any bridges." So, we began to pray about the next move earnestly.

We were contacted by pulpit committees from Metropolitan Baptist Church in Wichita, Kansas, First Baptist Church in Euless, Texas, First Baptist Church in Midland, Texas, and First Baptist Church Van Nuys, California. We had never made it a horse race between churches, so we knew we had to consider them one at a time. Metropolitan Baptist had contacted us first, so we dealt with them first.

Three members of the committee from Wichita flew in a private jet to Love Field to meet with us. They were remarkable. They told us that they had been meeting regularly, praying, and listening to sermons of various pastors but had not contacted anyone yet. They said they had listened to my sermons, and all believed I should come in view of a call to Metropolitan. No church could ever have done a more disciplined and prayerful search than the committee from Metropolitan had done. It was so impressive that we agreed to go to Wichita in view of a call.

Around this time, First Baptist Church of Euless had also contacted us. My college classmate, Bill Anderson, had served First Baptist Euless for ten years and had just moved to Calvary Baptist Church in Clearwater, Florida. When he left, he recommended me to the pulpit committee. When they called me, I told them that we would meet with their committee but first had to settle whether we would go to Wichita before we could consider coming to Euless.

Early the week before we went to Wichita, we met with the pulpit committee from Euless. They knew we were going to Metropolitan

NEW ROLE IN BIG "D"

Baptist Church in Wichita the next weekend and that we could not consider Euless until we had determined what we would do with the Metropolitan Baptist. We met in a small church parlor; the meeting was awkward and did not go smoothly. It started with one of them saying, "We don't know much about you, so tell us about yourself." Our first time together was not very impressive.

During a break, they took us to see the auditorium. The thing that caught our attention was the pulpit. It was no ordinary pulpit, but a replica of the balcony rail from which Charles Spurgeon preached in his church at Metropolitan Tabernacle in London in the 19th century. I did not think much about that at the time but would shortly!

The day we were leaving to go to Wichita for the weekend, two men came from Euless to see me. One was Harold Samuels, a deacon at Euless, a member of the pulpit committee, and the mayor of the City of Euless. The other one was Jim McKinney, the associate pastor at Euless. In our brief visit, Harold told me of his desire for us to come to Euless and not go to Wichita. Without fanfare or hurry, he said what he had come to say, and the two of them left. I told him I would let them know what happened at Metropolitan when we got back.

On Sunday, October 5, 1975, I preached in view of a call at Metropolitan Baptist Church. I met with the Sunday School leadership and deacons on Saturday afternoon and evening. The first meeting was packed with scores of the Sunday School leadership and children. I then met with the deacons that night. The next day I preached both morning and evening services.

At the deacons' meeting, I remarked about the enormous marble pulpit that was in the sanctuary and expressed concern because it was like being in the prow of a ship that separated the preacher from his congregation. Press Houston, who was president of Coleman Lanterns there in Wichita, raised his hand and said, "Bro. Jimmy, I put that pulpit there years ago. Where would you like for it to be moved?" Everything about that weekend was met with a positive response from the people.

I never talked to any church about my salary throughout all of my ministry. I never knew what I was going to make until I got my first paycheck, so I refused to talk with them about it. For us, the real issue was not what I was going to be paid but having confidence that it was God's will for us to serve there. Though I would not talk salary with them, they told me they knew what I was making at Dallas and that they would beat that salary.

At lunch at a private country club after the morning service, they promised us incredible provision for our family. They told us they would provide a car for us each year, pay tuition for our children to go to private school, give us a down payment for a home, give us a country club membership, and so on. The committee provided everything and more we could ever have asked for.

When we got back to our adjoining hotel rooms for our family, the phone was ringing. I answered it, and it was a long-time friend from my seminary days, Roy Fish. You could look the world over and not find a more gracious Christian gentleman or friend than Roy Fish. He apologized for calling and said that he did not want to interfere with our lives, but that he had a deep conviction that I

NEW ROLE IN BIG "D"

should come to First Baptist Church Euless. At that time, he was the interim pastor at Euless, as he had been before Bill Anderson had come ten years earlier.

Roy said he had preached at Metropolitan Baptist in Wichita some months before. The church had put him in the same Holiday Inn downtown near the church. He called there, not even knowing if they had done the same for us. He said what he had to say fairly quickly, and the conversation was over. When I hung up the phone, I turned to Carol Ann. She appeared asleep but was actually playing possum and was wide awake.

"What do you think about Metropolitan," I asked her. She asked if I really wanted to know and then sat up. She looked at me and said, "Two times while you were preaching behind that big marble pulpit, I saw you preaching behind the Spurgeon's Rail at First Baptist Church in Euless. I have never had a visual moment like that before."

I had to confess to her that although the church had done everything possible to appeal to us, I had the feeling all day of "What in the world are we doing here?" I preached that night to a packed house of over 1,000 people. I was called by over 950 secret ballot votes with only two negative votes. No minister could ever expect or require a better vote than that. It is rare for a Southern Baptist Church to have that strong of a vote to call a pastor.

But despite the overwhelming vote, our hearts were still not settled on coming to Wichita. Having lived in Kansas City, we loved the Midwest, and it was a great way for us to get away from Dallas. The church was the leading church in the city. And yet we still had no peace about coming. Saying "no" to that church was one of the hardest decisions we ever made, but we just could not get peace about it. With the many doubts we had, there was no way we could accept that call.

When we returned to Dallas from Wichita, I met with Dr. Criswell as we were preparing for the evening service on October 12. I told the pastor that something needed to be said by him about all the rumors that were flying around prompted by the Dallas Morning News article. Dr. Criswell replied that he would just tell the church that I needed my own church. I told him that he could do that, but it would not be the truth. God had called me to serve with him, and I was happy doing that. He then told me to tell them whatever I thought was best.

That evening the building was packed when we entered for the service. When I rose to preach, I wanted to relieve the tension in the air, so I started by saying, "I understand you are here tonight to hear me resign. I feel kind of like Mark Twain, who was in Europe when he read his obituary in the newspapers. He sent a cable back to the United States stating, 'The news of my demise is greatly exaggerated.'" Then I continued, "I have no intention of resigning."

As I said that, the entire congregation rose in a standing ovation. That is, all but Mrs. Criswell, her close associates, and Dr. Criswell. What I meant as a light way to begin the service, they had taken it very seriously. When I got home, I told Carol Ann, "If it wasn't over before, it is now!" And it was!

The next week the pulpit committee from First Baptist Church in Midland, Texas, called and wanted us to come out to Midland to meet with their committee. I told them I had agreed to preach in Euless in view of a call. They insisted that we at least come out

NEW ROLE IN BIG "D"

to Midland and meet with them before we preached at Euless. We obliged, and on October 21, 1975, before we preached in Euless, we made a quick trip to Midland. They knew we were committed to preach in Euless and were willing for us to make that decision, but still wanted us to come anyway.

The same day we agreed to come in view of a call to Euless, I received a call from the First Baptist Church in Van Nuys, California, inviting us to come to California and meet with their committee. I told them I had just accepted an offer to preach in Euless and that we could not come.

On October 26, we preached in view of a call at First Baptist Church in Euless. I had agreed to come with the stipulation that they had to vote on Sunday morning so I could resign at First Baptist Dallas on Sunday night. They were happy to do so. By this time, Helen Parmley, the religion editor for the Dallas Morning News, had written two front-page articles speculating about our potential move. I called her and asked her not to write any more articles and assured her I would call her as soon as a decision had been made.

After I preached that morning at Euless, we had lunch with the chairman of the Pulpit Committee, Bob Eden, and his family. True to my word, when the votes were tallied, and I had been called to First Baptist Church of Euless, I called Helen Parmley to give her the information.

To say that leaving Dallas was a period of incredible turmoil would be a gross understatement. It truly was a continuation of a whirlwind of action that seemed to characterize our lives all through the years.

WHO BUT GOD! RIDING THE WHIRLWIND
JIMMY AND CAROL ANN DRAPER

Martin Lovvorn was president of a local bank in Dallas, and when we prepared to leave First Baptist Dallas, he offered Carol Ann a job as his executive assistant. He told her that he knew she did not have any experience but that he would train her. He knew we might need help in making the move and this was his way of loving us and trying to help us. Though Carol Ann declined the offer, it was a remarkable offer from a dear friend.

Some of the most exceptional individuals I have ever known were at First Baptist Dallas while we were there. Some have passed on to Glory, and some are still serving today. Some of them include Martin Lovvorn, Clarence Bentley, Jack Pogue, Orville Rogers, Ed Yates, Ed Farrow, Del Rogers, Dean Willis, and so many others. Women like Mary Crowley, Martha Branham, and Marilyn Goff were just a few of the outstanding women in leadership in the church. Staff heroes of mine were many as well, including Leroy Till, Dan Beam, Jack Byrd, Libby Reynolds, Millie Cohn, Ruth Swanson, Mel Carter, among others.

One other thing about our leaving Dallas was both interesting and disappointing. As I was getting ready for the evening service when I would resign, I asked Dr. Criswell when I should resign in the service. Dr. Criswell replied that it didn't make any difference and that I should do whatever I felt best. I had preached for over two years on KRLD radio every Sunday night, and the service was always broadcast live.

The service itself was not unusual, but we were on a strict schedule for the service. Dr. Criswell had told me that I should always get into the invitation while we were on the air, so I knew that was a priority. My sermon that night had to be one of the worst I have ever preached

NEW ROLE IN BIG "D"

as I scrambled to complete it before the end of the broadcast. At Dr. Criswell's instruction, the music for the evening was much longer than usual. The other thing I did not know was that Dr. Criswell told the media director, Jack Byrd, to put on a tape of one of his sermons when I got up to preach. As it turned out, I had preached a very poor message in the short time I had been given and had not even been on the air.

The next day, the pastor asked me, "Lad, do you really want to help me?" I replied that I certainly did. He said, "Then don't come to church here next Sunday morning. You can teach your class, but don't come to the morning services." Sadly, on my last day in Dallas, I was asked not to even come to the worship service on Sunday morning. For the evening service, I did not preach as the church observed the Lord's supper, but I was asked to voice one of the prayers in the service.

I never felt the decisions that were made in those last days reflected the desire or attitude of Dr. Criswell. I understood that there were many factors involved in his requests, and I did not take them personally or reflective of what he wanted. I told Carol Ann that the internal struggles at the church were strong and divisive and that I was determined that I would not defend myself or fan the flames that were beginning. I loved Dr. Criswell and still do today! I know he did not like the way it ended with us there, but I knew God was still on His throne and in control of our lives.

A hastily planned reception was planned for us after church that Sunday evening, and over a thousand people crowded into the dining area to tell us goodbye. The Chairman of the Deacons presented me with all 69 volumes of Spurgeon's Metropolitan Pulpit sermons as a gift.

When we got home that night as we got in bed, Carol Ann burst into tears and cried, "I'm so glad it is over!" I was glad too. It had been a difficult few months, but we had not betrayed our integrity, nor had we tried to defend ourselves or hurt the church in any way. Dr. Criswell was never my accuser or adversary, and we remained friends until he died.

Dr. Criswell and I appeared on many programs together after we went to Euless. He always called me, "my young Timothy." He was cordial and affirming at every possible chance. A few years after we came to Euless, Del Rogers, one of the FBC deacons called to tell me, "You got the closest thing to an apology from Dr. Criswell last night that you will probably ever get." He went on to say that the pastor had mentioned in deacon's meeting about a young man who had come to be his associate but had not stayed long. He was obviously referring to me. He said the biggest mistake he ever made was to let him go.

Near his death, I met with Dr. Criswell when he was failing rapidly. I had come to Dallas to meet with Bill Pinson, Executive Director of the Baptist General Convention of Texas. I called Jack Pogue, who was providing a place for Dr. Criswell to stay in his home during his last days. I told Jack I was coming to Dallas and wanted to come by to see the pastor. He eagerly responded for me to come.

When I got to Jack's house, I found the pastor in a hospital bed in the living room. O.S. Hawkins, who had been pastor at Dallas for several years, and was now president of the Southern Baptist Convention's Annuity Board, was there. I suppose that Jack had told O.S. I was coming. He had remained close to Dr. Criswell since leaving the church.

NEW ROLE IN BIG "D"

As we stood beside Dr. Criswell's bed, O.S. said, "Pastor, you know no one loves you more than Jimmy does." To which Dr. Criswell replied, "Yes, and he has every reason to hate me." O.S. had obviously had this conversation with him before, and he said, "Why pastor, why would you say that?" And he replied, "Because when he was with me, some people came against him, and I did not stand with him."

What a special time it was for me as I told him that I believed in the Sovereignty of God and knew that God had called me there to serve with him. I added that, if I had known then what I knew now, I would still have come to serve with him. We shared some incredible moments of tears and rejoicing in the faithfulness of God. We shared our love for the Lord and each other in those emotional moments. That was the last time I saw him before he died.

To this day, some of our best friends are folks from First Baptist Church Dallas. One of my greatest privileges was later to be interim president of Criswell College for nearly a year. We continue to interact with so many of the people who became friends while we were in Dallas. One special friend, Jack Pogue, was fiercely devoted to Dr. Criswell. I told the pastor one day, "Pastor, any man who has a friend like Jack Pogue is a rich man!"

Jack has poured his life into one of the most creative and innovative websites in the world. You can go to wacriswell.com and get thousands of messages of Dr. Criswell online, free of charge. If you can remember two words from any of his sermons, you can enter those two words, and the software will find the sermon in which that was said. Over 4,000 sermons are there online, each complete with audio, video, transcripts, and Dr. Criswell's notes on each sermon. While he rarely used notes, he did write out notes on each sermon. It is one of the most remarkable websites I have ever seen and is a fitting tribute to one of the greatest preachers I have ever known and heard.

Jimmy preaching

Bailey, Jimmy & Randy

The Family

First Doctorate - Howard Payne University

NEW ROLE IN BIG "D"

Billy Graham & Jimmy
Easter 1974

Randy with Grandparents
and Carol Ann at
High School
Graduation

Ed McAteer, W.A. Criswell & Jimmy

House in Dallas

WHO BUT GOD! RIDING THE WHIRLWIND
JIMMY AND CAROL ANN DRAPER

First Baptist Church
Euless, TX

14

IN THE HEART OF DFW

FIRST BAPTIST CHURCH EULESS, TEXAS

Euless began as a cotton gin community built on land owned by Elisha Adam Euless. He was a Tennessee native who moved to Texas in 1867 and bought 170 acres. The city developed around the land Euless owned, so locals named the city in honor of him.

Much of DFW International Airport is located on land originally part of the City of Euless. The original runways and terminals were all in the city limits of Euless. It was and is a bedroom community for both Dallas and Fort Worth. It is a wonderful community to live in, and First Baptist Church was the most influential church in Euless. The mayor and many of the city council belonged to First Baptist Euless. The church averaged 950 in attendance for Sunday School in 1974-75.

The church was founded in 1904 as the Candon Baptist Church; most recently, it has become known as Cross City Church,

First Euless. This is the fifth name the church has had in its 115-year history.

Trinity High School is located across the street from the church. Today the school still allows the church to use their parking lot on Sundays, and the church allows students and others to use church parking during the week. At one time, we rented 41 classrooms at Trinity for Youth Sunday School. There has always been a close tie between the church and the school.

We moved into the church parsonage in Euless. It was a smaller home than what we previously had, but we lived there for five years. Our second house in Euless was built at 700 Bent Tree Drive and we moved in on February 1, 1981. We had lots of help to move from others in the church. We had an inside crew and an outside crew. That helped because of the snow and ice that fell that day. The crews took turns working inside and out: when the outside crew got too cold, they would trade with the inside crew. It was wet and cold, but lots of fun and remarkably our furniture got placed in the right rooms.

My first Sunday at First Baptist Euless was November 26, 1975. It began 16 years of exciting and satisfying ministry in a great church! Well-known evangelist, Vance Havner, was preaching a revival at the church that week and was supposed to preach through that Sunday. He had been a cherished friend of mine since he ministered to the pastors and staff of the churches in Kansas City back in the late 1960s when I was Chairman of the Evangelism Committee for the Kansas City Baptist Association. We met for lunch on Saturday and he informed me that I should preach that Sunday and that he was going home. I wanted him to preach that Sunday, but he strongly felt I should preach for my first Sunday. So, he returned home, and I preached that Sunday.

Something special happened that Sunday. In the evening service, I looked up and saw Clarence and Mary Jo Bentley in the service. Clarence was the chairman of the annual pledge campaign to underwrite the church budget at First Baptist Dallas and a past chairman of the deacons there. It was a shock to me because I knew that his committee was to have presented the report on the pledge campaign that night in Dallas. When I asked him about that, he shared that he had gotten someone else to do it because, as he said, "I just wanted to make sure that you got off to a good start!" What precious friends they were.

One of the funniest things that happened while we were in Dallas involved Clarence and Mary Jo. I was interviewed on the radio one day and spoke of my love for Carol Ann. Mary Jo just could not wait for Clarence to get home that evening to tell him about it. She described the interview and then said, "Bro. Jimmy said he didn't just love Carol Ann; he liked her!" To which, Clarence replied, "Well, I like her, too!" Mary Jo said that was not the response she was looking for! We all had a good laugh when they shared this story.

Bill Anderson had done a wonderful job as pastor of the church, and Roy Fish followed up as a strong interim pastor. The church had an excellent staff when I arrived. Bill Fowlkes was the Minister of Education and had excellent pastoral skills. After several years of our ministry together, he became our Associate Pastor and Minister to Senior Adults. Bill was a tremendous friend and partner in ministry.

He was an excellent Minister of Education, but when the need for an associate pastor to do hospital visitation and senior adult ministry developed, he was a natural to move to that position.

Under Bill Fowlkes' leadership, we had a small group of skilled craftsmen who would travel to the churches we were supporting and help on the construction of buildings and with repairs and maintenance problems that were too much for small churches to tackle. This group stayed active and very busy for years.

Bill and his wife, Jetta, remained friends until their deaths. Their oldest daughter, Lynn, married Mark Sostarich, a Southern Baptist pastor, and they had a great ministry in Houston. Mark and Lynn named their first child, "Carol Ann." That was such a blessing for us! Their youngest daughter, Jan, married Tim Viertel, who was the son of Southern Baptist missionaries. He later became a lead officer in the United States Secret Service and served for many years.

Don Wilkins, our Minister of Music, had been with the church for more than a decade. In 1980 Don and Ruth moved to a new position at First Baptist Church in Madisonville, Texas. Two months after he got there, the pastor died suddenly, and Don found himself in the primary leadership role of the church. We talked often during those first months about the expanded role he acquired. Don ended his active ministry serving for many years at Park Hills Baptist Church in San Antonio as Executive Pastor, working alongside pastor Robert Welch. Robert told me last year that Don was the best administrator he had ever seen and spoke so highly of his ministry at Park Hills.

Robert Wagoner became our next Minister of Music. Together with his wife, Anita, they served for ten wonderful years. Their daughter, Alecia, married an outstanding young man, Rob Olmstead, and they have spent over 15 years actively serving in China with the International Mission Board.

Their oldest son, Reagan, led a church plant in Cincinnati, Ohio several years ago. Although it is new, they have already launched another church plant. They are now in the final stages of completing their first building for the church. Robert and Anita's youngest son, Ryan, is a committed Christian and a coach at a Christian secondary school.

Robert and I served together again at the Sunday School Board/LifeWay when he came to serve in the Church Music Department. Anita also worked with us and wrote children's musicals that were published by the Sunday School Board/LifeWay.

Rick Braswell became our Minister of Evangelism early in our ministry at Euless. He had served with Bob Harrington during the years Bob was the Chaplain of Bourbon Street in New Orleans, Louisiana. He was strong on evangelism training for our people and a great witness. It was under his leadership that we adopted Evangelism Explosion (EE) as a training tool. We regularly had more than 200 people on Tuesday evenings being trained in EE. We were one of the few churches in the nation that held a special weeklong training session for leaders of other churches across the country to be trained in EE. They were equipped so they could return to their churches and start an EE program there.

During our 16 years at Euless, we hired 11 staff members from within the church membership to lead our various ministries. All of them proved to be incredible partners in ministry. Gary Phillips, Terry Barber, Gary Hill, Charles Thornton, Carey Rector, Bob Kaumeyer, Brian Lakey, Ted Groesbeck, Steve Smith, Jean Baker, and

Ann Hettinger all came from within our church membership and served faithfully.

We also had a remarkable team of women on our church staff who led in various areas of the ministry. Jean Baker led the preschool area when we first came to Euless. She served part-time for several years and then became the Director of Childhood Ministries at Riverside Baptist Church in Fort Worth. Ann Hettinger followed Jean to lead our preschool area of ministry. Jeanene Chumley led our ministry for children Grades 1-6.

In the spring of 1976, we began planning for a 24-Hour Intercessory Prayer Ministry. We began the ministry on May 24, 1976, at 9:00 p.m. when the first intercessor entered to pray. When we launched the ministry, Ron Dunn came on a Sunday evening church service and challenged us to fill every hour of the week. The rain was torrential that night, but by the time it let up, more than 180 people had signed up to fill the 168 one-hour prayer times every hour of the week.

The prayer room was located on the north end of our A-frame buildings across the street from Trinity High School. It had an outside door for people to enter from the street at the time of their prayer hour. God richly blessed our church through that remarkable ministry. By the end of the first year, 320 people had been involved in the prayer ministry. We had prayed for over 3,000 prayers requests and had specific answers to over 1,000 prayers. Connie Zirkle became the heart and soul of the Intercessory Prayer Ministry and remained with the program until she retired in December 1985. Carra Kumpe succeeded her for many years afterward. Both these special ladies were used incredibly of the Lord to keep the IPM moving forward in prayer.

In the first several years of the ministry, we had inquiries from 74 churches in 17 states, many from other countries and interest from associations, seminaries, and collegiate student ministries about how our program worked. We continued to have so many inquiries, we printed a booklet, 'How to Begin an IPM.' It was published in both English and Spanish. Byron and Connie Zirkle, along with Bill and Jetta Fowlkes, introduced the booklet at a pastors' conference in Chili. The pastors there presented an oxen yoke to our church as a symbol of the churches in Chili and FBCE working together in this ministry.

In November 1976, we brought Bob Bachman and his wife, Trudy, to serve as our first Minister of Childhood Education. Bob was one of the most highly respected men in that area of ministry in our convention. Under his leadership, we named our first Minister of Preschool Education, Jim Robinson, and his wife, Cindy. They came to us from Birchman Baptist Church in Fort Worth and were cherished partners in ministry. Jim resigned in July 1982, to take a similar position at Cottage Hill Baptist Church in Mobile, Alabama.

Jeanene Chumley became the Director of Childhood Education in March 1984. She had just completed 13 years in a similar position at First Baptist Church Irving. Ann Hettinger joined our church staff in November 1986, as Director of Preschool Education. By this time, we had over 700 preschoolers enrolled. Ann did a remarkable job of leading the ministry that included many, many childcare needs for special church events, as well as the ongoing staff required to meet these challenges.

Randy and Elizabeth were married while we were still living in the parsonage. The wedding was beautiful, but very, very hot on August 13, 1977. On Sunday after church, we invited all the out-of-town guests to come to our house for lunch. We fed 26 people out of a very small kitchen, but it was a very special memory.

One of the most important staff members we had at First Baptist Euless was Dr. William E. Bell. I met Dr. Bell when Rick Braswell took some classes at Dallas Baptist University. One of his classes was taught by Dr. Bell. I had heard about Dr. Bell from many fellow pastors over the years, and Rick was excited about him. He suggested that we should ask Dr. Bell to come on staff as a special assistant. Dr. Bell had a special ministry of providing tapes for Sunday School teachers to use each week that he offered at a modest price. He also was gone many week-ends in order to supplement his salary at Dallas Baptist University. I asked Dr. Bell how much money did he make on those weekend trips. When he told me how much he made by going out on weekends, I suggested that we would pay him that amount if he would just stay home and serve with us. He agreed to become our Theologian in Residence. I have never known a more gifted biblical scholar than Dr. Bell or a more unselfish ministry partner. He taught a very popular adult Sunday School class for many years and proved to be invaluable for our church and to me.

Dr. Bell was converted through the Old-Fashioned Revival Hour Broadcast out of Long Beach, California, during his freshman year at Georgia Tech University. He worked for a public accounting firm for some time before beginning his Th.M. at Dallas Theological Seminary. While at Dallas Seminary, his classmate Chuck Swindoll, introduced him to Martha Barret. They fell in love and were married in 1964 after he had been in New York for about a year.

After graduation from Dallas Theological Seminary, he taught at King's College in Briarcliff Manor in New York. While there, he earned a Ph.D. in religion at New York University. The Bells formally identified with the Southern Baptist Convention when they moved to Dallas and joined First Baptist Dallas and the faculty at Dallas Baptist University in 1967. He taught there for over 40 years and became the chairman of the Religion/Bible Department while there. They joined the staff at First Baptist Church Euless in October 1977.

Charles Thornton was led to the Lord by his sister, Kay Brassell. She was Rick Braswell's assistant. Charles came by my office one day about a year or so after he had been saved and told me that God had called him to ministry and that he had just resigned his job as a regional manager for a computer company. He jumped right in and began to help with our evangelism training, even leading the Evangclism Explosion training program at times.

In May 1980, Rick resigned to accept a similar position at the San Jacinto Baptist Church in Amarillo, Texas. Just two months later, we extended an offer to Mike Foster, who was serving as the Campus Evangelism and Single Adult Minister at Bellevue Baptist Church in Memphis. He had graduated from the University of Tennessee and Mid-America Baptist Seminary. He came to us as a single man, but was engaged to the daughter of Adrian Rogers, pastor of Bellevue Baptist Church, and was married later that year.

Nearly two years later, Mike and Gayle left First Baptist Euless to return to Bellevue to serve there. Shortly after they left, on a Sunday night, I suggested to the people that we call Charles Thornton to be our Minister of Evangelism. He had proven his devotion as a volunteer, and the church knew him well. The church responded with a standing ovation, and that is how we called Charles to our church staff. No personnel committee was involved as the people already knew and loved Charles. He served in that capacity for 25 years. He also began the position as a single man, but before long fell in love with Pat McCormick and married. They have ministered together ever since then.

In 1981, Dr. Ted Groesbeck began the ministry that became the Christian Growth Center and was later renamed Christian Counseling Associates. It all started on the third floor of our educational building when Dr. Groesbeck began counseling our church members. More space was eventually needed for the counseling center, so the ministry moved into office space in the Gill Savings and Loan Building across the street from the church property. It continued to grow and took even more space in the years that followed. Dr. Groesbeck was both a counselor and the director of the counseling ministry. With a sliding fee scale adjusted to reduce costs based on income and a shoebox full of record cards, Dr. Groesbeck's counseling ministry was a remarkable success.

Dan and Priscilla Taylor joined the staff in the early 1980s. He had been a Navy pilot and a star athlete for the University of Texas. Dan became one of my most valuable staff members. When I was elected president of the Southern Baptist Convention in 1982, he was invaluable to me. Dan carefully watched my mail as the volume increased tremendously. Because of the kinds of letters the president frequently received, he made sure that angry or inappropriate mail

IN THE HEART OF DFW

never reached my desk. We always responded to legitimate mail, but when a correspondence was just angry and railing against something inappropriately, he made sure I did not see it. Just this simple act saved me a lot of discomfort and grief and allowed me not to be distracted by unnecessary things during the two years I was president.

Over the years, we have had many opportunities to be with the Taylors. I was interim pastor at Dauphin Way Baptist Church in Mobile for nearly a year back in 2009-2010. Dan was on staff there. We flew into Mobile every Saturday and often stayed with the Taylors for the weekend.

We had a succession of Youth Ministers over the years at Euless. Richard Dateau was Youth Minister when we arrived. He was an outstanding young man with a heart for building relationships with the youth. His focus on discipleship and faithful obedience to God was remarkable and set an excellent example for our youth.

Tony Dyer came after Richard and was one of the most creative young men I have ever served with. It was through his leadership that we started Christian Family Day at Six Flags in Arlington. As I was writing these words in early April of this year, we were informed by his family that Tony had died. We had maintained a close friendship over all the years. At his suggestion, we went to Six Flags and asked to rent the park on the last Friday before the official opening, which was Good Friday. At that time, Six Flags did not open until after Easter and stayed open till late in November.

We asked them to have the park open with concessions and shops open with their staff, and we would provide personnel to take tickets at the gate. We also asked that we could use the entertainment areas for Christian entertainers and rallies. They agreed to our proposal and told us that the tickets would cost $7.00 per person. We could keep $2.00 of each purchase for our expenses, and they would take the remaining $5.00 for Six Flags.

We had to guarantee them $50,000, which meant we had to have 10,000 show up to cover our rental expenses. We also wanted to pay entertainers well for their concerts. Over the four years, we had many well-known Christian individuals and groups, including Dallas Holm, Tim Sheppard, The Imperial Quartette, Dino Kartsonakis, and many others.

When Good Friday arrived, it was a beautiful day, and 14,000 people came to the first-ever Christian Family Day at Six Flags. We had partnered with a Christian radio station in Dallas, and they had shared the event across the metroplex.

The next year we had thousands more attend, so we added Saturday also. By the second day, more than 39,000 attended that two-day celebration, but Six Flags had not increased the number of employees to work the rides and concession stands, so the waits were long and uncomfortable.

In the fourth year, we did not do as well, even though we had good crowds attend. The lower attendance was undoubtedly due, at least in part, because of the failure of Six Flags the year before to have adequate personnel in the park. They also failed to print and mail the information that year promoting it. When we lost several thousand dollars that year, I was convinced they were actually working against Christian Family Day.

When it came time for us to settle our account with Six Flags, I explained that they had failed to produce the needed advertising and material as they had in the past. I asked them to pay the losses we had incurred for that reason, and they agreed. I believe their failure to support us was because they saw what a huge success Christian Family Day was for the park. The next year, they began to have Christian Family Day at all the Six Flag Parks across the country and continued doing that for years. We pioneered it for them, and they took it and ran with it.

We also had Steve Knutz, and Greg Davis lead our youth for a season in the early years of our ministry at FBC Euless. Steve had been in our church while he attended Southwestern Seminary and knew our church well. He was serving at First Baptist Church in Broken Arrow, Oklahoma, when we asked him to come to Euless. He came and served effectively with us for a number of years.

Greg Davis came to us from First Baptist Church in Wichita Falls and was a very impressive young man. I don't believe I ever interviewed a more impressive young man over the years. Two months later we discovered he was bipolar, a condition that had not been diagnosed or treated before he came to Euless. Circumstances made it necessary for him to resign from his position in our church. Our church rallied around him and his family and paid his salary for nearly a year after he left and also provided the medical treatment needed for his condition. It was a gracious example of the incredible generosity and compassion in our church.

Our longest tenured Minister of Youth was Keith Moore. He and his wife, Allison, were solid in every way and made a tremendous impact on our entire church family. They were with us for five years. To this day, I still see adults whose lives were turned around, and their relationship with the Lord solidified from the years Keith led our youth. He made it a point to meet regularly with many of our youth and disciple them.

Keith began with us while he was attending Southwestern Seminary and continued with us for several years after graduation. When he did leave First Euless, he went back to his home state of Georgia and served with one of his close friends, Ike Reighard, who was pastor of New Hope Baptist Church in Fayetteville, Georgia. After several years, that church started a mission in Peachtree City, Georgia, and Keith led in its establishment and became pastor. He has been senior pastor there ever since, over 30 years.

We have kept up closely with Keith and Allison over all the years and still count them as very dear to our hearts. I have preached several times for Keith since he began that church.

By 1977 we realized that we needed to have additional printing capabilities at the church. Ted Mall became our first Director of Printing. His father had a print shop in Chicago, and Ted knew the printing needs thoroughly. He also was a skilled photographer. Ted was born in India and spoke six languages fluently. Ted and his wife, Claudia, served with us until 1983 when he became the Ambassador to the United Nations - sponsored by the Home Mission Board of the Southern Baptist Convention. His linguistic skills made him a great leader as he served effectively there for a number of years.

When Ted and his wife, Claudia, left for New York, Richard Hubley was ready to step into that role. He had served as Ted's assistant since January 1980 and assumed Ted's role in the fall of 1983.

IN THE HEART OF DFW

Bill Fowlkes had been serving as Minister of Education and Business Administrator for nearly two years when we called our first Business Administrator, Terry Barber. He had been a pitcher in the Los Angeles Dodger baseball organization for six years before settling into a career in the insurance business. Terry came to us at the very time we were beginning our two new buildings just east of our older buildings. He was tremendously helpful in guiding us through the difficulties of that project.

After Terry left, Gary Phillips came to be our Business Administrator. He and Teresa had come to First Baptist Euless several years earlier. He increased our efficiency in how we handled funds and brought us to a strong financial position. He was a valuable and cherished co-worker and friend. He did an outstanding job as our Business Administrator for a number of years and then left to enter private business. Gary loved to fix things, and when everything was fixed, he naturally looked to something else to fix!

Gary Hill joined our staff following the departure of Gary Phillips. Gary was raised here in the HEB area and played quarterback for the LD Bell Blue Raiders football team. He and Barbara made a great team, and we enjoyed some special years together.

Bryan and Jean Lakey came to assist in the Business Administrator office and became fast friends. They served with us for several years and then moved on to serve a church in Vidor, near Beaumont, Texas. Some years later they migrating to Memphis to be near their children. We recently learned they are moving back to our area and we are very excited to have them back.

One of the ministries that developed in our early years at Euless was for single adults. We were seeing such an influx of single adults in the church we knew it was an opportunity to serve them well and hired Bob Kaumeyer as our first Minister to Single Adults in 1981. He was a native of Santa Monica, California. In his junior year at Polytechnic University, he felt God's call into ministry and came to Dallas Theological Seminary following his graduation in 1967.

Bob worked for seven years for the Dallas County Juvenile Department and was a bi-vocational pastor. He and his wife, Jana, joined FBC in 1980, and he began to teach an adult Sunday School class. Bob was working as a counselor for Irving Christian Counseling and seeking God's will for a full-time ministry position. He served effectively for four years with our single adults and firmly grounded them in Biblical truth. He was passionate about a ministry that not only brought single adults to Christ but led them to maturity in their faith.

Steve Smith assumed the role in 1985. He had previously been a deacon and a teacher in our young adult couples class. At that time, Steve was one of the top salesmen in the country for the Levi Strauss Company. He had already felt God's call to ministry and was preparing to leave the business world to follow that call. Steve and his wife, Donna, worked tirelessly to connect with the single adults. The numbers of single adults involved in our church swelled to over 1,000 by the end of 1988.

Over the 16 years we served with the wonderful staff at the church, we were blessed by some of the most gifted and compassionate partners in ministry who served in the support roles for all the ministries. Each of these ladies who partnered in the ministries of the staff they served was outstanding. We could never have seen the remarkable growth that grew exponentially every year without those special ladies who undergirded all the ministries of our church.

A special word from Carol Ann and me must be said about Marilyn Novak. She had served as the receptionist in the last months of Bill Anderson's ministry here. When I came, I brought my special assistant, Lavern Moore, from First Baptist Dallas, to help get all my files and everything set up for me to be most effective. She stayed for two months, and then I asked Marilyn Novak to become my secretary. Marilyn and her husband, Bill, had been members of the church and became cherished friends.

It was great for me to work with Marilyn. She loved the people, had the respect of the church, and she loved chaos and confusion that often comes with ministry. The more complicated it became, the more she liked it. That was perfect for me, because I loved changes and challenges, too, and continued to have my share of chaos in the whirlwind of my life. Carol Ann and all our children loved and appreciated Marilyn for her service to the church and me.

Over the years we were at First Baptist Euless, we had many outstanding interns from students at Southwestern Seminary. One of the first was Ed Litton and his wife, Tammy. They became special friends until Tammy's death in an automobile accident some years later. Ed has remained a great friend, along with his wife, Cathy, whom he married several years after her preacher husband had been killed in a similar automobile accident. They are pastor and wife of Redemption Church in Mobile, Alabama. Both are in high demand across the country for speaking engagements.

Doug Walker served as an intern with Charles Thornton and handled all our details surrounding baptisms and assisted Charles in the ongoing evangelism training. Doug planted a church in north Tarrant County called Fellowship of the Parks, which has become a mega-church now with multiple locations. Charles Thornton is the campus pastor for the Grapevine location and additionally serves as a special assistant to Doug's ministry.

Todd and Sherri Bell came to be our associates in the music ministry while they were in seminary. Todd was one of the best I had ever seen in leading a choir, and the congregation is singing. Sherri was a wonderful soloist and musician. Todd went on to serve as Minister of Music at Dauphin Way Baptist Church in Mobile, Alabama, after graduation. When Jack Graham called me one day to see if I could recommend a Minister of Music to him for Prestonwood Baptist Church in Plano, I told him about Todd. He brought Todd and Sherri to Prestonwood, where they served for over 20 years.

Mark Loy came as a music intern and was with us for several years. He became our Associate Minister of Music. During his time with us, he met and married his wife, Connie. They have remained strong and effective in ministry over all the years and are now serving in South Carolina.

Every time God moved us to serve in a new church, we always had extra expenses. That's the way it was when we moved to Euless. I provided the basic income, but Carol Ann always prayed for the 'extra' we needed.

Our son, Bailey, had become an excellent football player and was an outstanding kicker in high school. We were getting the family settled into our new home and church in Euless when he was in the tenth grade. As a kicker, he needed a special kicking shoe. We never realized a kicker needed a particular shoe and that we needed to buy just one shoe! Carol Ann let him know that a kicking shoe was not high on the list of extras we needed but that it would be on our prayer list of things we needed. Often, sometimes twice a week, Bailey would ask, "Can we get my kicking shoe today?"

One morning while Carol Ann and Bailey were having breakfast, he asked yet again. Exasperated, Carol Ann replied, "If God gives us money out of the clear blue sky, we will go buy it." With that, she dropped him off at Trinity High School and came to my office across the street. When she walked into my office, she could see that I had a check on my desk that was made out to me. She asked me about it, and I told her that it had just come "right out of the clear blue sky, for no apparent reason." I later learned it came from a lady in Oklahoma City, but, to this day, I still don't know why she sent it!

Carol Ann began to rejoice and thank the Lord that Bailey was finally going to get his kicking shoe. The check was for $50, so Bailey got his kicking shoe for $20, and Carol Ann got a $30 bonus! We both rejoiced that God always gives us more than we ask for, as He promised in Ephesians 3:20. We were blessed once again with God's faithful love and provision.

In December 1976, a lady from the State WMU office in Dallas called and invited Carol Ann to be the speaker at their spring WMU House Party on April 28, 1977. She thanked her and said, "I will pray about the request," and asked the lady to call her back after Christmas. Carol Ann had bought a new 1978 calendar and circled that date in red. Carol Ann wasn't speaking much outside the church at the time and that weekend looked clear. Still, she needed to know if this was God's assignment for her. She prayed and read God's Word, and as always, was listening for God's answer.

One morning while reading through the Bible, she came to Genesis 26.:2. God said, "Do not go down into the land of Egypt." Since she always put her name in Scripture, she knew that was God's answer for her. The request was not God's assignment for her and so she declined the invitation.

She remembers being so grateful for a God who sees well beyond December to April, because she was greatly needed at home on April 28 due to a critical family emergency. Carol Ann's prayers went like this: "Thank you Jesus for leading me in your Word to hear your answer to my prayer. I praise God that He hears and answers my big and small requests." It also brought to mind the command and promise of Philippians 4:6, "Don't worry about anything but pray about everything. Tell God your needs and don't forget to thank Him for His answers."

In the spring of 1977, we began a special Women's Ministry. It began with Carol Ann leading the effort to provide some special events for women. The first women's banquet was in April, and Hannah Till from First Baptist Church in Dallas was the featured speaker. That ministry grew to include special conferences and seminars for women throughout the year and an annual Women's Retreat at one of the hotels near the airport for the women. These became some of the signature events in the life of our church!

One year, Carol Ann was invited to speak to a women's retreat at First Baptist Church in Borger, Texas. After the retreat, a dear couple drove her to Amarillo to catch her flight. The weather in Dallas was severe, so the connecting flight was late arriving in Amarillo. As she boarded, she saw the pilot and asked if he had flown the plane from DFW. He told her he had and planned on flying it back, too.

IN THE HEART OF DFW

Carol Ann found her seat on the plane and began to pray. The plane was a prop plane with two seats on either side of the aisle. Her seat was just over the wings of the plane. The flight was only about 40 minutes, but it was still a very windy and bumpy ride. She opened her Bible to get the comfort and peace she greatly needed at that time. She had been teaching in the book of Amos, and chapters three and four were scheduled for the coming Sunday's lesson. She began to read, and when she got to Amos 4:12, God seemed to speak right to her as it said, "Prepare to meet your God!" Since she always put her name in Scripture, she read it as a direct word from God.

She took a moment and checked her heart and then prayed, "Lord, if my feet touch the golden streets of Glory, I'm going to praise you. If they touch the asphalt of earth, I'm going to praise you. So, it doesn't matter to me because I am yours." At that moment, the peace only God can give settled down over her, and she sat at rest in Him all the way to DFW. The plane did arrive safely, and we all were very grateful.

Vernard Johnson, a great Christian saxophonist, became a close personal friend. I mentioned to him one day when we met at an event away from the church that I wanted him to come some Sunday to First Baptist Euless. We did not talk about when, but I wanted him to know I intended for him to come soon to our church. One Sunday morning, when we started our last service, I looked up, and Vernard was sitting on the front row with his saxophone. I asked a staff member to go find out why he was here, and the report came back that he thought he was going to play for our service that day.

It's important to know that Vernard has at least two significant achievements in his life and ministry. He was one of the absolute best saxophonists in the nation and he was the first African-American to gain a Ph.D. in Music from Southwestern Seminary. He was extremely intelligent and very musically gifted. On the spot, and in front of our congregation, I explained what had happened, and then I told Vernard, "We have 45 minutes left in this service. You take 20 minutes, and I'll take 20 minutes, and we'll get through on time. Our people thoroughly enjoyed our working it out before them, and we had a marvelous serendipity with Vernard that day!

I was elected president of the Southern Baptist Pastors' Conference in 1979. I presented the program in 1980 in St. Louis with Jack Price leading the music for the conference. He did a phenomenal job of helping make it a remarkable conference for all who attended. He had been a dear friend ever since our days in Del City when he came one summer to sing at the Starlite Crusade. He had gone to Ouachita with my brother Charlie and Charlie was the one who urged me to invite Jack. What a marvelous singer we found in Jack Price. For years he produced some of the greatest choral music arrangements for choirs in churches across America.

During my year as president of the Southern Baptist Convention's Pastors' Conference, I joined five other evangelical leaders in meeting with Governor Ronald Reagan for a special personal conference. He was seeking the nomination for the Republican Party at that time, and we wanted to know his familiarity with and openness to evangelicals. The meeting was with the six of us, the Governor, and one aide, at a hotel in Washington, D.C. I sat next to D. James Kennedy, the originator of Evangelism Explosion and pastor of Coral Ridge Presbyterian Church in Fort Lauderdale, Florida, when he asked the two Evangelism Explosion questions to Ronald Reagan.

IN THE HEART OF DFW

James asked, "Governor, if you died today, do you have the assurance that you will go to heaven?" He affirmed that he did have that confidence. Then James asked, "If God should ask you why He should let you into His heaven what would your response be?" At that moment, Ronald Reagan glanced up at the ceiling and then looked back at James, and said, "Well, I never have thought of it like that before, but I guess I would say, 'Because I pray to your Son, Jesus Christ, every day.'" After his response, I realized he was an honest politician who could be trusted. I have been a Ronald Reagan fan ever since. He was not a perfect president, but he did make us proud to be Americans again and brought great respect from around the world to America.

President Reagan had a wonderful liaison to the evangelical community named Carolyn Sundseth. She and her husband lived in Maui, Hawaii, where they served with Youth With A Mission. They moved to D.C. during the eight years of the Reagan presidency and we had an open door to Carolyn and her to the president. It was an incredible season for all of us as we had a channel to communicate with the White House.

I did not always agree with the decisions of President Reagan. At one point when he was considering appointing an Ambassador to the Vatican, Charles Stanley and I met with James Baker and Bob McFarland at the White House to urge them to share with the president our deep conviction that there should not be an official representative of the government to the Vatican or any other religious entity. Ultimately, however, the president did appoint an Ambassador to the Vatican over our objection.

Bailey and Kim met at our church when Jon and Phyllis Moore brought their two children, Mike and Kim, to Euless. Since Kim was the new girl, Bailey wanted to introduce her to the youth at church. Their initial friendship turned into love, and the rest is history as they married on October 4, 1980. It was a beautiful wedding, complemented by wonderful weather!

The year 1980 saw us make our first trip to the Hawaiian Islands. Fred Daniel, one of our deacons at First Baptist Church Euless was an employee at Delta Airlines. He set up a wonderful trip for us on our 25th wedding anniversary. We were at the Southern Baptist Convention in Los Angeles that June, and from there we went on to Hawaii for a wonderful week of vacation. While there we visited four of the islands and had a wonderful time. This was the first "real" vacation we had ever had. Normally we went to be with our parents on vacations, but now we had launched out into a whole new world of vacations.

Since that first visit, we have returned many times over the last 40 years. We have many cherished friends serving there and every time we go, we connect with them. My brother, Charlie and his family lived in Honolulu for five years and he served as pastor of the Pearl Harbor Baptist Church. Through him we became close friends with two wonderful Japanese American Hawaiian natives, Paul and Steve Kaneshiro. Both have served in Hawaii after their seminary days as pastors. I preached for them at their churches on all our visits to the islands, as well as other churches there.

Over the years I have preached in the big island of Hawaii, Maui, Oahu, and Kauai and always found a great fellowship of God's people in each church. We really have loved our years of travel to Hawaii and those who minister in that beautiful, but difficult paradise. Most come there to get away from everything and it is a tourist culture that makes it hard to capture the attention of both residents and visitors to the islands. We have some wonderful servants of the Lord whom we dearly love in the Hawaii/Pacific Baptist Convention. For two years at LifeWay I had as chairman of our trustees from Hawaii, George Iwahiro, who served as chairman in that key position. What a dynamic friend and servant of the Lord he has become over the years.

In 1980, Dallas Baptist University bestowed the Doctor of Humanities degree upon me. My good friend, Marvin Watson, was president of DBU at that time. He had been the Postmaster General of the United States when Lyndon B. Johnson was president back in the 1960s. One Sunday, I asked Marvin to preach in my absence. I had heard him give his personal testimony at an event held at Bunker Hunt's ranch in Keller, so I asked him to repeat his testimony for our people.

When the day arrived, he came with a multi-page manuscript and read his message, completely ignoring what I had asked him to do. Not only did he not give his testimony, he read a very long sermon from his manuscript. After a few minutes, Terri wrote on her bulletin, "Is he going to preach?" and handed it to Carol Ann. She wrote back, "I think he already is!" and gave it back to Terri. To which Terri wrote, "If my dad were here, he would be sweating!"

We had a good laugh about that, but the next Sunday, one of our deacons, Jiggs Wise, told me, "Preacher, I don't know what you owed that fellow that preached last week, but whatever it was you paid him last Sunday." Then he added, "Whatever I owed you, I paid you last

Sunday!" Marvin remained a good friend, but on that Sunday, he got carried away with a message I did not ask him to preach.

The church began a new ministry in 1982 when a member gave the church a three-bedroom home nearby. The home was to be used by visiting missionaries home on furlough. Various church members provided all the furnishings as well as a car for their use. A second home was later donated, and both homes were in such high demand, they were often booked two years in advance.

All three of our children went to Baylor University, but Terri was the only one who graduated. After graduation she moved home and began a job teaching elementary school in the Hurst-Euless-Bedford Independent School District. She attended our singles department and met Mike Wilkinson, who conveniently lived just around the corner from us. Their friendship soon turned to love, and they were married at First Baptist Euless on March 10, 1984.

Randy introduced the wedding ceremony, and I had the privilege of walking Terri down the aisle. After the introduction, Randy asked, "Who now on behalf of our Heavenly Father gives Terri in marriage to Michael?" I managed to say, "Her mother and I do," but didn't realize how hard it was going to be to say that simple line. After I placed Teri's hand in Mike's, I stepped up to the platform to finish the ceremony. After the ceremony, it was a wonderful celebration with many family and friends.

With our last child married, Carol Ann and I were officially empty nesters with one exception—we still had grandmother who continued to be one of the real blessings in our lives. We missed our children but praised the Lord that they were happily married to their

IN THE HEART OF DFW

God-given spouses for life. Each of them continues to serve the Lord in a very positive way today.

Carey Rector came on our staff in the mid-1980s. He had been a vice president for El Centro College in Dallas. As an ordained deacon and a great encourager to me, Carey did an outstanding job working with Dan Taylor in the Adult Sunday School area. He and Carolyn are still two special friends whom we see often as we are both members of First Baptist Euless again.

I was a trustee at Southwest Baptist University in Bolivar, Missouri, from 1982-84. I had preached a campus revival there many years before, and the seminary president had asked me to serve on the Trustee Board because of my reputation there in the Midwest. I only served one term as I was not able to attend trustee meetings regularly.

One of the most meaningful relationships developed in those early years at First Baptist Euless was my friendship with Tom Landry, head coach of the Dallas Cowboys. Tom and I shared a lot of things over the years. At one time, he helped us as we pioneered a special software system with the telephone that would let us make calls and record the responses from those we called. I used it to call our church members from time to time. Our system was so innovative at the time, it was featured on the front page of the Wall Street Journal.

Tom did a recording for the system, and we were given permission to call the guests at the nearby Holiday Inn Hotel. We always used a live caller who would explain that they had a call from Coach Landry and ask if they could receive the call at that time. If they agreed to the call, the recording played. On the recording, Coach Landry introduced them to our church and invited them to attend the next Sunday. It was a great experience of outreach for our church

I spoke to his coaching staff for their weekly devotional time together at the Cowboy offices. He came to Euless on several occasions to give his testimony. Once was during a revival when Adrian Rogers preached for us. We had invited the football teams and coaches from our area to the service that night. Coach Landry spoke of his faith and shared how Jesus Christ had changed his life.

His influence was a powerful force for good throughout his years with the Cowboys. Anytime there were issues in the public sector that needed someone to advocate or oppose a question of morality, Tom was always ready to step up. He supported pro-life issues and opposed abortion. He always stood on the side of his Biblical faith. He had not been saved until he was an adult, and he never got over it! He remained a good friend until his death.

The first mission trip we took church members on was in September 1981. We took a team of our members along with other church groups from the Tarrant Baptist Association to Belo Horizonte, Brazil. Carol Ann and I spent the week with the Agua Branca Baptist Church in the Contagem area of Belo Horizonte. The pastor, Jozely de Almeida, and his wife, Ruth, became fast friends and even came to Euless later to spend some time with us. Our translators for the week were our missionaries Don and Irma Highfill.

When we returned to Euless, we began to communicate with Pastor Jozely about buying a piece of property for their church one block away from their current location. Our church purchased the property, and they built a new auditorium and educational space there. They named the building 'The Jimmy Draper Building.'

IN THE HEART OF DFW

A year or so later, Pastor Jozely and Ruth came to spend ten days in our home in Euless. During their stay, Don and Irma Highfill, our missionaries in Brazil, were on furlough and were staying in our mission home. They were our translators again as Pastor Jozely and Ruth did not speak English, and we did not speak Portuguese.

That was the first of many mission trips by our church. By the end of our pastorate at Euless, we were sending over a hundred people a year on mission trips. We have a good number of former members who served as foreign missionaries, and many who still are serving on the foreign field today.

In 1982 I was elected president of the Southern Baptist Convention and served for two years as president. I was the third president during the conservative resurgence. It was a busy, challenging, and very special time for Carol Ann and me. During those two years, my travels took me over 300,000 miles around the world. There were three trips to the White House during those two years.

An interesting thing about my election involved the Sunday School Board, where I would serve as president some 9 years later. The president of the Sunday School Board was Grady Cauthen. We had been friends for many years and I had him preach on the Pastors' Conference that I led in 1980. The day I was nominated to be president of the Southern Baptist Convention Grady Cauthen nominated Duke McCall for the same office. Grady and I actually had breakfast together that morning as I found him sitting alone in the restaurant for breakfast. He told me he was going to nominate Duke and I assured him that was not a problem to me. He seemed really discouraged that morning, but I wanted him to know our friendship was secure.

After I was elected president of the convention, he invited me to come to Nashville to speak to his trustees for my first official presidential visit. I was preaching at a Sunday School conference in Mississippi that week but drove to New Orleans late afternoon and flew to Nashville to speak to the trustees of the Sunday School Board. I was taken in one of the south entrances, spoke to the trustees at their dinner, then flew back to New Orleans and got back to the conference there in time to get a good night's sleep.

I appreciated Grady's gesture of friendship more than I could express. When I was elected president of the Sunday School Board nine years later, the first call I had to congratulate me was from Grady Cauthen. Although he was totally opposed to the Conservative Resurgence, our friendship was not broken.

One unusual thing happened during my first year as president. I received an invitation to preach in Calvary Church in Charlotte, North Carolina. I accepted the invitation thinking it was Calvary Baptist Church in Charlotte. When Ross Rhodes met me at the airport, I discovered that it was just Calvary Church and was not even a Southern Baptist Church. However, it was a God thing for me. The church was a wonderful church and I was incredibly blessed to know Ross and to be in the church. And when I preached that Wednesday night, Grady Wilson was in the audience near the front of the church. He was in poor health but had made great effort to be there that night. It reminded me of the time when we met in ramp of Rice Stadium back nearly 30 years before at the Billy Graham Crusade in Houston in 1953. That was to be the last time I saw Grady before he died.

IN THE HEART OF DFW

During my first year as president of the Southern Baptist Convention, one of the most amazing trips was to Anchorage, Alaska, for their Evangelism Conference. Carol Ann and I were both going on that trip but had to begin the journey from different cities. She was to fly out of DFW and meet me in Denver, where we would then fly on to Anchorage. The night before our flights to Anchorage, I preached the Evangelism Conference in Pineville, Louisiana, at Louisiana Baptist College. Pineville is a suburb of Alexandria, so my flights were to and from Alexandria.

The morning I was to fly out of Alexandria, fog hung low over the airport and the rain was very heavy. I was to fly out at 7:30 to New Orleans and then on to Denver to meet Carol Ann. The connection in New Orleans was not long, so time was of the essence. As the time for our departure out of Alexandria neared, we were told the flight would be delayed. Visibility was virtually zero with fog and rain. The departure kept being pushed back until we had almost used up all of the time needed to get to New Orleans in time for the connection. Delta Airlines took my ticket on to Anchorage and gave me an alternate flight that did not include meeting Carol Ann in Denver. I called Carol Ann and told her it looked like I would not get to Denver and for her to go on to Anchorage and we would meet there.

Finally, we did take off from Alexandria, and we arrived in New Orleans exactly at the time my original flight was due to leave for Denver. When I got off the plane, the departure gate was right across from the arrival gate. I ran over to that gate, and no one was there. The plane had not left yet, so when the agent came back to the counter, I told him who I was and what had happened and that I needed to get on that plane to Denver. He recognized me and even said he had been at the convention in New Orleans when I was elected the previous summer.

I now had no ticket to fly through Denver, but he was able to put me on the plane to Denver. The agent said for me to just get on the plane and he would wire the agents in Denver, and they would provide me with a ticket on to Anchorage. That sounded like a perfect plan, and I was grateful to Delta for going to such efforts to make my original itinerary work. However, when I got to Denver, the agents at the gate had not received that word, so I still didn't have my original ticket to Anchorage.

The agents found the record of my original schedule and told me to run to the gate and get on the plane to Anchorage, and they called ahead to tell the agent to hold the plane until I got there. I raced to the gate, boarded the plane, and found my seat next to Carol Ann still vacant, so she was shocked to see me when I arrived!

The amazing thing is that due to the remarkable people at Delta who helped me, I flew from New Orleans to Denver to Anchorage without a ticket! Who but God could have worked all that out to get me to Denver and Anchorage on schedule! The Evangelism Conference in Anchorage was a great conference despite their frigid mid-winter weather. It was a wonderful blessing the Lord provided to get us together to our destination, and me without a ticket!

Campbell University in Buies Creek, North Carolina, voted to present me with a Doctor of Divinity degree in 1983. It is a unique university as the police department, and the water department were also the police and water department for the city itself. Carol Ann told me if she ever ran away from home, she would come to Buies

IN THE HEART OF DFW

Creek! Our good friend Norman Wiggins was the president of the school at that time. I teased Norman and told him that he was our Baptist "boss hog!" like that character on the TV show "Dukes of Hazzard." We had a wonderful graduation service at Campbell that year.

In 1984 I was chosen to serve as a trustee of Southwestern Baptist Theological Seminary. It was a bit of a homegoing for me as my earliest memories as a small child are of the seminary. My daddy took us to Southwestern when I was less than two years old. I was a trustee until 1991, serving as chairman the last two years I was on the board. When I accepted the presidency of the Sunday School Board and moved to Nashville, I had to resign from the trustees at Southwestern.

During my second term as president of the Southern Baptist Convention in April 1984, we began another ministry at FBCE. My good friend, Paul Carlin, had developed an incredible ministry in the prisons all over Texas. He had been urging me to come and preach in the prisons for several years, but it just never seemed to work out. He invited me to come with him to preach in the Ellis Unit of the Texas Department of Corrections. It was a maximum-security unit with death row for those awaiting execution.

On April 13, 1984, Paul arranged for a private jet to pick us up in Fort Worth and fly us down to Huntsville to preach at the Ellis Unit. Carol Ann and my Administrative Assistant, Marilyn Novak, flew with us and went inside the prison with us for the service. This was significant because the last women to enter as visitors at the Ellis Unit had been held hostage by inmates several decades before. The Warden's wife and Paul's wife also joined us. It was their first time inside the prison, too. The service was remarkable! The enthusiasm and response to the invitation was overwhelming.

We returned another time with a film crew from WFAA Channel 8 in Dallas to video our visit to the Ellis Unit. Peggy Weymeyer, a committed believer, was a featured reporter for Channel 8 and went with us for that special rally in prison. Peggy is a genuine believer and had attended Dallas Theological Seminary. It was very unusual for the prison to allow such access, but God opened the doors for a significant video of the ministry there.

That planted in my heart the desire to regularly participate in prison ministry with Paul. A group of our men began to go to the prisons in Huntsville to minister regularly. To this day, some of those men continue with the prison ministry.

I preached in all six of our Southern Baptist Seminaries and met with all the entities of the convention while president of the convention. I also traveled, by myself, to six countries in Europe, the Middle East, and Africa on a 26-day trip in May 1984. In Africa, I met with national leaders and missionaries. In every country I visited, I met with our missionaries. It was a monumental trip. I went through customs 11 times in those 26 days, sometimes in and out of the same country twice. So many challenging and exciting things happened on that trip.

My first stop was in Nairobi, Kenya. Upon landing, we went straight to the largest and oldest slum in Nairobi called Mathare Valley. It is one of the worst slum areas in Nairobi and in the world. People live in 6' x 8' shanties made of old tin and mud. There were no beds, electricity, or running water. People slept on pieces of cardboard on the dirt floors of the shanties. There were public toilets that residents had to pay to use. Those who could not afford to pay had to use the alleys and ditches between the shanties.

Approximately 600,000 people lived in an area of three-square miles, most on an income of less than a dollar a day. Crime and HIV/AIDS remain extremely common. Many parents die of AIDS and leave their children to fend for themselves. Upwards of 70% of Nairobi's population of 4,000,000 lived on 5% of the city's land area.

Today, Mathare Valley contains a population greater than the cities of Seattle, Denver, or Boston, yet the slum covers an area of only three-square miles. In comparison, Seattle covers 80 square miles, Denver 150 square miles and Boston 42 square miles. One of three adults in Mathare Valley is HIV positive. The average life expectancy for a person with AIDS in Mathare is five years or less. Other health problems, especially for children in Mathare Valley, include dysentery, malnutrition, malaria, typhoid, cholera, tetanus and polio.

There are an estimated 70,000 children in Mathare Valley, with only 3-4 schools to educate them. Many children do not attend school and often turn to a future of crime, prostitution, drug abuse, and disease.

I had been up for over 24 hours when we landed, so the fatigue had started to get to me. But seeing the extreme poverty first-hand was a definite wake-up to reality. I was grateful we had a strong missionary presence there with a medical clinic. I was blessed to share in that ministry with our missionaries. Our next stop that day was in Machakos, Kenya, where I preached a dedication for a church building that was just beginning to take shape. Since I was president of the Southern Baptist Convention, they wanted me to share in a special dedication for the yet to be finished facility. Their present building was only about 20' x 40' and was built like an apple crate with spaces between the slats on the sides of the building. The people were thrilled with that simple building but were really excited about the new one being built.

In most of the countries I visited, the missionaries were wary of my presidency. They had been told by some of the leaders in the Foreign Mission Board that I was one of those terrible fundamentalists who was trying to take over the convention. They had also been told that if we succeeded, they would all be unable to stay on the field or be supported by the convention. Of course, none of that was true, but that created a difficult challenge for me in every country I entered.

In Tanzania, the attitude was so bad that none of the missionaries wanted to meet or transport me around the country. Because of that, when I landed in Mwanza, they sent the newest missionary, Robin Hadaway, to be my escort in Tanzania. Robin and his wife, Cathy, had only been in Tanzania for two weeks and did not know much more than I did about the language or city itself.

I landed in Mwanza, Tanzania, via our 'Baptist Air' Cessna 210. Southern Baptists had several planes stationed in East Africa at that time. Our arrival was comical at best. The control tower for the airport was a platform about six feet above ground, built out of 4" x 4" corner wood beams. As was usual, there was no one on the radio or in the tower when we approached the area, so we landed without any clearance or assistance.

Upon landing, a neatly dressed customs agent met us at the plane and accompanied us into the small airport terminal. She ushered me into a room about 15' x 15' feet with a simple eight-foot table on one side. Nothing else was in the room or on the walls. I waited with no one in the room for some time. Finally, the man who would clear me through customs entered the room. He had a live chicken with its feet tied together under his arm. He tossed the chicken on the table, greeted me and went through my luggage. I had brought lots of candy for the missionary children, so he found that. He looked through it and took several pieces and said, "You can leave now," and pointed toward the doorway.

I looked over at the doorway, and there was no door at all. In that doorway was a door frame, like you would hang a door on, with curtains hanging down over that door frame almost to the floor. He wanted me to go through that. There were no metal detectors, or anything else, just hanging curtains. I think they had seen pictures of security doors with curtains in airports and assumed that was the way it was supposed to be! Needless to say, it gave me one of the more lighthearted moments on my trip.

As I exited the building, there was no one there to greet me or transport me. For a moment, I considered my predicament: I was now in a strange country whose language I did not speak or understand, and I had no way to contact anyone. Blessedly, Robin arrived a few minutes later, and that was the beginning of a great friendship with Robin and Cathy that still exists today.

Over the years that followed, I was privileged to spend many days with the Hadaways in both Kenya and Tanzania. We played golf together in Nairobi and traveled near the Ethiopian border to the Samburu National Park. Carol Ann and I were thankful to travel with their family to see the incredible sights and wild game.

WHO BUT GOD! RIDING THE WHIRLWIND
JIMMY AND CAROL ANN DRAPER

The longest portion of my trip was in Uganda. We flew into Kampala, where the airport was on an island a few miles out of the city. I stayed with missionaries Larry and Sharon Pumpelly. Larry was my transportation for the week we were in Uganda. We traveled up to the northern area of Uganda and stayed for several nights in Jinja, where Southern Baptists had a mission compound of several houses. Jinja is a town on the shores of Lake Victoria. The White Nile River flows out of Lake Victoria. To this day, there is a dispute about the headwaters of the Nile River. Further to the northeast, the Blue Nile River flows out of Ethiopia. Both of those rivers form the Nile River when they come together and flow down to the Mediterranean Sea.

We also traveled up to Soroti, where we met several missionaries there that have remained friends. Harry and Doris Garvin lived in Soroti. We were grateful to spend a couple of nights with them. Harry took us up into a dangerous area north of Soroti to meet with believers in the bush area. We had lunch with the believers, and then I preached to them. I preached about the 'one another's in the New Testament and spoke of how we needed to support and encourage one another. The men and women were separated in the outdoor area where we met as was customary in that tribe. When I finished preaching, a spontaneous response occurred. Men began to stand and confess their sins, and the people began to weep as the Holy Spirit spread across all of us.

It was a highly unusual thing for the men to speak so freely and openly; men of that area are traditionally very private about saying such things in front of the women. It just did not happen. The Lord touched the entire group of us there that day, and His presence was overwhelming. It was one of those unforgettable moments in my ministry to have the privilege of witnessing God's movement that day!

While in Soroti, I completed the sermon I planned to deliver to the Southern Baptist Convention in a few weeks in Kansas City, Missouri. I also preached in Kampala at a great church near the campus of one of the strong universities in Uganda.

As in each of the countries, the missionaries warmed up to me, but it never felt like a family reunion. In several of the countries, I was asked who would be elected SBC president following me. I always mentioned several potential candidates, but when I mentioned Charles Stanley as a possibility, it created a very uneasy mood in the missionaries. They were still under the false impression that if another conservative were elected, they would not have the support of the SBC any longer! True to my assessment, Charles was elected, and the missionary support among Southern Baptist churches has remained strong and vibrant ever since.

One of the high spots for me on this trip was to get to know the missionaries and national leaders in Kenya. It has become my favorite place to minister in the world. I have been to Kenya 16 times between 1984 and 2007. Most of those trips took place between 1986 and my retirement in 2006. I have not returned to Kenya but once since I retired.

From Nairobi, Kenya, I flew to Cairo, Egypt. Our hotel was right on the Nile River. Finley Graham, one of our missionary heroes in the Middle East, met me in Cairo, and we spent several days there. He was a regular runner, so we ran together in the city streets from the hotel, across the Nile River bridge and for a mile and a half and back. My normal jog was three miles, so I stopped at the hotel, but Finley waved at me and went on to run many more miles before he reached his daily distance.

In Cairo, it was the first time I preached with armed guards present. Even back then, there was concern that my presence at the Baptist Church might trigger some attack from Muslim extremists. We did not call violence terrorist attacks then, but that is exactly what they feared. I preached with armed police outside and inside the building. They stayed with me until I had safely left the church. We had a wonderful fellowship with the pastor and his wife in their home after we left the church.

From Cairo, Egypt, I flew with Finley Graham to Amman, Jordan, to spend several days with our missionaries there. We had a great group of missionaries with both a hospital and a seminary there. The hospital was up in the mountains above Amman, while the seminary operated out of Amman. When I retired from LifeWay, I sent about forty boxes of my library books to the seminary in Amman.

We visited our hospital in Ajloun up in the mountains. It was a great visit and a wonderful opportunity to see the great ministry taking place in that hospital and to visit with our missionaries in Amman. One of those missionary couples, Wilson and Sharon Tatum, would later come and spend a year in our missionary home at First Baptist Church Euless.

I was scheduled to fly out of Amman, Jordan, and into Casa Blanca International Airport in Morocco on Saturday. I was also scheduled to preach at the International Church in the capital city of Rabat on Sunday. Finley was to fly back home to Cypress. He had served among the Arab peoples in several countries during his

IN THE HEART OF DFW

storied ministry in the Middle East. He currently lived on Cypress but traveled in many of the Arab countries regularly.

We were both flying out of Queen Alia International Airport in Amman on the same day. The Amman airport is built in the shape of an oval with landscaping in the middle. As we parted, he went to his gate on the opposite side from the ticketing area, and I went to Royal Jordanian Airlines to check-in. When I got to the counter, I was informed that the Casa Blanca flight would not fly until the next day. Although I had tickets and a boarding pass that clearly showed it should fly that day, I could not change what I was told. These were the days of getting boarding passes ahead of the flights.

I did not know what to do, so I gathered my luggage and raced to catch Finley to see what he suggested. When I found him, he advised me to fly to Madrid, where I was supposed to be early the next week. The ticket agent changed my flight from Morocco to Madrid and told me to purchase another ticket to Morocco when I needed it. He took two legs of my tickets and gave me one ticket to Madrid. I would now have to arrange round trip tickets from Madrid to Morocco.

I made the flight, but somewhere around 35,000 feet I realized I was on my way to Madrid, and no one knew I was coming! I had no idea what I would do when I got to Madrid since no missionary knew I was coming.

Several experiences made this entire trip both remarkable and unforgettable. When I left on this trip, my administrative assistant, Marilyn, had put a special folder of information that I might need in my briefcase. It later became obvious that only the Holy Spirit could have orchestrated her choice of information.

When I got to Madrid, I tried to book a flight to Morocco, but was told, "Manana a la noche." My Spanish is very poor, but I understood that to mean they were making no more trips to Morocco that evening. I didn't know where to turn at that point except to the folder of information Marilyn had sent.

As I rifled through the papers, I found a sheet with the names and numbers of missionaries from only one country—Spain! She did not include any information about missionaries from any of the other 8 countries on that trip—just this one. The airline allowed me to use the phone in their offices, and I called the first number on that list. It turned out that to be the missionary who lived the closest to the airport. Who but God could have provided that?

The missionary graciously came for me, and I stayed with his family for the night. While there, I called Billy Wagner, the regional evangelism leader for Western Europe and the Middle East. Billy was supposed to pick me up in Casa Blanca, and I had to let him know I wasn't arriving as expected. Billy and his wife, Sally, had been friends since our early teenage years when I would spend the summers in Albuquerque, New Mexico, where he was raised. We later studied together in Baylor.

Billy suggested I fly to Tangiers on Sunday night, and he would drive over to Tangiers to pick me up. He said he would preach for me at the International Church in Rabat on Sunday morning and then come to Tangiers.

The next morning, I preached in one of the churches in Madrid that was not expecting me. It was the church in Madrid where the seminary held its classes. Though they did not know I was coming, they graciously had me preach that morning.

IN THE HEART OF DFW

One thing that was unusual for me was that the Lord's Supper was also observed that morning, and the church used real wine. The church was sensitive to my abstinence from alcohol, so that morning I was presented with a bottle of grape juice in a brown bag so I would not have to drink the alcoholic wine. I guess you would say I 'brown-bagged' it to church that morning!

After lunch and later in the afternoon, I came back to the airport to fly to Tangiers and Bill met me there. We stayed at a hotel in Tangiers and then drove to Fez on Monday. Fez has one of the largest universities in Morocco, so it was a bustling city, full of activities and energy. On the way to Fez, Bill told me we would be meeting with two of our representatives in Fez along with the wives of five native Moroccan men who had been arrested simply because they had converted to faith in Christ. The Moroccan authorities had a total of twelve believers in jail, specifically for that 'crime.'

We were joined that evening for dinner by two wonderful Anglican missionaries from England and several of the wives whose husbands were in jail. We had one of the most delicious meals I have ever tasted. It was one of those meals where we cooked our own meat on a surface that looked like a Chinese Coolie hat. The meat cooked on the side, and the juice drained down into an area where it remained until we dipped bread in it to eat along with our meat. We ate the entire meal with our fingers instead of utensils. It was absolutely incredible!

We ended the evening, praying for the husbands who were in jail. The next day Bill Wagner left to fly back to Brussels, and our representative in Morocco, who lived in Fez, drove me to Rabat. On the way, he told me that we were going to meet with the United

States Ambassador to Morocco that afternoon. He went over the cities where believers were in jail and told me to ask our Ambassador to work for their release. The embassy had intervened for some 'Moonies' six months earlier and facilitated their release. On the way to Rabat, I memorized those cities.

When we arrived in Rabat, we went to the United States Embassy for our meeting. Upon arrival, we were informed that the Ambassador had been delayed in Mali with the same problem I had encountered in Amman. He would not be able to meet with me, but his new Charge-de-faire would meet with me. He had only been at his post in Rabat for several weeks. We had a great visit as we shared about our travels, and he explained that he had just come from Russia, where he had spent five years in a similar position to the one he had in Rabat.

After getting acquainted, I asked him if he knew that Christian believers had been arrested in five cities just for being believers. He had not heard of that, so I continued. I reminded him that Morocco received more United States foreign aid than any other country in North Africa. I also reminded him of the efforts our Embassy made on behalf of the 'Moonies' who had been arrested six months earlier. When I asked him to intervene on behalf of the believers and gave him the names of the cities where they were jailed, he said that he was making official visits to the Moroccan government officials to introduce himself to them and that he would ask for the release of the believers who were in jail.

When we left the Embassy, the man who had taken me to the Embassy had tears streaming down his face. When I asked him why he was crying, he said, "You do not know what just happened, do you?" I told him I did not realize anything special had happened. He then told me that God had completely rearranged my schedule to bring me to Rabat on a different day than I had originally planned. He went on to explain that God rearranged the schedule of the Ambassador to keep him in Mali, so I would have to meet with his assistant. Then he said, "I have visited with the Ambassador many times. He would have listened sympathetically, but then do nothing. The young man we just met with will do something about this issue!"

He was right. I received a letter from the Charge-de-faire several weeks later telling me the believers had been released. Bill Wagner also let me know the good news. Who but God could have arranged such a thing for me? It was one of the most awesome experiences I have ever had as I realized all that God had done to get me there at just the right time to present the request to intervene on behalf of the believers who had been arrested.

I flew back to Madrid the next day and had some time to spend with the missionaries. They were such a great group and had a celebration reception for me with all of our missionaries there. Spain was a bright spot on the trip because of its flexibility and welcome!

While president, I represented Southern Baptists at the African-American National Baptist Conventions, the European Baptist Convention meeting in Germany, and preached in many conventions and conferences throughout the Southern Baptist Convention.

While at the National Baptist Convention USA meeting in Kansas City that year, S.M. Lockridge entered my life again. I had landed in Kansas City without anyone meeting me. I rented a car and drove down to the Music Hall in downtown where the convention was being held.

When I got there, no one knew I was coming. I had no contact person to connect with, and they had not planned for me to be there at that moment. Looking back, I'm not sure how that happened, but that's how it was when I arrived at the convention that year. I was also the only white face in the entire crowd. The convention was in some sort of recess while the delegates caucused in various places to discuss the election of officers. Nothing was happening on the platform as I arrived in the Music Hall.

I went down to the platform and got the attention of one of the men on the platform. He didn't know what to do with me, and none of the officers were on the platform. As he tried to figure out what to do, S.M. Lockridge came walking down the outside of the Music Hall toward the platform, but he had not yet seen me. As soon as he saw me, he came up and gave me a big bear hug and rescued the poor man I had been talking to.

When the program reconvened, the president of the convention asked S. M. Lockridge to introduce me. He did a remarkable job in presenting me to the convention. He rattled off the names of the places I had served beginning with Red Bridge there in Kansas City, First Southern in Del City, Oklahoma, First Baptist Church Dallas, and First Baptist Church in Euless. I have no idea where he found all that information about me, but I was really introduced properly at that convention.

While president of the Southern Baptist Convention, I spoke at all six of the Southern Baptist Seminaries, plus meetings like the State Evangelism Directors at their annual meeting in San Juan, Puerto Rico, and many other such meetings across our convention. I also visited each of the twelve entities of the convention meeting with the staff of each entity.

One of the most remarkable ministries ever begun at First Baptist Euless opened in 1984. In January of that year, on the first "Sanctity of Life" Sunday, I preached a sermon entitled 'Abortion: The Death of America.' It was the first time I dealt with abortion as a pastor. I had always been pro-life but had never addressed it in a message. I did careful research on the issue and brought the message with conviction and passion. That sermon moved our congregation in a way that no other sermon had ever done.

A small group of people began to meet and pray about finding practical ways to address the abortion issue. Staff members Gary Phillips and Charles Thornton began to meet with the group as they prayed. The group prayed, but also researched what other churches were doing to deal with this challenge.

Virginia Reedy, in her history of First Baptist Church Euless, reported, "One night as this group met to pray and discuss possibilities for addressing the problem, a man showed up. No one had ever seen him before, and no one has ever seen him since. During that meeting, he wept as he told about his two adopted children and explained that because of his children, he was strongly opposed to abortion. He said he traveled a lot and stayed very busy, so he could not give his time to help establish a crisis pregnancy center, but before he left, he handed the astonished men a check for $2,500."

Other church members gave, and soon this group of praying believers had $6,000 to begin a special ministry to deal with the issue. It wasn't long before they presented me with the check, and plans began for a Crisis Pregnancy Center. When the United States Congressman from Arlington, Tom Vandergriff, heard about what we were doing, he sent a sizable check to add to the funds being gathered.

The group continued to pray for guidance on how to begin such a ministry. The answer came from Andy Merritt at Edgewood Baptist Church, who led a Crisis Pregnancy Center in Columbus, Georgia. He sent materials to the group, and they studied and prayed about using that example to begin the Crisis Pregnancy Center. Soon the church rented space in the Euless Town Center on the southwestern corner of the Airport Freeway and Highway 157, just across the freeway from the church property. On opening day, a young woman was waiting for us to open the center when the doors were unlocked.

Over the 35 years of this ministry, we have seen over 35,000 women come to the center and the great majority of them choose life for their babies. From the beginning, the overriding purpose has been to both encourage alternatives to abortion and to share the Gospel with the women who come to the center.

The center has now expanded to new facilities in Bedford and has another new location in Irving. We also have a medical service involved in the centers, including sonogram machines for both of the locations. We have a medical director attached to the centers to guide in the physical issues related to the women who come to the center. A staggering 85% of the woman who see their sonogram choose not to abort their babies.

Our first director was Betty Crumpler, who gathered a network of volunteers to staff the center. Jane DeLaney became the next director for the center as the number of women who came to the center soon reached over 300 per month in the earliest years. We were the first evangelical church in America to begin such a ministry west of the Mississippi River.

Every Sunday, we reported in a unique way on the babies born the previous week. A row of bud vases holding pink, blue, and white carnations lined the rail in front of the organ at the altar of the church. The pink and blue carnations represented babies born to our church members, and the white carnations represented babies born to women who came through our Crisis Pregnancy Center.

Soon, it became apparent we needed to begin another ministry to work in tandem with the CPC; we needed an adoption agency for the women who choose to have their babies but wanted to place them up for adoption. At that time, there was an adoption agency in East Dallas and one in west Fort Worth, but none in between. We received encouragement from state officials and many others to begin this ministry. Rhonda Vaughn was the adoption specialist who directed the day-to-day operations of the agency. During our time in Euless, this ministry was able to place 42 babies into homes of loving parents.

In May 1985, Dub Jackson set up a trip to Taipei, Taiwan and Seoul, Korea. Carol Ann and I flew to the far east with the chairman of our deacons and his wife, Wayne and Berna Dean Lee. The purpose of the trip was to greet missionaries in Hong Kong and Taiwan and to lead a conference for pastors at a retreat center up in the mountains out of Seoul, Korea. I spoke six times that week to about 150 Korean pastors. What a great encouragement that was to my own spirit! I felt then and now that we have much to learn about prayer from Korean believers.

One really funny thing happened to us in Taipei. Dub Jackson always set up appointments with governmental officials wherever he led a partnership mission trip. On this trip, he had arranged for us to have dinner with the vice-mayor of Taipei and her husband in the City Hall. She was the highest-ranking female leader in Taiwan. Her husband was the representative of Taiwan to Japan. He would have been the Ambassador to Japan, but Japan, at that time, did not recognize the legitimacy of Taiwan.

We ate at a large table in a broad hallway right outside of Chiang Kai-Shek's office. His office was still furnished as it was when he was alive, and we got to visit inside that office while there. He was the leader of the Republic of China from 1928-1975. He first led on mainland China from 1928-1949 and then in Taiwan from 1949-1975. He was the leader who led in moving his government to what was then called the island of Formosa, now Taiwan. He was a legendary leader in every way.

We had been traveling for several days, and fatigue began to set in during dinner. The dinner was exquisite and fancy and included many, many courses. The meal was to be topped off with Peking Duck as the entrée. The duck was traditionally cooked slowly for a full 24 hours and was a delicacy in Taiwan.

Berna Dean was sitting right across from Carol Ann at the table. Carol Ann had quite a time getting the black mushrooms in one of the courses of the dinner to stay connected to her chopsticks. She tried several times to pick it up but, just before she could get it to her mouth, it would fall and splatter down on her plate. The last time she tried, it happened again just as she looked up to see Berna Dean was looking right at her. The two of them lost it. They were about to burst out laughing!

That might have created an international crisis as our hosts did not understand English, and we could not explain anything as we did not speak Chinese. We had no interpreter for the meal. Before they started all-out laughing, I looked at Carol Ann and gave her my very best 'not here and not now!' look. Somehow, she and Berna Dean pulled it together, but we had lots of laughs afterward and still laugh about it today.

We flew from there to Seoul, Korea, where we arrived late in the evening and had missed the evening meal. After checking into one of the fanciest hotels in Seoul, the Shilla Hotel, we went downstairs to a restaurant and ordered a little food. We didn't want a big meal that late but needed something to hold us over. Wayne ordered a fruit cocktail thinking it would be like what we can buy in cans in the United States. However, this was fresh fruit that had been washed, chopped and served.

By the next morning, Wayne had become deathly sick. Berna Dean is a registered emergency room nurse and took care of him in the hotel room for much of the week. He was finally able to get out toward the end of the week but was still very sick when we began the trip home. If the airlines had known how sick he was, they might not have let him fly. We had to change planes in Narita International Airport in Tokyo, and it was hard to get Wayne transported from one plane to the other. Dub Jackson was able to get us upgraded to Business Class on the return flights, which helped make it a bit easier on the way home.

WHO BUT GOD! RIDING THE WHIRLWIND
JIMMY AND CAROL ANN DRAPER

When we arrived at DFW airport, Wayne was immediately taken to the H.E.B. hospital in Bedford, Texas. He had contracted a virus from Korea that was very difficult to diagnose. He remained in the hospital for almost a week. One day, he called me to say, "Now I know why I had to get sick in Seoul. My nurse is from Korea, and today she prayed to receive Christ as her Savior!" What a wonderful silver lining we found in that difficult time with Wayne's sickness.

One of the great things God allowed us to do while in Euless was to begin to take our members at FBCE on overseas Mission Trips. We began making overseas Mission Trips in 1981. By the time we left for the Sunday School Board, we were taking over 100 people a year on such ministry efforts.

Several of our members followed the Lord's call to serve overseas as full-time missionaries. The Mission trips were the catalysts that stirred their hearts to be open to God's call. Today we have missionaries in countries around the world as a result of what God did in us and through us on those mission efforts.

In the late spring of 1985, I went back to the 700 Club, where my good friend Pat Robertson was still the host of the show. I had been on the show with Pat previously, so it was good to renew that friendship. The battle was raging in the convention over the inroads of liberal theology into our institutions. This was also the time when Southern Baptist Convention entity presidents were openly campaigning against Charles Stanley's re-election. Adrian Rogers and I were interviewed extensively by Pat, with us sharing some written and public statements made by liberal seminary professors and other Baptist teachers across our convention.

IN THE HEART OF DFW

Pat allowed me to read the statements and then we discussed what I had read live on Pat's television program. This was a big help to us in maintaining the momentum of the conservative resurgence, as Charles Stanley was reelected in 1985. We heard from many people across the country expressing gratitude for our appearance on the 700 Club.

In April 1986, we had Ralph Bethea, a Foreign Mission Board missionary in Mombasa, Kenya, to speak at a Wednesday evening prayer service. Dub Jackson had urged me to have him, although I had never met Ralph. He quickly connected with our church and concluded with an invitation to come to Kenya for a special crusade in late August. Churches who do go on partnership mission trips will tell you that it takes many months to prepare for and conduct such an effort effectively. However, the Holy Spirit was so strong that night, that I responded immediately by saying, "We'll be there!" And in less than three months, we had 47 people in Mombasa, Kenya.

That week in Kenya began a wonderful ministry for us. Kenya was a relatively new nation, having only been established near the end of 1963. It had become a Protectorate of the British Empire in 1895, and officially a colony in 1920. The population of Kenya today is over 52 million people from at least 29 different tribes.

Joma Kenyatta became the first president of Kenya when it was established. Daniel arap Moi became the second president in 1978 and remained in that position until 2002. I had the privilege of meeting president Moi several times. He was a strong evangelical who was very committed to Christ and often spoke very naturally with biblical messages.

WHO BUT GOD! RIDING THE WHIRLWIND
JIMMY AND CAROL ANN DRAPER

The missionaries at that time did not support our efforts. In fact, when I called the then-president of the Foreign Mission Board, Keith Parks, and told him what we were going to do, he told me we couldn't do it. I shared with him that we were happy to work with the Foreign Mission Board, but that as a local Southern Baptist Church, we would not allow them to forbid us to minister there. We were absolutely going whether he approved it or not! Looking back, that may have been one reason we felt he did everything he could to sabotage not only that trip, but also subsequent trips we made while he was president of the Foreign Mission Board.

On Sunday morning of our week there, I preached at the First Baptist Church of Mombasa, where Dickson Wanje was pastor. The building was packed. When I gave the invitation, 52 people were saved, including Ralph, Jr., son of missionaries Ralph and Lynda Bethea. Sadly, most of the missionaries got up and left the building when I began to extend the invitation. Fortunately, the Mombasa missionaries would come around to be strong supporters for the 1990 Kenya Coastal Crusade, but they did not support our efforts that week.

After that Sunday service, Pastor Wanje took us out into the streets and walking paths for us to preach everywhere people gathered. I didn't preach another sermon in the church building during that week!

After a day or so, we settled in at a special area near the bridge that carried people north from Mombasa. The city is on an island and can only be entered or exited by ferry boats or bridges. We took an old pickup truck and parked it near the north bridge, where thousands of people walked by daily. We had not planned to have

IN THE HEART OF DFW

that kind of mission opportunity, but it was wonderful and exciting. We were literally flying by the seat of our pants!

Without a script or even much thought, we decided to use the puppets we had brought. Even though none of us had ever used puppets, we made-do. We put a sheet up to cover the ones using the puppets, and the puppets peered just over the top. We had no program or dialogue rehearsed, but the people stopped to watch and pay attention to the puppets. They absolutely loved the puppets!

Our team improvised, and those who spoke the language said whatever they could think to say. It wasn't pretty or profound, but it worked. After the impromptu puppet show, one of us would present the gospel in about three to five minutes and give the appeal for response. We took those who responded around the other side of the truck to counsel with them, and the 'program' began again.

That week was one of the most incredible mission trips we ever made. God was all over the preparation and the efforts that we made in Mombasa that week. Over 6,000 professions of faith came out of that effort. We had names and addresses of everyone who indicated that they had made a profession of faith, so the churches in the area could follow up on them.

Southwestern Seminary named me a Distinguished Alumnus in 1987. It was a great honor to receive the designation from the school that had such a remarkable influence on my entire life and ministry.

In August 1987, our church sent another group to Taipei, Taiwan. Several dozen of our church members made that trip with us. Several days before we were to leave for Taiwan, Carol Ann's mother died. We prayed and agonized over what to do. We knew that her mother would have wanted us to go on to Taiwan for the ministry, but we could not get complete peace to do so knowing that we wanted to be there for her coronation service.

The group went on ahead of us, and we arrived a day late following the service for Carol Ann's mother. I preached seven times that week in churches in Taipei. While in Taiwan, we met with governmental officials and leaders. We traveled to the mountain headquarters of the Taiwanese government and met many of the leaders there. Much of the time, the government met in the City Hall in Taipei, but more strategic meetings were held at the mountain property. The week was such a blessing to all of us, and God moved to bring many into the Kingdom during those two weeks.

In November 1987, Terry Horton and I traveled back to Nairobi, Kenya. This time I preached at Parklands Baptist Church in Nairobi and a Maasai church that met in the rural area east of Nairobi. Then I led a pastors' conference of over 100 pastors at the Brackenhurst International Conference Center in Limuru, Kenya. It was a former English plantation during the time when Kenya was a colony of England. It is a beautiful conference center that sits 6,000 feet above sea level and has been greatly used of God over the years.

I spoke to the group at Brackenhurst five days that week. At the conclusion of our services, the pastors presented me with a beautiful painting of a Baobab tree in the foreground and Mt. Meru in Tanzania in the background. It is on the wall in my study today, along with many mementos from Kenya.

The exciting thing that week for Terry and me were the many tribes represented at the conference. Nearly all of the 29 tribes were represented that week. In the evenings, the groups would start to sing, each one in its tribal language. To see the Christian fellowship

IN THE HEART OF DFW

with all the tribes together singing in their own languages of their devotion to the Lord Jesus Christ is a vivid picture I will never forget. It was what I picture it will be like in glory when all the redeemed of every nation will sing before the throne of God!

Another partnership crusade was conducted in Kenya in August 1988. Terry and Sammy Horton went with us a week early to Paris. We rented a car and drove down to Brussels, then through Luxembourg, Austria, and Southern Germany, before ending up in Munich. We met our mission team in Paris a week later. I preached at the International Church in Brussels the first Sunday we were there and in a German Baptist Church in Munich the second Sunday.

When we drove back into Germany from central Austria, we had planned to drive east to reach Salzburg. The rain was so hard we decided not to go to Salzburg since we had received word that crossing the border that day was a very slow process. Instead, we turned west and went to Munich even though we had not originally planned to go there. On this European portion of our trip, we did not have any accommodations reserved but stayed mostly at bed & breakfast inns along the way.

We got to Munich late Saturday afternoon. We actually found a Pizza Hut and had a great reminder of being home with pizza. My good friend, Paul Box, was serving as pastor of the English-speaking German Baptist Church in Munich. There was a small park across the street from the Pizza Hut that had a public telephone booth and I found Paul's name in the phone book. I had no idea how many coins to put in the machine, so I just put a bunch in, and the call went through.

Paul immediately took it upon himself to help us find lodging and found nice rooms at the Holiday Inn. When I told him we were going to hear him preach in the morning, he corrected me and told me he was going to listen to me preach! It was a great opportunity to preach in Munich even though we hadn't even planned to go there.

After that Sunday, we traveled back to Paris and met up with our mission group from First Baptist Euless before heading on to Nairobi. The trip to Nairobi was greatly blessed of God and deepened our relationship with the missionaries and national leaders.

Terry and I returned to Kenya in January 1989 for me to preach in Nairobi. I spoke at the annual meeting of our missionaries from Kenya and Uganda five times at Brackenhurst that week. The bond between us and the missionaries had grown stronger. The Kenyan missionaries appointed me an honorary missionary and presented me with a certificate they had all signed.

On February 1, 1989, my brother, George, died of complications from several heart attacks. He and his wife, Beverly, had moved to Euless when we first got there. George had graduated from East Texas Baptist University in Marshall, Texas, and gone into the pastoral ministry. Beverly was one of his fellow students at ETBC, and they married on August 26, 1967, my dad's birthday.

George and Beverly served churches in Genado, Texas, and Fort Worth. Then the Lord led them to North Dakota to have some remarkable years serving the First Baptist Church in Devil's Lake and the First Baptist Church in Wolf Point, Montana. George suffered two heart attacks while serving in North Dakota and Montana.

In 1984 we brought him and his family back to Euless. Doctors were not optimistic about his physical condition and did not give him long to live. However, the Lord gave us five years together before his death, and we are grateful. When they first came to Euless, they adopted two beautiful Korean girls; they named them Rebecca and Elizabeth. Both these young ladies married and have children of their own now. We continue to be so proud of them! Beverly and the girls are still cherished family to us.

A smaller group from FBCE accompanied Carol Ann and me when we returned to Belo Horizonte, Brazil, in 1989. It was such a great trip returning to Agua Blanca Baptist Church and Pastor Jozely and Ruth de Almeida. I had the opportunity to preach for our dear friends there and to see the almost-completed new Jimmy Draper' building. From there, we went on to preach in Uberlandia, Brazil, where Don and Irma Highfill were serving. He interpreted for me twice that day – first at Agua Blanca on Sunday morning and then at their church in Uberlandia for the evening service.

In July 1990, I led the Kenya Coast Crusade in Mombasa, Kenya. Ralph and Lynda Bethea spent the year before that crusade in one of our church mission homes. Ralph spent most of the year traveling across America, enlisting participants for the crusade. We enlisted 536 people to go to Kenya that July. They came from 16 states and 82 churches. Half of the group went for the first two weeks, and the other half came for the second two weeks.

The month began when the first group arrived in Mombasa. Carol Ann and I were already there and deeply involved in the logistics of the crusade. Several great things happened that first week of the crusade. Morris Chapman had just been elected president of the Southern Baptist Convention. He was pastor of First Baptist

Church in Wichita Falls, Texas, and was a very close friend. He had nominated me for SBC president when I was elected in 1982.

We had arranged for Morris to meet with President Moi when he arrived. I flew from Mombasa to Nairobi to meet Morris. The rest of his group from Wichita Falls flew directly to Mombasa. When I arrived at the Nairobi airport, President Moi had his staff pick me up and deliver me to the hotel where they had chosen for us to stay. At the time, Nairobi was in a state of chaos with riots throughout the city, so I was instructed not to leave the hotel at all.

Morris arrived with the same instructions, so we settled in for the night. Before bedtime, there was a knock at my door. When I opened it, Morris was standing there, holding a cable message that had just arrived for me from our team in Mombasa. The hotel had delivered it to Morris instead of to me. The cable simply said, "Bro. Manley went to be with the Lord today." Manley Beasley, one of the all-time great revivalist/evangelists in Southern Baptist life, had been a member of our church for 13 years. We knew he was very ill but did not have any thought that he might die while we were gone.

Morris and I sat in the room and wept together. Both of us had such a close relationship with Bro. Manley. Interestingly, there were six other pastors involved in the crusade in Mombasa at that time. On the day of Bro. Manley's celebration service, all of us were able to be in a hotel room in Mombasa and participate by phone in the coronation service held at First Baptist Euless. Every one of those pastors had a special connection to Bro. Manley.

The next day Morris and I had a private meeting with President Moi in his residence, which is the equivalent of our White House. He

IN THE HEART OF DFW

was very kind and welcoming, which we greatly appreciated. He was grateful for what we were trying to do for his country.

The Kenyan missionaries had become great friends by this time and jumped in to assist us for the entire month we were involved in that Crusade. Kenyan Airlines actually put on special flights from London to Mombasa to accommodate the travel for the many participants who filled each plane coming and going between Mombasa and London for the crusade.

When the first two weeks were finished, the plane from London arrived with our team members in Mombasa. The arriving team of 250+ deplaned and the 250+ leaving boarded the plane to return to London. It was a spine-chilling moment to watch the team leaving march out onto the tarmac from the plane to meet the new team preparing to leave while all the while singing 'Victory in Jesus' and 'To God be the Glory!' Ralph Bethea and I watched this passing of the teams with tears of joy!

The entire Kenya Coast Crusade was handled out of our church offices. By this time, Carey Rector had come on our staff with many different talents. One was that he loved details, the more detailed, the better. He arranged all of the travel for the crusade, including ground transportation to and from Mombasa, and hotel accommodations. It went like clockwork with Carey in charge of the details! He worked closely with my assistant, Marilyn, and between the two of them, everything was taken care of.

God blessed our efforts like we were experiencing the 29th chapter of Acts. When the month was over, we had seen over 65,000 professions of faith that were documented with names and addresses for follow-up with the Mombasa churches. Without a doubt, that was a month we will never forget.

It was a tragic day about a year later when I received a phone call one Wednesday evening just before prayer meeting. Lynda Bethea had been killed near the Rift Valley Academy in Kijabe, Kenya, in a violent attack as Ralph & Lynda drove to the school property. Ralph was beaten badly, and Lynda had been killed. This shocked all of us who had been so close to the Betheas and the Kenyan missionaries.

The family had a difficult time getting Lynda's body released to be returned to the United States. I called President Moi's son-in-law, Stephen Kasatani, and asked him to please help facilitate her release. The body was released quickly, and the family returned home through Chicago. Terry Horton and I flew to Chicago to meet the plane when the Bethea family landed in the United States on their way back to their home in Oklahoma. Pastor Joseph Maisha at the Ushindi Baptist Church in Mombasa was with them. He had come to comfort and encourage the family on their journey.

Terry and I went with the family to Tulsa, Oklahoma, where I preached the first funeral service for Lynda at First Baptist Church in Tulsa. Warren Hultgren, pastor of the church, and I conducted that service. Then we came back to Euless and had a great celebration of her life at First Baptist Euless and I preached a second message.

From there we went to First Baptist Church of Jackson, Mississippi, and I preached a third message, followed by a brief message at the graveside at the family farm outside of Jackson. Those days were memorable days and are forever etched in our hearts and minds!

IN THE HEART OF DFW

The mission trips transformed our church in a special way. It created a personal bond between those who went and brought back a more global perspective for those who supported the effort, but stayed home, gave funds to cover expenses, and prayed. It got the focus off us and onto the purpose for which the church was originally created by our Lord.

While we had at least one mission trip a year, I traveled extensively during the last five years I was pastor at Euless. Terry Horton became my closest friend during those years as his business allowed him to take off whenever I made trips to Europe, Africa, the Middle East, or the Far East. We spent 17 weeks together, traveling all over the world. Many of the trips were to prepare the way for our mission teams to come for a formal witnessing crusade.

Terry Horton and I had an incredible time during our trips overseas. Every trip seemed anointed by the Holy Spirit as we shared many special times together on our travels. One year after our team had been back to Mombasa, Carol Ann and Sammie returned home from Mombasa, but Terry and I flew on 'Baptist Air' to Mwanza, Tanzania, for a special time to hunt with missionaries and nationals there.

The hunt itself was remarkable as 21 of us went in numerous vehicles hunting. The wives and children stayed in camp while the men went to hunt. In Tanzania, many of our missionaries would hunt and then use the meat for their food supply at home. The hunt was exciting, including the drive across a wide river in a Land Rover with the water all the way up to the hood. While watching the group get a bull Cape Buffalo, I was nearly knocked off the top of the Land

Rover by a tree branch. That tree didn't knock me off but did give me a black eye!

Flying home gave us one more good laugh. Dr. Carlton Pittard had given us some Halcion to help us sleep on the trip home. It is not available now but was widely used then. On the plane, I took my Halcion when we left Nairobi, and apparently didn't remember it. Terry said I took another pill midway through the trip. Though I'm not sure that is true, what happened in the Paris airport could confirm Terry's theory.

When we got to the airport, I found a men's restroom that included a shower, so I took a shower and changed clothes while Terri guarded the door so no one would disturb me. After that we shopped at the airport since we had some time before our flight. In one of the shops I bought several things. I bought three ladies watches and three sweatshirts with Paris, France printed on the shirts. I'm still not sure why I bought only three as I had Carol Ann, Terri, Elizabeth, and Kim all back home. I don't remember much about my shopping spree, but that is how Terry tells it anyway.

Overall, we had 16 wonderful years at First Baptist Euless. Leaving was more than difficult. The night I resigned my emotions were so intense that my heart went out of rhythm. The doctor told me that sudden emotional events could trigger such a thing. It took 24 hours in the hospital to get it back in rhythm. After that, I had medication to take, when it went out of rhythm, to bring it back.

After a year or so, my heart refused to return to regular rhythm even after two cardioversions, which are electrical shocks to get my heart to return to rhythm. My heart would just not remain in normal rhythm. My condition is more of a concern than anything as the

IN THE HEART OF DFW

doctor has assured me it is not life-threatening. He must be right as it has been out of rhythm now for over 28 years!

The sadness of leaving First Baptist Euless was and still is there, but we never doubted that God had led us to the Sunday School Board. As in our churches, the years we were at the Sunday School Board, now LifeWay, gave me the privilege to work with some of the greatest people anywhere. But, as has always been the case, the best part of everyday was coming home! Carol Ann and I have now been married over 63 years, and our love has deepened each day. I had rather be with her than anyone else!

Randy & Family

Bailey & Family

Terri & Family

Carol Ann & Jimmy

WHO BUT GOD! RIDING THE WHIRLWIND
JIMMY AND CAROL ANN DRAPER

Grandmother Draper

At Jimmy's 50th birthday banquet

House we built

Our vacation Maui, HI

Jimmy with Tom Landry

IN THE HEART OF DFW

Parasailing in Hawaii

Carol Ann & Wanda Jean
Two Friends Retreat

Jimmy & Steve Kaneshiro
Kahalui, HI

Draper ladies

WHO BUT GOD! RIDING THE WHIRLWIND
JIMMY AND CAROL ANN DRAPER

Preaching at the SBC

A HILL WORTH DYING ON

THE CONSERVATIVE RESURGENCE

In 1974 I was elected to serve as a trustee of Baylor University. Baylor had always had someone from First Baptist Dallas on their board, and deacon Jim Irwin was rotating off the trustee board. They asked Dr. Criswell to recommend someone to be a trustee, and he recommended me. I considered it a great privilege to serve the university that had meant so much to me.

About eight or ten of the 48 trustees were pastors; the rest were laypersons from across the state. We met several times a year, and in time I became chairman of the Academic Affairs Committee. It was my responsibility to lead that committee and then report to the full board and make any recommendations that came out of our committee. We had a vice president assigned to our committee who also arranged our agenda for committee meetings and mailed them to our committee a week or so before the trustee meeting each quarter.

Several months before the trustee meeting in the fall while I was chairman of that committee, Herb Reynolds, Executive Vice President of Baylor, met with Jim Irwin and me in Dallas for lunch. Herb had already been designated the approved successor to President Abner McCall. Our chairman of the Religion Department at Baylor was Ray Summers, who had been one of my professors at Southwestern Seminary back in the late 1950s.

Knowing that Ray Summers was nearing retirement, I told Herb Reynolds how important I believed it was to have a well-known conservative scholar as chair for that department when Ray Summers retired. I believed Baylor should be the very best conservative school for teaching the Bible in the world.

Two months later, at our trustee meeting, the vice-president assigned to our committee informed me that President McCall and Executive Vice President Reynolds wanted to present something to our committee. Not anticipating anything unusual, I saw no problem with them doing that even though it was not on our agenda.

When they came to our committee, they presented the retirement letter of Ray Summers as chairman of the Religion Department at Baylor and at the same time brought a recommendation from the two of them as well as the faculty of the Religion Department, that Jack Flanders be named chairman-elect of the department.

I turned to Herb Reynolds and said, "Herb, we just had a lunch a few weeks ago where we talked about the time Ray Summers would retire and how important it was to get the proper person in that position. You never mentioned any of this to me at that time, or since then, that you knew it was coming." He did not offer an apology or explain why they had violated committee policy by bringing in something for consideration without prior notice to the committee. I wanted to know more and asked him, "Who in the world is Jack Flanders?"

Jack Flanders had been pastor of First Baptist Church in Waco just before coming on the faculty at Baylor. He was a recognized scholar who had taught at Furman University prior to coming to Waco and had co-authored two books dealing with the Scripture. Those books were 'The People of the Covenant' and 'Introduction of the Bible.' Abner McCall praised him as his pastor when his wife died and shared what a great comfort he had been to him and his family. Committee members present echoed the praise that the president bestowed on Jack Flanders. I knew nothing about him.

The committee approved the recommendation to accept the letter of retirement from Ray Summers and to designate Jack Flanders as chairman-elect of the Religion Department. I presented the recommendation to the full board, even though I was opposed to it. The committee had spoken, and I had no choice but to present it to the full board.

Since I did not know Jack Flanders, he called and wanted to meet me at a restaurant in Dallas soon. We met at the Cattlemen's Steak House near downtown, and he presented me with his two books. He inscribed both of them, 'To my new friend, Jimmy Draper' and signed his name.

When I had a chance to read 'People of the Covenant,' I was mortified. As I read, I became physically nauseated. I thought I had really lived a sheltered life theologically after reading just a few pages.

I had never heard such attacks upon God's Word. In his preface to the book, Jack Flanders had declared that the Bible was just Israel's concept of God, and it went downhill from there. In this same book he either ignored or explained away as myth every miracle of the Old Testament. The description of God's Word was that it was a purely human book subject to the same scrutiny and limitations as any other book.

I immediately called Herb Reynolds and told him what I had found and that I was writing a review of the 'People of the Covenant.' Herb offered no comment, but he urged me to complete my review and let him know. It took me several weeks to get it finished, and in the meantime, Herb had called several times, urging me to complete it quickly.

After I had completed my review, a meeting was set up at Baylor to discuss my review with Herb, Dr. McCall, Jack Flanders, and the pastors who were on the committee. Innocently, I went into the meeting expecting it to have a positive outcome. But when I entered the meeting, I realized that not only were those men present, but also the outside legal counsel for Baylor from Dallas. I realized this was not going to end well for what I had hoped to accomplish.

I had written one letter to Jack Flanders after we met for lunch in Dallas but did not receive a response. A week before the meeting, I had sent a second letter to Jack Flanders to try to get an opportunity to meet with him. In the letter, I told him I did not believe that 'People of the Covenant' represented the historic Southern Baptist belief and teaching concerning the Bible. I further told him that I felt the book should be removed from the curriculum as a textbook. I expressed my belief that it was intellectually dishonest as it did not

A HILL WORTH DYING ON

build faith in the Scriptures but created doubt about the divine nature of Scripture. I went on to explain I felt it ignored an entire segment of conservative scholars who had given their lives to pursuing their understanding of God's Word.

I did not hear back from him nor get to see him until the meeting. In the meeting, Jack Flanders had brought a good number of volumes of the Broadman Bible Commentary published by the Sunday School Board as a means of support of his view of Scripture. At that point, I realized that the commentary was not one that should have been produced by a Southern Baptist entity. Later I would be able to do something about that when I became president of the Sunday School Board, but not at the moment.

I opened the meeting with a few words for Jack Flanders. I told him that I did not really know him and had no personal vendetta against him, but that I had read 'People of the Covenant' and did not believe he should be chairman of the Religion Department at Baylor. The meeting adjourned with no action of any kind taking place. But the turmoil was just beginning.

Another meeting was called a few weeks later, but this time it included the entire Board of Trustees, the faculty of the Religion Department, and the university administration. By that time, I knew where we were headed. We met to spend the day to deal with my concerns. By noon, we had just walked around the entire issue. At the lunch break, I told Trustee Chairman, Milton Cunningham, that he needed to let me say something as we finished lunch and got back to the meeting. He did exactly that and called on me at the first of the afternoon session.

I told the group, "I know we are all aware of why we were there. We are here because of the issues I had raised about Jack Flanders." I stated my convictions simply that I did not believe Jack Flanders should be chairman of the Religion Department, and the book should not be a textbook.

I had talked to all the pastors who came that day, and they all promised to support my proposal. To a man, they said, "We are behind you." All of the faculty and the administration rallied around Jack Flanders, insisting that the book had been used for 16 years and was also in use at 72 other universities. They insisted they only had one complaint about the book concerning its orthodoxy. Their collective comments were largely fear-based and focused more upon providing academic freedom for the faculty and students at Baylor than what was being presented as truth.

By this point, I began to realize just how far behind me the pastors were in their support of my position—way behind me! When the vote was taken that day, only one other trustee voted with me, Paul Martin, a committed lawyer and lay leader from Houston. I was discouraged not only about the message of Flanders' books but also how the matter was dealt with.

In a surprise development on October 26, 1979, the faculty of the Religion Department sent a memorandum to the Academic Affairs Committee asking for our advice regarding the choice of textbooks to be considered and the direction the department should take in the coming years. The offer seemed too good to be true, but I was encouraged by it.

Regrettably, and in spite of this offer, Herb Reynolds launched an attack upon me and anyone else who shared in my concerns. In his

A HILL WORTH DYING ON

newsletter column on January 28, 1980, he referred to "the organized fundamentalist movement among Southern Baptists which seeks to impose upon our teaching institutions, in particular, a strict doctrinal (and creedal) position of biblical inerrancy...." He went on and fired every bullet in his arsenal, "...the power that they seek can be achieved only if all our Southern Baptist teachers believe the same way and teach their students to do likewise until everyone is properly indoctrinated...Then we would not have to be responsible for reading and interpreting our Bibles for ourselves under the Holy Spirit...It would all be conveniently laid out for us by the priestly group who believe that they are doing for us what God would do if He was just privy to all the facts."

On July 18, 1980, the trustees approved the report on the Religion Department that had been requested by the department at the previous trustee meeting in October. It was a genuine disappointment to me. By that time, I had become persona-non-grata at Baylor. I told my children, two of which were attending Baylor at the time that they were not to defend me and to stay out of any conflict focused on me. To be treated as an enemy to the school I dearly loved was a bitter pill to swallow. But I would not change anything I did in relation to the issue. I took to heart the words my dad always told me, "If something is right, stand by it, and if it is wrong, stand against it." Though professors were given the right to use or not use the books of Jack Flanders, nothing had essentially changed.

I had given my children good advice. I was subtly but effectively shunned from the Board of Trustees. I became the butt of jokes in the classroom, and my children were teased. Jack Flanders threatened to sue me. I told him, "Go ahead, you wrote the book; I didn't!" To this day, I have never been invited back to Baylor.

The theological concerns in the Conservative Resurgence centered in the faculties of our Southern Baptist Seminaries. While we had some great conservative professors in our seminaries, there were many on those campuses who were theological liberals. When many professors would go out from those seminary campuses to preach, they sounded like conservative crusaders. When they returned to campus, they would often brag in faculty lounges about what they preached in the churches and how it directly opposed what they taught in the classroom. What Baptists didn't know would protect their influence across the convention.

We had no state paper that would give us any favorable reporting except for a small paper in Indiana. Otherwise, we had no advocate in the Baptist Press across the convention. As a result, Robert Tenery published 'The Advocate,' a conservative newspaper, on newsprint, in his garage in North Carolina. That was our only option within our convention. Throughout this season, many of us continued to stand strong for the inerrancy of the Scripture in meetings and conferences around the country.

Our critics accused us of coining the word 'inerrancy.' They claimed it had not been used before in Southern Baptist life. That charge was completely destroyed when we produced a book by J.M. Frost, the first president of the Sunday School Board, written in 1903 entitled 'Baptist, Why and Why Not?' In that book, Frost specifically referred to Scripture as the inerrant Word of God. Our view of Scripture was the traditional view of the Southern Baptist Convention and of believers throughout history.

A HILL WORTH DYING ON

At the Southern Baptist Convention meeting in Los Angeles in 1980, I nominated Bailey Smith for president. He won handily on the first ballot against Abner McCall, former president of Baylor. Upon my dad's death, Bailey had become pastor at First Baptist Church in Warren, Arkansas, and followed me as pastor of First Southern when I left there. He always said, "I am the only man to follow Jimmy Draper twice," speaking of following my dad and then me.

Bailey and Sandy have been close friends ever since we met in 1966 when he came to Warren, Arkansas. We traveled together to Baptist World Alliance meetings around the world for 13 years while I was president of the Sunday School Board. We have also vacationed together in Hawaii and consider their children to be as our own children. That relationship now continues after Bailey's death in January 2019.

I was first asked to consider being nominated as president of the Southern Baptist Convention in September of 1981 by Bob Eklund. He was a dear friend and pastor of the First Baptist Church in Hurst, Texas. He asked if I would allow him to let the word out that I would be nominated at the next convention.

I immediately went to the deacons and told them about it. I emphasized to them that this was not my decision alone because the president of the convention would spend most of his time as president away from his church. I told them that this was 'our' decision, and I would not consider it without their approval.

At the same time, I asked Bob Eklund to contact a list of names of prominent Southern Baptist leaders and ask their opinion of me allowing my name to be presented. I made sure the deacons were alerted to the possibility that key people across our nation would voice their opinions about the possibility.

I presented this information at the September deacon's meeting. At our following monthly meetings, the deacons would ask for an update on my possible nomination. During this same time, Bob and some of his friends spent several months contacting approximately 50 key leaders in our convention.

Bob reported back to me that every one of the men they contacted thought my nomination was something I should allow. In May 1982, when our chairman of the deacons, Harold Samuels, again asked what the status was, I told the deacons that if the election was held at that point in time, I would probably have the green light to be nominated.

At that point, Harold asked me to leave and let the deacons meet. I was happy to give them time to thoroughly discuss my nomination as president of the convention. They remained there for several hours before adjourning. When they dismissed, every deacon signed a remarkable letter letting me know that they supported me in my nomination. They also declared that if I was elected, they would step in and take up many of the things I did as pastor to free me to meet the expectations and demands of being president. The deacon meetings until then included budget and financial information and other business items. At that point, ministry teams were formed in the deacon body and the business information was greatly reduced with ministry reports being the focus. Those ministry teams still exist today as the deacons stepped into their important role of serving the people in the church!

A HILL WORTH DYING ON

Ed Young, pastor of Second Baptist Church of Houston, has been a dear friend for 45 years. He was also being mentioned that year as a potential candidate for the presidency of the convention. We met for an extended time to talk about what both of us were facing as the convention drew near. He was at a place in Second Baptist where he felt it was not the right time for his nomination. He told me that he would not comment on his personal candidacy for the position but would remain as a 'stalking horse' to make it difficult for our critics to determine who would be nominated.

He was president of the Pastors' Conference of the Southern Baptist Convention in 1982 and had a tremendous program set up for the pastors, including Billy Graham, to close out the conference. Vice President George Bush gave his testimony, and Johnny Cash sang to the nearly 50,000 people at the conference that night. There was no doubt he could be elected in a landslide. I went to his room that night to express that conviction to him and offered not to be nominated. He still was not comfortable with letting his name be presented, so I was nominated and elected the next day in the convention.

The growth of our church during the two years I was president of the convention was amazing. I traveled most weeks between Sundays, but actually missed fewer Sundays than I would in a normal year as pastor. The supernatural result in the two years I was president of the convention saw our church add over 2,500 new members to the church. I give all the glory to God and praise our deacons and staff who gave their utmost to free me up to be gone while the church continued to grow!

WHO BUT GOD! RIDING THE WHIRLWIND
JIMMY AND CAROL ANN DRAPER

In 1983, the first year of my presidency, Bailey Smith came to preach a revival at First Baptist Euless. We were well prepared, and the excitement was high. Carol Ann had prayed that God would not let Bailey come to preach unless he was anointed for the week. He came, and he was! Bailey preached Sunday through Saturday evening and then caught a plane back to Oklahoma City. I extended the invitation after he left for the airport and many more made professions of faith. We had seen over 300 professions of faith that week.

The next day when I preached, we saw over 30 professions of faith, so we extended the services until Monday. When we had a full house on Monday, we extended to Tuesday. We continued to extend the service one day at a time all the way to Friday with 512 professions of faith for the two weeks of services. It was in these services that my son Bailey was saved, as was his wife, Kim, and my brother's wife, Retta.

The church continued to grow and prosper in the ensuing years. We completed a new 100,000 square foot educational building with new office space for the staff. The spirit and culture of the church was positive and exciting. It was such a blessing to serve in such a church during those exciting times.

My first focus as president was to reach out to both sides of the denominational controversy. There had been concerns about liberalism in the convention going back to the early 1960s. Ralph Elliott, professor at Midwestern Seminary, wrote his book, 'The Message of Genesis,' which portrayed the first 11 chapters of Genesis as mythological and not actual history.

K. Owen White, president of the convention at that time, wrote an article entitled 'Death in the Pot,' which was printed in most State

A HILL WORTH DYING ON

Baptist Papers. It referred to an Old Testament moment in the life of Elijah in 2 Kings 4:38-41, where Elijah told the sons of the prophets with him to make a stew. In the process, some inedible herbs were put in the pot of stew, and when they began to eat it, they cried out, "There's death in the pot, man of God." They were unable to eat it until Elijah sprinkled some flour in the stew, and the stew became good to eat.

The response around the convention among most scholars and prominent leaders was to express confidence in Elliott, and most were undisturbed about 'The Message of Genesis.' The issue finally came to the trustees of Midwestern Seminary. I obtained copies of the responses sent to Elliott from all across the convention and most of them were supportive of him, even to the point of praising him for his courage in printing the book. I realized our denomination just was not willing to call it the heresy it was.

When Elliott was finally terminated at Midwestern Seminary, it was not for heresy, but for insubordination. He refused instructions by the trustees to release a reprint of his book. That was the reason given for his termination, not for the content of the book.

This issue continued to create a restlessness in the convention, compounded by the Genesis volume of the Broadman Bible Commentary by G. Henton Davies, which had been released in early 1970. The book's release resulted in a hotly debated motion at the Southern Baptist Convention that year. The convention voted to recall the Genesis volume that Davies had written and have it rewritten by Clyde Francisco, an Old Testament professor at Southern Seminary. Although it was rewritten, Francisco was hardly an improvement on Davies' volume.

This concern was present throughout the 1970s, and the Conservative Resurgence was formally begun in 1979 with the election of Adrian Rogers as president of the convention. He served for one year and then declined another year, likely due to health issues earlier in the year. Bailey Smith was elected in 1980 in Los Angeles, and I was elected in 1982 in New Orleans.

The friendships I had made over the years found friends on both sides of this issue. My dad had always told me to be firm but kind in all matters. He often reminded me that convictions did not have to be brutal. Because of strong relationships across the theological spectrum at that time, I felt I could at least bring the sides to the table to discuss the issues.

I tried energetically to bring the two sides together to see if there was any common ground that could be found. I called 40 leaders together, representing both factions of the convention at the DFW Airport. I met with the seminary presidents. I had meetings at various points with many leaders. In 1981, I had gone to Israel with a group of Jewish leaders and Southern Baptist leaders led by Bailey Smith. It was such a success in the eyes of the Jewish leaders that I was asked to bring another group in the late fall of 1982.

I deliberately invited an equal mixture of SBC leaders from both elements of the controversy. I felt that if we could get them together for the trip, that some progress could possibly be made. We had a remarkable trip with the group. In October of that year, I was scheduled to fly to Los Angeles to meet with the Prime Minister of Israel, Menachem Begin. His wife died the night before our scheduled meeting, and he flew back to Israel immediately, so we did not get to meet.

A HILL WORTH DYING ON

It is the Jewish custom when a spouse dies for the surviving spouse to grieve for a specified period of time. Prime Minister Begin's first meeting following his wife's death, with anyone outside his family and closest allies, was with our group when we arrived in Jerusalem. It was a solemn meeting. It gave me an opportunity to thank him for his efforts to make peace with Egypt and to assure him of our prayers for him, his family, and for the nation of Israel.

Prime Minister Begin made arrangements for me to go into Lebanon accompanied by armed soldiers to meet with Southern Baptist Missionaries in Sidon. It was in the midst of the Peace for Galilee War between Israel and Lebanon. The Israelis had marched into Southern Lebanon all the way to within a short distance of Beirut. Later this incursion into Lebanon was renamed the First Lebanon War. The Israelis told us to rent two cars. I drove one and Baptist Press reporter, Dan Martin, drove the other. We drove to an Israeli military camp on the Lebanese border.

An armed officer with an Uzi machine gun rode in the car with me. Dan had an armed soldier in his car also. We were preceded and followed by Israeli jeeps with soldiers and mounted machine guns. After getting our clearance at the Israeli military camp, we proceeded to Tyre and on to Sidon, where we had lunch with missionaries who had driven down from Beirut. It was a special time of fellowship with those courageous missionaries living in war-torn Beirut at the time.

One interesting sidelight of this trip was that the Israeli Major who rode with me was also an acknowledged tour guide when he was not in active army service, so he took the time to give us a thorough tour of ancient Tyre and Sidon.

WHO BUT GOD! RIDING THE WHIRLWIND
JIMMY AND CAROL ANN DRAPER

Though the trip with the Jewish and Southern Baptist leaders was successful, and my visit with our Lebanese missionaries was such a blessing, we made no progress toward easing tensions within the Southern Baptist Convention.

During the years of the Conservative Resurgence, our concern was for the integrity and sufficiency of God's Word. We could not give that up. Our critics did not have biblical ground to stand on, but they saw their efforts as necessary to protect the denomination. The advantage that we had was that the issue was the Bible, and our leaders were the most popular and widely heard preachers around the country. They had the denominational strings to strum, but we had the preaching of those revered preachers declaring our position.

Longtime conservative pastor Jerry Vines liked to refer to our everyday conservative congregation members as 'Billy Baptists.' Jerry believed when the 'Billy Baptists' understood the issues, they would see things as we did. Apparently, a good many of them did as we were able to elect the president of the convention from among strongly conservative candidates for the rest of the 20th century.

The battles continued to be intense and continuous, but, in the end, we were able to gain ascendancy over our critics. Unfortunately, families were split, and friendships destroyed in the process in many instances, but we could do no less than stand our ground for the Word of God.

I preached in all six of our Southern Baptist Seminaries in the two years I was president of the convention. Two of those stand out in my mind still today. Those two were Southern Baptist Theological Seminary and Southeastern Baptist Theological Seminary.

A HILL WORTH DYING ON

One of the first I visited was Southern Seminary in Louisville, Kentucky. After preaching in Chapel, Carol Ann and I were taken to one of the larger classrooms with risers for each row of people. I stood before about 150 faculty and administrators of Southern Seminary and answered their questions for over an hour. One of the questions I was asked was what my definition of a liberal was. I replied simply that anyone who denied any portion of Scripture would be a liberal in my estimation. I was then asked to give a Scriptural illustration of liberalism. I recalled the story in Joshua 3, where Scripture says God stopped the waters of the Jordan so the children of Israel could cross into the promised land on dry ground. I said I believed that anyone who explained this to be simply a mudslide or some other natural explanation would be a liberal.

There was no sense of support or approval of our presence there that day. It was the only place we traveled while I was president where Carol Ann cried. The atmosphere in that classroom was cool and formal without any sense of prayers for me as I served as president. Everywhere else we went, the attitude of most seemed to say, "we may not have supported your candidacy for SBC president, but we will pray for you." That was not true at Southern Seminary.

There were, however, some supportive exceptions in Louisville, including Lewis Drummond, Wayne Ward, and Phil Roberts. Phil and his wife, Anya, were our transportation for our visit in Louisville. When the day was over, and Phil and Anya were taking us back to the airport, Phil said to me, "If you had said that anyone who denied the bodily resurrection of Jesus would be a liberal," you would have nailed 85% of the faculty!" The next week, I called Lewis Drummond, who was the head of the Billy Graham School of Evangelism and

Missions and asked him if that was true. He hesitated a moment and then said, "Yes, it is!" That is just one of many examples of what we faced in the early days of the Conservative Resurgence.

Armed with this understanding, I realized the great need for a simple understanding of the issue. In response, I wrote 'Authority: The Critical Issue for Southern Baptists.' I asked Herschel Hobbs, who was generally accepted as the best theologian among pastors in our convention, to write the forward which he did with a glowing endorsement of my book.

The book was published by Revell, who described the book as one showing that the belief in the authority of Scripture is at the core of doctrinal purity, evangelistic and mission outreach. I raised $80,000 and mailed every pastor in the convention my book. One thousand or more were returned because of bad addresses I had been given. The overwhelming majority of Southern Baptist pastors received the book. 65,000 books were distributed.

Sometime later, I was between planes in Charlotte, North Carolina, on my way to a meeting at the Foreign Mission Board in Richmond, Virginia. I checked in with my office, and Marilyn Novak told me that Herschel Hobbs was trying to reach me. With several hours before my plane, I had time to return his call. When I got him on the phone, he told he that he had been asked by the Baptist Standard newspaper in Texas why he had written such a glowing endorsement of my book, and he wanted to read me his response to the Baptist Standard.

After hearing his response, he asked me what I thought about it. I replied, "It sounds like you are trying to apologize for writing the forward to the book." He assured me that was not his intent and tried to explain what he was trying to say.

At that point, I told him the story of what Phil had told me at Southern Seminary. I knew he would have some familiarity with the seminary since he was a graduate of Southern. When I finished my story, I said, "You know that is true, don't you?" His simple reply shocked me. He said, "Yes, I do." I asked him why he would not say anything about it publicly since he was one of our most popular pastor/theologians in our convention. He simply said, "Because it is not common knowledge."

His answer is the simplest way to respond to the question of why we had the Conservative Resurgence. Herschel Hobbs was no liberal, but he valued protecting the bureaucracy of the convention over the integrity of the Scripture. I was disappointed that a man whose words could have gone a long way in resolving our controversy had refused to do so. I still love Dr. Hobbs and remain grateful he wrote more materials for the Sunday School Board over the years than any other author, but his response was a painful revelation to me.

I was the target of many accusations and criticisms during that time. At Baylor, while my children were attending there, I was often ridiculed in the classrooms and widely mocked by those who did not appreciate my stance. One prominent leader in the Southern Baptist Convention, who was an outspoken and aggressive spokesman for the opposition, told me, "We know you have skeletons in your closet, and we are going to find them and ruin you." That was the spirit of many of those who opposed the Conservative Resurgence.

WHO BUT GOD! RIDING THE WHIRLWIND
JIMMY AND CAROL ANN DRAPER

One of the first assignments we had after I was elected president was to attend a Spiritual Awakening Conference in Ridgecrest Conference Center in North Carolina in the fall of 1982. We had attended the conference center in Glorieta, NM, many times, but never been to Ridgecrest. It turned out to be another of those "Who But God" encounters. The young couple who provided our transportation for the conference was John and Connie Powers, who were serving a church in Tennessee. The friendship that was formed has endured and matured over the years. We have shared many things with them. We have vacationed together, stayed in their home, celebrated special occasions together and kept in touch at least each month for over 35 years. I have preached in churches he has pastored and when they came to Southwestern Seminary, they were faithful members of First Baptist Church in Euless. God has given us a relationship that continues to be a remarkable blessing over these years.

While I was president of the Southern Baptist Convention, I had the privilege to meet Chuck Colson. We became friends, and not long after my election, he put together a special trip to Washington, D.C. for us to be introduced to many of the leaders of our nation. He planned a special banquet at a luxurious residence in D.C. and invited us as his special guests. We sat at the table with Texas Senator Lloyd Bentsen and his wife, Beryl.

We had lunch with Senator Strom Thurman of South Carolina while there and enjoyed meeting with one of longest termed senators ever to sit in the U.S. Senate. It was a great delight for me to have Chuck Colson bring the final message to the Southern Baptist Convention in Pittsburg in 1983.

A HILL WORTH DYING ON

While I was president, Harold Bennett was president of the Executive Committee of the Southern Baptist Convention. He was a close, personal friend of mine and always treated me with honesty and fairness. At one point, he arranged a meeting with Cecil and Bill Sherman, leaders in the liberal segment of the convention. We met in the Executive Committee's offices in Nashville. Cecil and Bill wanted me to endorse a by-law change to take away from the president of the convention the power to appoint convention committees. Their desire was to make it necessary for the president to have the approval of his vice presidents before making the appointments.

I told them they were trying to change the rules of the convention in the midst of the struggles over the nature of the Bible and that I could not do that. They were furious with me, but I could not bow to their pressure on that issue. I realized after that meeting that the liberalism in our convention was so entrenched that there was no common ground to be found.

I deeply felt that the vast majority of Southern Baptists were strong conservative people who were committed to the total reliability of the Scripture. I further believed that the forces at work in our convention to deny that truth were contrary to our historic Southern Baptist belief. In my book, I pointed out that we had not demanded immediate termination of personnel who disagreed with us, nor had we presented a 'creed' all had to adopt. By this point, we primarily wanted to have our right to be heard as contributing, cooperating, and loyal Southern Baptists.

We were denied access to the normal communication channels in our convention. We were accused of trying to destroy academic freedom and excellence. The view of those who opposed us was that we and other conservatives were ignorant and opposed to genuine education and free inquiry. In reality, the opposite was true. Textbooks often used in our schools, and the positions presented by professors, often gave no place for traditional Biblical views.

Under the guise of academic freedom and free inquiry, many professors took license to intimidate students and to ridicule conservative beliefs. This ideology was very prevalent in our state Baptist Schools. We had no connection to the colleges and universities as they belonged to Baptist State Conventions, but the theology presented in those institutions was also present in our seminaries.

We were accused of trying to reject the biblical doctrine of the Priesthood of the Believer. The issue was not the Priesthood of the Believer. It was the matter of professors receiving salaries from the cooperative funds of the Southern Baptist Convention to teach liberal views that contradicted not only our Baptist historic position but the Bible itself! Our view was that if a person wanted to be paid by Southern Baptist funds, they should subscribe to certain foundational Southern Baptist doctrines. The integrity of the Bible was certainly at the top of those doctrines.

I even suggested in my book that a 'blue ribbon committee' be appointed to draw up a set of such parameters that we could all agree upon and have those parameters presented to the annual convention. Finally the Peace Committee was appointed by the convention in 1989 to deal with the issues before us. That committee confirmed that the issue was, indeed, concerning the doctrinal integrity of the Bible.

A HILL WORTH DYING ON

The battle over the integrity of the Bible continued throughout the 1980s. Both the administration at Baylor and Southwestern Seminary saw me as an adversary rather than a friend. Meanwhile, I became a trustee of Southwestern Seminary in the mid-1980s and was elected chairman of the trustees in 1989.

At one point in 1985, leading up to the Dallas Convention where Charles Stanley was reelected, Russell Dilday, president of Southwestern Seminary, campaigned against Charles Stanley actively. On two occasions he went to a city and made his charges attacking not only Charles, but conservatives whom he referred to as 'Fundamentalists.' I would visit the same city a week or two later to present the conservative viewpoint. This happened in Wichita, Kansas, and Shreveport, Louisiana.

Russell and other opponents to our efforts stressed that, as Southern Baptist leaders of convention agencies, they had the responsibility to speak out. I did not disagree that they had a responsibility to speak on certain issues, but that they should not be allowed to attack someone who might be elected to the presidency of the convention. I never did that as president of LifeWay and continue to believe that entity presidents should be nonpartisan.

Nothing would stop Russell's public rebuke and attacks upon those he considered opponents to his own view. He even went so far as to label conservatives as 'clones' of W.A. Criswell and called pre-millennialism a heresy. His anger and attacks were personal and painful because it did not accurately represent who we were or what we were trying to do.

The heat of this struggle continued until the election of Jerry Vines as president of the convention in 1988. After that, no more candidates were nominated to oppose the conservative nominations. We had finally arrived at the point we had hoped and prayed for: to have a good slate of conservative candidates to choose from for the presidency of the convention. That has continued to this very day. I was fortunate to preside at two conventions—one in Pittsburg, Pennsylvania, the other in Kansas City, Missouri. I was followed in office by Charles Stanley, one of my dearest friends.

It was just before his reelection in Dallas in 1985, when I made headlines without even intending to do so. I was speaking at a meeting of Southern Baptist journalists/media meeting in Richmond, Virginia. The group included national and state Baptist journalists. After my message to the group, Craig Byrd, a good friend of many years and a reporter for Baptist Press, asked me this question: "What will you do if Russell Dilday succeeds in defeating Charles Stanley's bid for reelection in Dallas?" It was a private conversation between Craig and me. I replied that if that happened, we might escrow our funds at First Baptist Church Euless IF it would bring us together to settle the issues that had been raised.

Craig wrote his article and then sent it to me to read. I examined it, and what I had said was correct in the context. He had made clear my desire to bring Southern Baptists together, but I did not realize that the context of my statement would not be included by many news outlets. Those opposed to our conservative convictions immediately accused me of "holding the SBC hostage" and "blackmailing" the convention. This was a serious charge because First Baptist Euless had consistently been in the top 20 churches in the convention in annual Cooperative Program giving.

A HILL WORTH DYING ON

What I was accused of was not what I said or intended. I had no desire to permanently hold back funds. Even the word 'escrow' certainly indicated any withholding would be temporary. I responded and made clear that I had no intention of permanently withholding funds from the convention, nor did I have any intention of allowing partisanship among the presidents of SBC entities to weaken the Southern Baptist Convention. I pointed out that three seminary presidents and the president of the Foreign Mission Board had publicly attacked Charles Stanley and called for a convention-wide campaign to deny him a second term.

I wrote a response to the criticism I was receiving to clarify my desires with that statement. I pointed out my great dissatisfaction that leaders paid by cooperative funds would mount a campaign against the reelection of the president of our convention. My statement about "escrowing funds" was only to be done if such action would be leveraged to arrive at a solution to the tensions in the convention. I stated that we would continue to support the convention but demanded that our denominational leaders be responsible and act in a way to lead us out of the denominational dilemma we faced, rather than further dividing the convention.

The tensions continued to rise as the liberals threw their support behind Winfred Moore, pastor of First Baptist Church of Amarillo, Texas, and president of the Baptist General Convention of Texas. Forty-five thousand Southern Baptists showed up in Dallas for the convention. That was more than three times the number who attended in Kansas City when Charles was elected. In Kansas City, Charles had won with three candidates nominated with 52% of the vote. In Dallas, he won against a single opponent with 55% of the vote.

WHO BUT GOD! RIDING THE WHIRLWIND
JIMMY AND CAROL ANN DRAPER

Jimmy & Carol Ann During presidency

Campbell University Doctorate

Mission trip partner, Terry Horton

George, Charlie & Jimmy

At Superdome - New Orleans

Jimmy testifying before Senate Foriegn Relations Commiittee, D.C.

A HILL WORTH DYING ON

Jimmy with Chuck Colson

Jimmy at the White House with President Reagan

Praying at SBC Pittsburg, PA 1983

Jimmy with Israeli Prime Minister Yitzhak Shamir 1990

Jimmy with Jerusalem Mayor Teddy Kollek 1990

WHO BUT GOD! RIDING THE WHIRLWIND
JIMMY AND CAROL ANN DRAPER

At the home of Billy & Ruth Graham

MUSIC CITY USA

SUNDAY SCHOOL BOARD PRESIDENT

I had always said that being a 'pastor' was not something I did but was who I truly was. That was all about to change.

Carol Ann and I found ourselves at 53 and 55 years old, respectively, serving at one of the truly great churches in America. It had never entered either of our minds that we would leave First Baptist Euless before we retired. Although we had been approached over the years about denominational positions, we never seriously considered leaving the pastoral role.

As early as February 1991, we were told that my name had been rumored to be a prospect for the presidency of the Sunday School Board of the Southern Baptist Convention. One of our former members at Euless, Jim Fleming, and his wife, Anna Mae, were visiting one Sunday early in February after they had moved to Nashville. They were among the first to tell us about the rumors coming out of Nashville that I was slated to become the next president of the Sunday School Board. In a lighthearted moment, I mentioned it in the service and even announced, "I have no plans to move to Nashville and the Sunday School Board."

Later that February, I was contacted by the Presidential Search Committee from the Sunday School Board. They told me they had agreed not to consider anyone who did not want to be interviewed or would not submit a resume. I told them simply, "I have never had a resume, and I am not interested in the position." That didn't stop them from calling me every two to three weeks throughout March and April even though my answer was always the same.

Not to be deterred, they finally tricked me into meeting with them. Early May, Wayne DuBois, chairman of the Presidential Search Committee, called to ask again if I had changed my mind. I had known him for years and had preached in churches he pastored on several occasions. I knew most of the committee members and had a personal relationship with several of them. Bill Anderson, Chairman of the Trustees of the Sunday School Board, and I, had been close friends since we were 18 years old and students in Baylor. My friendships with some of the other members did not go back that far but were still cherished relationships.

Wayne assured me that he was not trying to force me to consider the position, but he said that the committee was meeting at the Amfac Hotel at DFW Airport in a week or so and that it would be helpful to them if I could meet with them and possibly offer some guidance to the committee.

They had planned to meet from the afternoon into the evening. I had an hour or so that was not booked that day, so we agreed to a 4:00 meeting at the hotel. Wayne met me at the door to give me a bit of a head's up. He said, "Before we go in, I need to tell you something. Even though you would not provide a resume or agree to be considered, you have never been off our list of candidates. We have talked to scores of leaders from across the country, and your name is always in the top three names suggested. This is not just a casual meeting today; it is an official meeting for you with the committee in consideration of becoming the president of the Sunday School Board."

And then he opened the door to the entire trustee committee. I was seated at the end of this big table with about a dozen people around it. Bill Anderson was present as chairman of the trustees though he was not a committee member.

At my seat, there was a very nice leather-bound notebook filled with all kinds of information about the Sunday School Board, complete with colorful charts and reports. Looking back, Bill and I can now laugh at this as he remembers that I crossed my arms and pushed the notebook away like it was a rattlesnake. And then the interview began.

I don't recall much about the interview except that they asked me what my dreams were for the Sunday School Board. I told them that I had only been to the offices of the Sunday School Board one time while I was president of the Southern Baptist Convention. I had flown in one afternoon, addressed the trustees, and then flown back home that night. I'd had no tour or met with anyone else. They were stretching it because I had no dreams at the time. We talked for an hour and a half, and the meeting concluded.

I went home and told Carol Ann, "They are really serious at this. They're trying to make us pray about this!" I told her they would call-back for a second interview in a week or two. We honored the committee's request and began in earnest to pray for God's clear will to be realized. True enough, they called about a week later.

The committee had plans to meet in San Antonio and asked me to attend. Unbeknownst to them, God had been working in our hearts and created an interest in finding out more. After returning from that visit, I told Carol Ann, "They will call us before the convention in Atlanta and ask us to meet with them before or after the convention." One week later, Wayne called and asked us to stay after the convention for an extra day and visit again with the committee. By that time, I felt that if they offered me the position, I should accept it. Carol Ann agreed, although neither of us wanted to leave Euless.

The extra day with the search committee gave us a strong affirmation that God had led us to accept the presidency of the Sunday School Board. The Presidential Search Committee voted that day to ask us to come and made plans for a called trustee meeting in July in Nashville. At that time, they would recommend that I be elected president of the Sunday School Board. Next up, they wanted to discuss salary, but I refused. I told them I had never discussed salary with any church I had ever served and would not start now. They persisted, and I simply told them to provide the salary for me that they provided for the previous president.

I never did know what I would receive until a front-page article in the Nashville Tennessean gave details of my salary package. I had not yet received my first paycheck when the article came out. Just as we had always done previously, we knew the important thing was if

God wanted us there, everything else would take care of itself. And it did.

Nashville was incorporated as a city in 1806 and became the county seat of Davidson County. It was named the permanent capital of Tennessee in 1843. In 1831 the City government owned 24 slaves, and that number increased to 60 prior to the Civil War. The city was largely built on the backs of slaves and the slave market was in the heart of the city.

The city was named for Francis Nash, a hero during the Revolutionary Army in the 18th century. He was a general in the Continental Army. Founded in 1779, Nashville grew rapidly due to its strategic location on the Cumberland River. By the 19th century, it was also a center for rail traffic as railroads crisscrossed through the city. By 1860, it had become a very prosperous city.

When the Civil War began in 1862, the State of Tennessee, including Nashville, seceded from the Union. That same year, Nashville became the first Confederate capital to fall to Union troops. The state was occupied by Union forces for the remainder of the war. The battles of Nashville and Franklin were pivotal battles in the war, and thousands of troops on both sides were killed.

Those battles were closely connected as they were less than 30 miles apart. On Nov. 30, 1864, in the Battle of Franklin, the Southern forces suffered the worst defeat ever for the Confederacy. In that battle, 14 Confederate Generals were killed, seven were wounded, and one was captured.

The Battle of Nashville followed quickly on December 15-16, 1864. It was the most decisive tactical victory gained by either side. It was also the war's final major military action in which Tennessee regiments played a large part on both sides of the battle. Nashville and Franklin both still have historical sites that are prominent all across the area. Scars and prejudices from the Civil war died hard in Nashville. As late as 1960, Nashville still had racially segregated public restroom facilities, lunch counters, department store fitting rooms, hotels, and restaurants.

By the 1990s, Nashville had become a strong center for music, healthcare, publishing, education, banking, and transportation industries. There are at least 19 colleges and universities within a 40-mile radius. It is also home to many national businesses with companies such as Bridgestone, Hospital Corporation of America, Nissan, Dollar General, and Gaylord Industries.

Nashville is the national headquarters for the Southern Baptist Convention, Cokesbury Publishing (Methodist), Thomas Nelson Publishers, the National Baptist Convention USA, Inc., the Church of Christ, and the Sunday School Board, now renamed LifeWay Christian Resources.

The Sunday School Board of the Southern Baptist Convention was founded in Nashville in 1891. It became the largest distributor of Christian materials in the world and remained so during our time there. The Sunday School Board has remained in downtown Nashville over all these 129 years.

When we arrived in Nashville, the Sunday School Board had over 1.1 million square feet of space on 14 acres of prime property in downtown. Over 1,700 people worked in Nashville. Total employees at the bookstores and conference centers raised that number to 2,500.

In recent years, the 14 acres were sold for a special development group created to develop that property. LifeWay took the funds and purchased a three-acre tract of land just north of I-40 and less than half a mile away. A new LifeWay building was built on that property to maintain a downtown presence. Indoor parking was added to the office space. The beautiful nine-story tower is a great example of contemporary technology and operational strategies.

We moved to Nashville in August 1991 to an adventure that lasted 15 years. It started with a whirlwind of decisions and activities and never let up! When the previous president, Lloyd Elder, was encouraged to retire by the trustees, a motion was made to let him remain in office for 30 days after a new president was elected. That meant I could not come to Nashville until those 30 days had passed. Lloyd did not completely move out of his office until midnight on the last day. I could not get into my office until that Saturday morning. My first official day in office was on the next Monday when the trustees convened.

When I was elected back on July 18, I met with Lloyd and his executive assistant. She had resigned as secretary of the board, but not as executive assistant to the president. She wanted to remain in that position and expressed that to me in the meeting. I told her that I would not have accepted the invitation if I could not bring in my own executive assistant. Still, both of them asked me to pray about it over the weekend and let them know on Monday my decision.

I called on Monday after praying much about it and told Lloyd that when he left, she needed to leave also. He insisted that I tell her myself, which I did. I have never known why they were so insistent about her remaining there. It was doubly strange because I do not know of any president of any company who was pushed so hard by his predecessor to maintain the closest assistant to him.

I brought in Shirley Favazza, our long-time friend from our Red Bridge days in Kansas City, to be my executive assistant. Her arrival absolutely revolutionized the president's office. She was warm and caring, gentle, but effective. She changed the atmosphere from being cold, icy and forbidding, to being open, accepting, and gracious. Up until her death, whenever I would see folks who were there when we served together at LifeWay, they always asked about Shirley. Her 27 years of experience as the executive assistant for the regional office of Chrysler Corporation made her an excellent co-worker at the Sunday School Board. I had the privilege of preaching Shirley's funeral in September of 2019 in Kansas City.

Linda Rogers had been Shirley's assistant during her years as executive assistant to the president. Shirley told me that Linda was ready and well-trained to assume her position, so I asked her to take Shirley's place. She served in that capacity the remaining eight years of my time at LifeWay and was an excellent partner in ministry. We still keep in touch with Linda and her husband, David, each year.

When it was announced publicly that I was to be recommended as the next president, even critics of the Conservative Resurgence told me the Sunday School Board was top-heavy and needed to downsize. That was one of the first issues I faced.

Since my first official day was a trustee meeting, I jumped right into the midst of things and watched with great interest what took place during that meeting. There were two issues that stood out during the trustee meeting. First, there was some concern about the philosophy of teaching children. The Sunday School Board had developed a strategy that had concluded that certain doctrines of our faith could not be understood by young children.

MUSIC CITY USA

The leadership of the children's division had begun to teach that the issues of sin, repentance, grace, Christ's death on the cross, the resurrection, and other vital doctrines, could not be understood until a child was at least nine years old. I quickly let the children's division know that the issue had to be addressed and that nothing taught in the Bible was harmful for children.

The second issue was presented by a trustee who shared that he had just come from our Baptist Book Store and found a book for sale by Benny Henn, 'Good Morning Holy Spirit.' After telling the trustees about that, he made a motion that the trustees instruct the Sunday School Board not to sell that book. I asked them to allow me to deal with the issue, but to not even vote on that motion. They agreed to let me handle it. Our bookstore leadership had already removed the book, and we added to our guidelines that we would not carry any prosperity gospel/charismatic books. Over all the years since, LifeWay Bookstores upheld the strongest guidelines for inventory of any bookstore in the country.

After the trustees left, I learned that the past president always had a debriefing session with his executive leadership team after each trustee meeting. I will never forget that debriefing—it was my first and my last such meeting. I was told that the former president had instructed each of them to make sure that one of their staff was seated at every table during meals and sessions, and the debriefing session was their report of what they had heard. I also learned that trustees had been forbidden to speak to any Sunday School Board employees, and the employees were told not to answer any questions about the Sunday School Board if asked by the trustees.

In that debriefing session, I was asked what I thought about the trustee meeting and my opinion of the performance of the staff before the trustees. My reply was simple, "I never saw so many smoke and mirrors in my life." There were few straight answers given to trustees in the meeting. That was the last of those debriefing sessions while I was president.

I went further and made the decision that trustees could talk with any employees they wanted to engage and that employees could talk with trustees whenever approached. I also did away with planting staff at each table during trustees meetings. The strategies I inherited did not reflect even a remote respect for the integrity or devotion of the trustees to their responsibilities as trustees. Those changes had to be made.

One of my first decisions was to bring two of the trustees on as vice-presidents to serve with me. Gene Mims had been vice-chairman of the trustees. Since he served nearby at First Baptist Church in Cleveland, Tennessee, he had an active involvement in the activities at the Sunday School Board. I brought him on to help with relationships with pastors and churches. He led the Church Resource area of the Sunday School Board. Chuck Wilson was an MBA graduate of the Wharton Business School at the University of Pennsylvania. His business expertise was greatly needed to lead our ministry across our nationwide chain of bookstores.

My most important decision was to ask Mike Arrington to leave his job as one of the leading officers in the Texas Utilities Company. Mike is the consummate team builder whose expertise was in bringing consensus. He had been one of our deacons at First Baptist Euless, and we had developed a close relationship. His wife, Paula, and Carol Ann became good friends. When the trustees told me to,

"Bring someone to watch your back," I chose Mike for that job. He never disappointed me one time in the 15 years we served together!

He was a master at building relationships and willingly did whatever he was asked to do. I shifted him around in his roles several times, and he never complained. It was his leadership that brought about the name change to LifeWay. I did not think it was possible to do that and told him, "That just can't be done; it would be like trying to move a country graveyard!" The name change turned out to be one of the best decisions we made from a visibility and marketing standpoint. It was picked up immediately and praised from the very beginning.

I was harder on Mike than any of the other vice presidents. We were such good friends that I did not want it to look like he was my favorite vice president. He understood and never complained when sometimes I made it difficult for him, even though I wanted to be more visibly supportive. Truthfully, I trust Mike with my life and would never have succeeded at LifeWay without him!

Carol Ann was suddenly no longer the first lady of the church. There was no place for her in the organization of the Sunday School Board and was without any specific responsibilities. I had two desks put in the area where I spent most of my time, so she would have a desk to work from, but there was never an opportunity for her to use it. Paula Arrington stepped in as their friendship deepened in giant steps over the 15 years we lived in Nashville. Carol Ann and Paula were inseparable and remain staunchest friends now. Mike and Paula have been cherished friends, cheerleaders, and encouragers over all these years. We will always be more indebted to them than we could ever express.

WHO BUT GOD! RIDING THE WHIRLWIND
JIMMY AND CAROL ANN DRAPER

When I arrived at the Sunday School Board, the president's office was on the eleventh floor of the Sullivan Towers, and new employees were told to never go on that floor without an invitation. This created an immediate separation of the president from the employees. I immediately made plans to move down on the first floor for better accessibility. I wanted to be closer to where most of the employees passed every day and wanted to make it easy for them to come to see me. I let it be known that, "If the door is open, come on in. If it is closed, someone else is in there, so wait or come back later." I never understood why any president would not want to have regular contact with his fellow workers.

It took about five months to get it all done, but shortly after January 1, 1992, I was on the first floor. The hallway in front of my office led to the front door on the north end of the building. It was six feet wide, and we widened it to 10 feet. The halls which had been dimly lit, were now brightly lit. The entire entrance and hallway were now inviting and provided easy traffic for those busy hallways.

When we came to the Sunday School Board, we had a remarkable group of technical personnel who led our Information Technology department. At the time, technology was exploding around the world and even though our IT department had done a great job keeping us going, they lacked the expertise to meet the speed of changes.

My first out of town assignment after I became president was to fly to Miami to preach at a Florida Baptist Sunday School Conference. It was a great day, and one I thoroughly enjoyed with over 1,000 people present. I had been given a new laptop by our IT department before I left and had worked on a message during my flights. When I got back, I gave the laptop to our IT leadership and asked them to get it out of the laptop and into our internal computer system so it could be printed for my use. It took them 8 hours to figure out how to do that, including several hours studying the operational manual for the laptop. It was not their intention to limit us, but they were just not up to the speed we needed to be effective.

Our computer services and systems had to be changed. Some of the computers at that time were the first ones the Sunday School Board had purchased over 20 years before. We had at least 25 different mainframe systems throughout our buildings. That entire technology had to be restructured. One of the first changes was to bring in top quality experts in the developing technology that bombarded us every day.

That was when we brought Gerald Shields in to head up our IT department in 1995. He was a computer genius and able to lead us to the next level of expertise and do so in a remarkable way. The first big challenge Gerald faced came when he realized our infrastructure was grossly inadequate to continue to serve our customers and meet their needs.

After much research on the subject, he recommended a completely new software system called Vista. The cost of installing that system was almost $5 million, but it was worth every penny. The installation was excruciating. We did not miss a shipment during that process, but it required all our personnel to make it happen. We had to make up for what was lacking in our technology during the weeks Vista was being installed. Ask any employee who was with us during the installation of Vista, and you will get a big smile and perhaps a grimace!

WHO BUT GOD! RIDING THE WHIRLWIND
JIMMY AND CAROL ANN DRAPER

During the Vista installation, Gerald said it was like changing a tire at 60 miles per hour! Gerald and his entire IT team did not go home from Thanksgiving until Christmas, working around the clock and sleeping in their offices during that month. But when it was completed, we moved forward with a new excitement and strength with the increased capacity in our software.

We moved from having an IT department filled with good people who did not have the expertise to meet the challenges of new technology to a world-class IT department. Under his leadership, we moved up to the next level of IT expertise. When Gerald left, he became the IT director for AFLAC and its nationwide medical insurance supplements.

Gerald's standard of expertise was continued when Tim Vineyard became our Chief Information Officer and Vice President in 2002. He had been vice president of a firm specializing in computer sales, networking, and the Internet. Under his leadership, his team was responsible for maintaining and continually improving the quality of our website and adding a consistently growing long list of services, including online Bible Studies and websites for churches.

Our ability to take advantage of new technologies impacted us in several ways. As an example, in 2002, we sent out almost 21 million packages, but we had 30-40% fewer people in the warehouse than we had in 1997. Technology was changing the way we communicated and how we delivered our product. We were able to pull an order, box it, weigh it, put postage on it, and ship it all completely automatic.

One of the first things I did when I got to the Sunday School Board was to declare the Broadman Bible Commentary out of print, along with the Layman's Bible Commentary. Existing copies were destroyed except for one copy kept for historical purposes. Both of them contained elements of the things that made the Conservative Resurgence necessary.

We worked hard from Day One of our time in Nashville to change the culture of the Sunday School Board from discouraging to encouraging, from the mid-twentieth century to the coming twenty-first century. The previous president had often told the employees that the Sunday School Board was a dying organization. That attitude had to be removed!

I soon learned there was quite the bureaucracy involved in bringing both our Sunday School curriculum and mass-market books to market. In talking to Harry Piland, the head of our Sunday School area, I learned it took four-and-a-half years for Sunday School materials to move from concept to distribution. And Harry was proud of that! I also learned that it took three years and 15 signatures to publish a book.

Harry and I had been friends for years, but I told him that I did not believe we should be proud of this timeline. This production schedule had to change, or we could never produce relevant materials for current needs. One of the challenges is that personnel at the Sunday School Board did not write most of the materials, but only edited them for publication. Thousands of individuals around the country in our convention did the writing. It took some effort, but we were able to get the literature development process down to 18 months and book publishing down to one year with less signatures required. Once this happened, we were confident the culture change at the Sunday School Board was complete, and we could move ahead with developing a new vision statement.

When we had reached that point in our restructuring, and in a miraculous time of just three hours, we developed the following vision statement: "We will assist local churches and believers to evangelize the world to Christ, develop believers, and grow churches by being the best worldwide provider of relevant, high-quality, high-value Christian products and services."

For the first eight to ten months, I tried to get to know the Sunday School Board and its employees thoroughly. Then it was time to face the issue of streamlining the organizational strategy for the Sunday School Board and begin the reorganization. Our Executive Leadership team set up four task forces to consider the structure of the Sunday School Board and how we did business. There were about 25 people on each of those groups, and I wanted them to tell us what worked and what did not work.

I asked them to give us suggestions on what changes needed to be made in order to improve our service as a company and how to best communicate their findings so everyone could know the results. The four task forces were (1) the External/customer group, (2) the Organizational option group, (3) the People resources group, and (4) the Communications Strategy group.

The task force members were not the officers at the board, but supervisors and line workers who actually were doing the work. We provided one outside consultant for each task force, not to direct them, but to help them stay on task and to answer any questions. None of us on the Executive Team attended any of the meetings of this group. They were given 60 days to do their work. We put them in an area across the street in a building we owned but were not using.

MUSIC CITY USA

These task forces focused on restructuring to improve quality, promoting flexibility, understanding how to better serve the needs of our customers, and on downsizing and reorganizing the Sunday School Board. They ultimately recommended early retirement options with special financial incentives. For eliminated positions, the law required us to offer the same package to everyone qualified to receive the offer. We lost some employees we did not want to lose, but everyone who qualified for the early retirement had to have the opportunity to accept.

We were told that the average number of employees who accept such offers was about 30%. But of the 191 employees who were offered the early retirement, 159 accepted! We lost some of our best employees because they were free to accept the offer.

On November 1, 1992, 159 employees left the Sunday School Board. Some of our employees were angry as signs appeared in some parts of the buildings with a caricature of me on it and the words 'King Jimmy.' Other signs had somber representations and the words, 'Black Tuesday.' I never took any of those signs personally because I understood the employees had gone through a very difficult time before I came. I also knew that time would heal their wounds, and they would gain confidence in me.

One really hilarious thing happened as a result of those signs. We were able to trace the signs to the exact printer and employee. We decided to make a statement that needed to be made. Mike took the signs and went to the floor of the department where the man worked. He waited until it was close to time for employees to start going home. He rode the elevator up to the printer's office in the

Sullivan Towers, and when the doors opened, he was met with a whole lobby full of employees from that department waiting to get on the elevator. Looking really stern, Mike mentioned the man's name who had printed the signs and asked if he was in that day and held up the pictures. Stunned, someone in the group finally said that he was not in that day.

At that point, Mike said, "Well, tell him when he comes in tomorrow to clean out his desk and leave his keys and that he is fired." The crowd was shocked and silent. Mike waited a few moments before he burst out laughing and said, "No, I was just kidding. We got a good laugh out of this but tell him he might want to go down and apologize to Dr. Draper!" It was an excellent opportunity for us to further develop the relationships we were building with employees.

For most of our employees, there was no crying because what was done was the recommendation of the employee task forces we had formed. Some of those who accepted the offer did not like the feeling of being pushed out, but no one ever was unhappy with the way they were treated. It was an expensive step for us to take as we spent nearly $15 million on the early retirement offer, but it did allow us to right-size and move forward. From that time on, we saw a great improvement in the overall attitude of the employees that continued until the time I retired.

After the reorganization was completed on Nov. 1, 1992, we moved forward to get the best possible people in each of the top positions. Mark Scott, who had been with the Sunday School Board for many years, became our Vice President for the Baptist Book Stores. An accountant by training, Mark had a great ability to see through issues and to move forward in dealing with them. Under his leadership, the number of our bookstores increased from 63 to over 175 stores.

Ken Stephens was a top administrator at Thomas Nelson Publishers. He came in to direct our retail publishing arm, Broadman Press. He did a remarkable job of turning what had been a 'vanity press' for mediocre books into a truly great publishing arm of the organization. Ken helped us discover that Broadman Publishers never even had a strategy to actually publish what the industry called an 'A book,' which refers to top-selling books. As a result, most of Broadman's books were 'C books' when sales were tallied.

During these years, B & H stepped out on some creative and risky projects. One that was exciting, but had limited success, was a video production of what was called 'Secret Adventures.' It was built around a family with teenagers and was perfect for children of all ages. It was filmed in California by top professionals and included classic-style hand-drawn animation sequences. Each episode had a guest star on the program. Michael W. Smith made his acting debut on one show. John Tesh, the popular TV host of Entertainment Tonight and A.C. Green, an all-star NBA player, also appeared in episodes.

This project won many awards for its high-quality, family-friendly entertainment value, including a Gold Camera Award from the U.S. International Film and Video Festival. Each show contained a biblical lesson for the teenage star in the show to learn. Although highly acclaimed, it was not received well enough for us to continue that project.

B & H also produced a video called 'Storybook Tree,' which was a fanciful series for young children featuring Henry Cory and multiple puppet characters. B & H, also, gained exclusive religious distribution rights to the hit CBS television show 'Christy,' based on a novel by Peter Marshall's wife, Catherine.

During the same year, we became a distributor of Billy Graham's Worldwide Film catalog of inspirational movies and documentaries. By 1995 the Sunday School Board was the largest distributor of Christian videos in the world. We also got into the record business by launching Genesis Records to go along with our Genevox music publishing efforts.

We had two books make it to the New York Times best-selling list. One was 'Payne Stewart: The Authorized Biography,' written by Ken Abraham, a Tennessee author with strong connections to Payne's wife, Tracey. In 2000, that book spent 13 weeks on the New York Times best-selling list and sold nearly a half-million copies.

Payne was a top PGA golfer known for his knee-length knickers, colorful socks with unique golf shoes with silver tips, and a British golf hat. Known, also, for his bad temper and strong language, Payne had been led to the Lord and experienced the transformation of his life. His conversion became his passion, and his golf game was reinvigorated. That book took his Christian testimony to the Today Show, Sports Illustrated, and other major secular media outlets.

The other major success for B & H was the novel by Colonel Oliver North in 2002 named 'Mission Compromised.' It also made the New York Times Best Selling list and sold over 300,000 copies in the first year. Ollie was a Marine and a former National Security Council officer. He was a controversial leader who had become involved in the Iran-Contra Affair as instructed by his superiors. He also became known as a devoted and passionate follower of Jesus Christ and an outspoken supporter of a biblical worldview.

MUSIC CITY USA

Not long after I got there, Richard Ross and Jimmy Hester came to my office with a new idea to promote sexual purity in young people prior to marriage. They sketched it out on a napkin from the cafeteria and called it 'True Love Waits.' Richard had already successfully tried it out at his youth group at First Baptist Church in Mt. Juliet, just east of Nashville. It was a remarkable plan that we did implement. I really thought they wanted my advice but found out quickly what they really needed was $25,000 to kick it off, and they knew I had a budget that could provide it!

I gave them the go-ahead and provided the cash from my presidential budget. It was launched at the National Youth Ministers' Conference we had each year at the Sunday School Board. Richard had his youth come and celebrated embracing the concept. It went viral quickly among the youth ministers. Many of them went back and introduced it to their own youth groups.

We had a nation-wide launch for 'True Love Waits' on July 29, 1994, on the Mall in Washington, D.C., with 210,000 cards displayed on the National Mall. On that same day, the nation of Uganda launched the same emphasis in Kampala in a grand parade filled with bands and the military. The president of the nation, Yoweri Museveni and his wife, Janet, led and promoted 'True Love Waits' in Uganda. Years later, I met with Mrs. Museveni, and she told me that both of their children had taken the pledge and married spouses who had made the pledge. Part of both wedding ceremonies was to exchange their 'True Love Waits' pledge card.

She also reported that since 'True Love Waits' was launched in Uganda, there had been a large reduction of AIDS cases there. Though there were other ministries addressing the AIDS issue, she credited 'True Love Waits' as being the primary reason for the decline AIDS cases in the country.

On April 1, 1993, the Sunday School Board released a series of six studies dealing with the Christian understanding of sex. On June 14, 1994, 'True Love Waits' was presented to the Southern Baptist Convention meeting in Orlando, Florida. During my report to the convention, a thousand students rushed the aisles to the platform waving their 'True Love Waits' cards in support of that effort. At that time, 102,000 students had taken the pledge. That number continued to grow dramatically. By July 29th, thousands of students swarmed all over the Washington Mall and planted stakes with 210,000 cards stapled on them in the ground.

On October 29th, Richard Ross appeared on the Today Show to promote 'True Love Waits,' and the first 'True Love Waits' newsletter was released.

In February 1995, 'True Love Waits' launched the 'Through the Roof' campaign and rally in the Georgia Dome. There were 18,000 students at the rally with the goal to stack their commitment cards so high it would go through the roof! A year later, over 340,000 more students joined the movement. Two years later, rallies across the country over brought in 500,000 additional pledge cards.

At the Baptist World Alliance in August 1995, meeting in Buenos Aires, Argentina, I preached the main message of that BWA. At that meeting hundreds of thousands of 'True Love Waits' cards from 13 different countries were displayed. The 'True Love Waits' emphasis was presented to Congress in Washington, D.C., in 1998, and in the fall of that year, the website was launched.

'Crossing the Bridge' was the emphasis in 1999 as over 1,500 teenagers carried over 100,000 cards across the Golden Gate Bridge in October. In December, the 'True Love Waits' movement promoted a fantastic prayer meeting asking for God's blessings on the students who made those 100,000 pledges. In February 2001, the challenge was issued for teens to 'Seize the Net' and were invited to sign the pledge online. An additional 31,338 youth signed up online from that campaign.

The Olympics were held in Athens, Greece, in 2004, and students displayed 460,000 pledge cards from 20 countries around the world. In 2005, 'True Love Waits Takes the Town' was launched in Nashville. In 2007, it was officially introduced throughout Africa.

In 2008, the emphasis was on the distribution of a 'True Love Waits' New Testament; it was launched in Africa and the Philippines. Another theme was introduced later that year, 'A Path to Purity,' and it was successful as well. From its beginning in 1993 until today, 'True Love Waits' has been a shining beacon calling teenagers to a biblical view of the sacredness of sex.

The purpose of 'True Love Waits' was simple. It was a challenge to teenagers to understand the value of remaining sexually pure until marriage. It was designed to assist parents and churches in addressing biblical standards of sexual behavior. The ultimate goal was to communicate to the world a preferred alternative to the secular 'safe sex' message.

'True Love Waits' was not a virginity campaign. Richard Ross said, "We want young people who have made serious mistakes in their lives to be welcome to pledge abstinence from this day forward until marriage." It was a campaign for all who had found forgiveness of past failures.

'True Love Waits' was one of the most important things that happened while I was president of LifeWay. 'True Love Waits' emphasized a lifetime of purity despite a secular environment that opposed this whole concept of remaining sexually pure until marriage.

In 1993, we completed a new parking garage that could accommodate 800 cars for our employees, along with a new cafeteria, and space for the Human Resources Department. Now employees could have indoor parking in times when weather conditions made outdoor parking difficult. We also opened the Harry Piland Prayer Chapel on the upper level of the new entry that was created by the new building.

In October 1993, I preached in a celebration of 100 years of Sunday School work in Brazil. It was a nationwide conference called 'Celebrando la Biblia.' The Maracanã Soccer stadium in Rio de Janeiro holds over 100,000 people. Right beside it is a smaller arena that seats 5,000-6,000. I preached in the smaller arena every night Monday through Friday. The pastor of the First Baptist Church in Rio de Janeiro, Fausto Vasconcelos, was my interpreter. He may have been the best translator I have ever had!

I was assigned five topics dealing with the Bible's position of five key issues facing the churches there. I sent manuscripts to them, and they printed books of my messages in Portuguese to give away to the thousands who came each night. That book was entitled "O Desafio da Palavra."

MUSIC CITY USA

From 1993-94 we appointed a Sunday School Task Force that surveyed 13,000 people to ask them what they needed and wanted in their Bible Study materials. As a result, we took our main three curriculum materials and completely reconfigured two of them to respond to the task force findings and made a major change in the third set of materials. These were our changes: (1) The Bible Book Series was renamed Explore the Bible. (2) The Uniform Series was an effort to join denominations all over the country so that all our churches would be studying the same Scripture each Sunday. We had provided most of the funding for this effort, but we did not want to continue in that effort but concentrate on our three curriculums. We withdrew from our commitment to the Uniform Series, and (3) named its replacement the Family Bible Series.

Carol Ann and I returned to Korea, along with Kirk and Dana Humphreys, in November 1994. I had known Kirk since our Del City days when he was a student at the University of Oklahoma. He was the current chairman of our trustees, and we were excited to share the trip with him and Dana. He was a prominent businessman in Oklahoma City and would become mayor after he completed his trustee term.

It was a hectic and frantic pace during our week there. I preached seven times at a Pastors' Retreat in the mountains near Seoul. While there, I preached for my friend, Han Ki Man, pastor of the great Yoido Baptist Church in Seoul. He later would visit me in Nashville on one of his trips to the United States to get his two children in American universities. We also rode over to Tajon for me to speak at the seminary there. I had the privilege of preaching for my dear friend, Billy Kim, at Central Baptist Church in Suwon, Korea. They had seven services each weekend, and the same choir sang at all of them. That choir considered those seven services their service for the Lord in the church.

Around this time, I was facing a huge decision concerning the structure of our leadership team at the Sunday School Board. I had set up a consensus leadership strategy when I arrived that allowed me to have the final authority if an agreement could not be reached. That had worked for the first couple of years, but it became more and more difficult to navigate the waters of that strategy. On this trip, I was considering whether or not to create the position of Chief Operating Officer and put Ted Warren in that position or just continue as we were currently structured.

On a single day while in Korea, I received 54 pages of faxes from my vice presidents, urging me not to make the change. I asked Kirk to read the faxes, which he did, but without any comment. He later told me he already knew what I would do and didn't want his opinion to enter into making the decision. After much prayer, I asked Ted to assume that role and things really begin to move forward in a big way. It was one of the best and most important decisions I made while at LifeWay.

Ted Warren came to work for us as our Chief Financial Officer in 1994. He had an MBA from Harvard University and had been an executive at several oil companies since graduation. He had been leading the 'Experiencing God' Bible study on weekends at local churches and realized one day he had not been practicing what he was teaching. Up to that point, he had never considered finding where God was working and joining Him in ministry. When God laid this on his heart, we were blessed to have him join our team.

At the time he came, the Sunday School Board had just had two consecutive years of losses that totaled over $13 million. Within 90 days, Ted had us back in the black, and we never returned to operating in the red during our 15 years there. Ted was a gifted leader, and his effectiveness was obvious.

In June 1995, I returned to Kenya. Another great crusade was being held at the Uhuru Park in downtown Nairobi. A prominent African-American pastor from the United States was scheduled to preach in the park, which included one grandstand behind the platform for the crusade. I was not involved in the preparation or details of the crusade but was there as a participant.

Carol Ann and I joined some friends at the crusade and were sitting high in the grandstand behind the platform for the crusade. President Moi and his entourage were in an area to our right as we looked out over the platform. Some of the participants in the crusade from the United States were seated in a tented area. Before the service got underway, a messenger came up to find me and told me that President Moi wanted me to sit by him in his tent. I was surprised but grateful for his invitation to join him there at his side.

During that crusade, I preached five times in the Kayole Baptist Church and the Riruta Baptist Church in Nairobi on Sundays. I also met with key national leaders and missionaries to encourage them and discuss discipleship partnership with them and LifeWay.

Jim Carter was recommended to us several years before he joined our staff as Chief Financial Officer. We weren't ready for him the first time he was recommended but followed up with him when the time came. He was a career military officer whose last assignment had been at the Pentagon. He came out of First Baptist Dallas, where he was a deacon and a very active leader. He brought a skill and passion that was greatly needed.

Jim's wife, Jeannine, was deeply committed to partnership missions, and had been on scores of mission trips over the years. When we began to send our employees on overseas Partnership Mission trips, Jim and Jeannine led that emphasis. While Jim took care of all the details for the trips, Jeannine was a super participant and cheerleader in promoting the trips.

Our partnership mission effort began in 1996. Over the ten years we sent employees on overseas partnership mission trips, we had 115 total trips with 130,529 professions of faith reported on those trips. There were 1502 participants who went on those trips, most of whom were our employees. There were 280 churches planted as a result of those mission trips.

During those ten years, we had a mission trip display just inside the main entrance to our LifeWay building so everyone who entered could see the display. The missions display included a list of the countries and participants, the proposed trips for the current year, as well as application forms for individuals who were interested in participating in one of those trips.

This mission trip strategy was pivotal in creating a new spirit in what was now called LifeWay. We offered our employees paid leave to go on the trips, and we paid half the costs for the trip if they would raise the other half. Our first year, the mission trip had nine people go. At our highest, we had scores on each trip and an incredible boost to how our employees saw their work when they returned.

It helped our employees realize that the work they did at their desks was not just 'busy work,' but was actually impacting over 125 nations around the world. It created a sense of purpose and community that was greatly needed. It is difficult to imagine LifeWay today without the mission trips!

In 1996, we took over the Wounded Heroes Ministry of Freddie Gage and changed the name to LeaderCare. We held conferences across the country for ministers and staff who were having burnout or faced challenges that were overwhelming. Brooks Faulkner and I did conferences frequently to deal with those issues. We called them 'Strength Under Stress' conferences. It was amazing how many hurting pastors and staff leaders were really at the end of their rope.

In 1996-97, I was on the road for 144 days. Those days led me to 29 states in that two-year period. With Ted Warren effectively leading internal operations, I was free to continue building relationships with Southern Baptists and other evangelical believers across the nation.

After we went through the restructuring of the Sunday School Board, Mike Arrington began to urge us to consider changing the name of the Sunday School Board. Initially, I was opposed to it, but James Sullivan, who had been president of the Sunday School Board from 1953-76, told me he had wanted to change the name when he was president. He felt that when the Southern Baptist Convention assigned Church Training (Discipleship) to the Sunday School Board, the name became outdated and obsolete. Dr. Sullivan encouraged us to examine the name change issue closely. We worked with an outside firm to meet with groups around the country and considered many possible names. Mike Arrington led the study team that looked into all that would be involved in a name change.

We knew we wanted a name that was Biblical and one that would be a good tool for witnessing. The name that emerged was LifeWay Christian Resources. When someone would ask what that meant, we would point them to John 14:6, "Jesus said, I am the Way, the Truth and the Life, no one comes to the Father but through Me." We surveyed over 600 ministers, and the majority approved that name.

We had opened two bookstores back in the 1970s named LifeWay Stores, but the name failed to gain traction then, and the stores didn't keep the name. Years later, we felt it was a great descriptive name for us. God has blessed the name from the beginning. The name was formally approved by the Southern Baptist Convention in June 1997 and 1998. It required approval by two successive conventions to be official.

The Sunday School Board was originally charged with publishing Bible study materials. And while we had been highly successful in doing that, we had never owned a Bible translation of our own. Holman had published many translations but had to pay royalties on most of those translations. We would not have completed a new Bible Translation if it had not been for the strategy that the New International Version put in place in the mid-1990s.

The Zondervan Publishing Company owned the copyright for the NIV. They released a politically correct translation in the United Kingdom called the TNIV. It catered to the 'diversity" and inclusiveness' sweeping the world at that time. I called a meeting of the Zondervan leadership and the International Bible Society who had produced the TNIV, and we confronted them with our concerns.

In 1973, when the NIV translation was released, we placed it in our Bible Study materials, and it had been there ever since. I believe we had a large part in the popularity of the NIV, which accounted for 43% of the Bible sales in America at the time we met with Zondervan and the translators.

At the meeting, I informed them that if they published the TNIV, we would take the NIV out of our literature. They promised us they would not release that translation in America, but then did so six months later. At that point, we realized if we were going to have a strong, accurate translation that was true to the original languages of the Bible, we would have to do it ourselves.

We absorbed a group that had begun a translation from the original languages in 1984. It was a team of 78 translation scholars who were experts in ancient Hebrew, Greek, and Aramaic and was led by a brilliant scholar, Art Farstad. Sadly, Art died two months after our partnership, but Ed Blum stepped in to complete the project.

We had a tremendous advantage in the translation as new technology allowed us to work at a remarkable speed in completing the translation. The New Testament was released in 2001, and the complete Bible was released in 2004!

How we named the translation is a story on its own. About a dozen of us met at a small retreat center north of Nashville for one afternoon and evening and into the next day until noon. As we discussed names for the new Bible, it began to dawn on us that we were going to name a new Bible translation. Up to that point, I don't think we all had grasped the solemnity of what we were doing, but when we did, it felt as if a Holy hush dwelt with us all evening.

We began to list the names we might consider and discussed them in the evening session. During that process, we realized that none of the Bible translations at that time contained the name

'Christian' in them, so we gradually moved toward naming it the Christian Standard Bible.

Deeper into our discussions, we learned the Standard Publishing Company in Cincinnati, Ohio, had produced a weekly newsletter by that name for over 100 years named the 'Christian Standard.' Standard Publishing had joined us in a research project several years before dealing with the use of names for Bibles. That project concluded that a newsletter or magazine name should not prohibit naming a Bible translation by the same name. Thus, we didn't see a conflict between a newsletter and a translation having the same name.

Just to be sure, I flew to Cincinnati and spent the day with Gene Wiggington, the president of Standard Publishing and his staff. They were strong and committed believers, and our meeting was the beginning of a wonderful relationship. They had little concern for us using the same name, although there was a slight hesitancy due to its long-standing use with their newsletter.

Although they had participated in the original survey with us, we were surprised when they later opposed the use of the name Christian Standard. We learned that in the time before the translation was completed, Standard Publishing had been bought out by a large conglomerate in New York. As soon as the new owners took control, Standard Publishing told the new owners about the matter of our new translation and the use of 'Christian Standard.'

The new owners insisted that the Standard Publishing Company protest the use of the name and even threatened to file a protest if we used the name. Their protest led to an agreement to engage in binding arbitration with mediators presiding over the proposal. The agreement was that we would split the cost of the mediation, and that we would abide by the decision that was made by the arbitrators.

We chose one of the lawyers for the mediation, Standard chose a lawyer, and then those two lawyers chose a third lawyer for the mediation panel. When I flew to Atlanta to give my deposition, I walked into the room and saw Gene Wiggington. He winked at me and smiled slightly. I knew then that he did not want to be in the room and was forced to make the protest, which led to the mediation.

When all depositions were presented, we won all aspects of the mediation. The decision was made to give us permission to use 'Christian Standard,' and all the costs were to be paid by Standard Publishing. We agreed on two conditions: first, we split the cost of the mediation because we had agreed with Standard in advance to do that; second, we had such respect for the men from Standard Publishing that we chose to name the new translation 'The Holman Christian Standard Bible.'

We knew in time the word 'Holman' would be dropped, and it would become known as the Christian Standard Bible. That happened in 2018 when a new revision of the translation was released. It is a faithful translation of the original languages and has maintained a strong presence in the Bible market here in the United States.

I now believe that the most significant thing we achieved at the Sunday School Board/LifeWay during my time as president was the new translation of the Bible. Some have asked, "Why a new translation? There's been a large number of new translations already during the 20th century!" But that statement was simply not true. There were only two evangelical translations done from the original languages in the 20th century—the American Standard and the New International Version. All the other 'new' Bibles were revisions of versions that did not go back to the original languages to translate; they simply revised existing translations. To be clear, there were many revisions, but only two evangelical translations from the original manuscripts in the 20th century.

We had one very exciting trustee meeting in our February 2000 meeting. During the first day of the trustee meeting, the weather changed drastically as snow and ice were quickly developing. Carol Ann had driven to LifeWay for her meeting with the trustee wives, but as the conditions worsened, several of our LifeWay wives opted to leave early. By the time our meeting ended, things had gotten even worse. When I suggested to Carol Ann to follow me home, she and Paula Arrington thought better of that and decided to leave their cars and ride with me.

Mike Arrington had planned to finish up a few things before he headed home. We headed out on I-65 toward our home when we realized we were driving on a road that was completely covered with 'black ice.' We could not see it, but there was no doubt an invisible layer of ice had formed on the road. After a harrowing three hours, we finally made it the 13 miles to get Paula home and then to ours. Mike had taken a different route than we had and got home several hours after us. Over 10,000 cars were stranded on the highways in Nashville that night.

Our September trustee meeting in 2001 was held at our Glorieta Conference Center. When we greeted the new day on September 11, we were faced with the terrorist attack on the World Trade Center that killed more than 3,000 people. There was nonstop coverage of the

MUSIC CITY USA

attacks for that day and for weeks afterward. We brought televisions into the trustee meeting to stay informed throughout the day.

We watched in disbelief when we saw American Airlines Flight #11 crash into the North Tower at 8:46 a.m., followed by United Airlines Flight #175 hitting the South Tower at 9:02 a.m. These were followed by American Airlines Flight #77 as it hit the Pentagon at 9:37 a.m. and United Airlines Flight #93 that crashed in an open field at 10:03 a.m. This last plane was prevented from harming any people on the ground or buildings due to the heroism of the passengers who charged the terrorists to keep it from hitting another target, likely the Capitol Building or White House.

We spent much of the time that day praying for our nation and for all the victims of the attacks. There is no way to adequately describe the emotions and atmosphere coming from the terrorist attacks. All flights within the country and coming into the country were immediately canceled. The only plane in the air after a few hours was Air Force One, which was carefully guarded as it remained in flight most of the day. The public did not know the exact location of the president's plane at that time.

We ended our trustee meeting on time, but now we faced the challenge of transportation home for the trustees. Air travel was still canceled, so most of the trustees drove rental cars home. We chartered a bus to get many of our LifeWay personnel home. One group of three trustees from the Philadelphia area drove over 40 hours just to get home. Many chose to remain at Glorieta until the restrictions on air travel were lifted, which finally happened on Friday evening that week.

WHO BUT GOD! RIDING THE WHIRLWIND
JIMMY AND CAROL ANN DRAPER

Carol Ann and I did not leave Glorieta until all the trustees were safely on their way home. On Friday evening, we flew out of Albuquerque to Dallas to connect with a flight on to Nashville. When we landed, we made our way to the terminal for the connecting flight, but when we got to the terminal, it was empty. DFW Airport police met us as we entered the terminal and informed us that we would have to go outside as there had been a bomb threat in that terminal.

We joined hundreds of other passengers waiting outside the terminal for further instructions. In the meantime, I called our airline contact to let them know our flight had been canceled. When I explained our situation, the airline representative announced to everyone around her, "He says there is a bomb threat, and all the passengers are outside the terminal in the street." Obviously, that telephone center had not yet been told about the bomb threat.

We booked a flight back to Nashville on Saturday and called Randy to come get us and we would spend the night with them. His family was glad for the visit, and we were glad to be with them after such a long week. It was an unforgettable week for all of us and one we will never forget.

Another important goal of our time at LifeWay was to build strong relationships with the state conventions across the country. I knew most of the state executive directors but had never been in most of their offices. It took three years and 103 days of travel to visit each state convention office personally. I never went to two states on the same trip as I wanted each of them to know that they were important enough for me to make their stop the only one on my trip.

Their response was such a rewarding part of my years at LifeWay. In those visits, we discussed the cooperative agreements we had with each state convention. We asked of them to promote our materials, and in return, we gave each state annual funds. We instructed the money to be used on conferences and for activities that we wanted them to conduct and to report back how it was spent.

After my visits to the state offices, I realized that our 'one size fits all' approach was not a good fit for our state conventions. Even though they all had the same instructions for the funds we provided, I realized that we really needed to ask each state where they saw the funds were needed most and how they would like to spend the funds. By placing each state in control of the funds and the activities, we created huge loyalty across the state conventions.

My relationship with the state convention executives was one of my greatest blessings. Many of them have either retired or been transferred to heaven, but those still alive are great friends today. When I retired, the state convention executive directors presented me with a riding lawn mower and a Benelli Shotgun as a token of their esteem and friendship. There are still stories floating around about how John Sullivan, Executive Director in Florida, tried to get through security with that shotgun!

There was general consensus we needed a strong evangelism emphasis in our Sunday School strategy, so we began the FAITH Sunday School/Evangelism emphasis. We had tried unsuccessfully to get D. James Kennedy, pastor of Coral Ridge Presbyterian Church in Fort Lauderdale, Florida, and president of Evangelism Explosion, to let us use his Evangelism Explosion materials in our FAITH Sunday School/Evangelism effort.

We met several times with him and worked hard to make it happen. Our trustee, Bobby Welch, had been on the board of

Evangelism Explosion since its inception and worked hard to get James to allow us to use Evangelism Explosion as our evangelistic piece in our strategy.

James was sympathetic to what we were trying to do, but he could not come to the point where he would allow us use of the materials with our new strategy without requiring everyone to buy one of his Evangelism Explosion books. In the end, we couldn't reach an agreement acceptable to both parties, so we stepped back from it.

While Bobby was still on James' board, he wrote the FAITH strategy and tested it out in his church in Daytona Beach, Florida. When he was satisfied that worked, he came to Nashville to talk with Gene Mims and me about adopting the new FAITH Sunday School/evangelism strategy.

It was amusing to watch Bobby present his strategy with his usual passion and excitement. Even after I said, "We'll do it!" he kept right on talking before he realized what I had said. He stopped and asked, "You what?" Gene and I had a good laugh out of that. When Bobby gets to going, you can't slow him down! That's what makes him one of the best pastor/evangelists in the Southern Baptist Convention.

When we launched the FAITH strategy in Bobby's church, in Daytona Beach, Florida, Coral Ridge Presbyterian Church sent a special message from James Kennedy and Evangelism Explosion congratulating us on the launch and assuring us of their prayers. Even though we could not complete a partnership with them, James Kennedy remained a fast friend in every way.

We inaugurated LifeWay International in 1998. Though it was difficult to launch this global ministry, by the time I retired, we were serving believers in over 125 countries. Luis Aranguren, a Cuban immigrant, led those first years in a very effective way.

When we arrived in Nashville, the Sunday School Board had just released Henry Blackaby's 'Experiencing God.' It was a fantastic study that has been used all over the world since its publication. That was the beginning of many great discipleship studies. T.W. Hunt's 'Mind of Christ' was published in 1994. In addition to 'Mind of Christ,' many other discipleship books have come out since 1991, including those by Beth Moore and Priscilla Shirer. Both of them were signed to publish through LifeWay while I was president.

It is interesting how we signed those two outstanding women authors. Carol Ann had spoken at a Women's Conference that Joyce Rogers, Adrian Roger's wife, planned and directed at Bellevue Baptist Church in Cordova, Tennessee. When she came back from the conference, she told me about a wonderful speaker with her at the conference. Her name was Beth Moore, and Carol Ann advised me to get our folks busy and sign her on as an author for LifeWay.

I passed that word along to our Church Resource people and was told they had already looked at her materials and had rejected her as an author. When I told Carol Ann, she said, "You better tell them to reconsider and sign her!" Carol Ann rarely makes such a strong suggestion, so I did exactly what she told me to do, and we signed Beth. The last year I was president, we sold over $26 million of her books! She is, without doubt, the leading author today at LifeWay.

When we first learned of Priscilla Shirer, we wasted no time in setting up an appointment for her to come to Nashville to meet with us. I did not know her, but did know her father, Tony Evans, pastor of Oak Cliff Bible Church in Dallas. We set up a private lunch in one of our smaller dining areas. On the day she came, we not only met Priscilla, but her husband, Jerry, and a two-month-old baby. Together they lead their special ministry called 'Going Beyond Ministries.' We had a great meeting and soon signed her as a LifeWay author.

In 1998, Southern Baptist Theological Seminary in Louisville, Kentucky, surprised me when I spoke at their chapel service. They presented me with the E.Y. Mullins Distinguished Denominational Service Award, the highest award Southern gives that rarely goes to anyone not a Southern graduate. Southern's president, Al Mohler, has been a good friend since he was the editor for the Georgia Index paper for Georgia Baptists.

A year later, Southwestern Seminary honored Carol Ann and me with the L.R. Scarborough Award. It was yet another example of how God has been so gracious to us in bringing so many opportunities into our lives.

In February 2001, we launched LifeWayLINK as a way to order our products online. This has become even more important now than it was then since the closing of all LifeWay brick and mortar stores.

One of the assignments that fell to me as president of the Sunday School Board was to be on the Executive Council of the Baptist World Alliance, which met each year. Carol Ann and I attended those annual meetings for 13 years. During those years, we attended BWA meetings in the United States, Germany, Sweden, Jamaica, Argentina, South Africa, England, Hong Kong, Canada, and more. We always were able to enjoy those times with friends like Bailey and Sandy Smith, Paige and Dorothy Patterson, Chuck and Rhonda

Kelley, Jim and Jeanette Henry, Morris and Jodi Chapman, and Richard and Becky Land.

In August 1995, I was asked to preach the main message at the Baptist World Alliance in Buenos Aires, Argentina. That remains a vivid memory because it is winter down there while it is summer up here. The facilities did not have heat in the building, so it was a cold-weather meeting!

While in Buenos Aires, several of us rode a hydrofoil boat over to Montevideo, Uruguay. It was a windy and cold day, but we enjoyed walking around the streets of Montevideo. When we arrived in Montevideo, it was to a shipyard area with only a small facility to check passports. We had to walk about a quarter of a mile to get out of the gates of the waterfront buildings.

None of us spoke Spanish, nor did any of us know where to go. Fortunately for us, there was a gentleman walking nearby who spoke English who gave us directions to the best part of the downtown area. We enjoyed a windy but wonderful day in Montevideo and found our way back to the boat and back to the hotel safely.

As the 21st century began, the whirlwind continued. In May 2003, I was asked to preach the commencement for California Baptist University. I didn't know it at the time, but they also had plans to present me with another Doctor of Divinity degree during the ceremony. University president, Ron Ellis, had been a good friend for a number of years. A couple of years later, I was asked to serve on the Board of Trustees for CBU and did so from 2005-2011.

Union University in Jackson, Tennessee, announced in 2004 that I would be the recipient of the M.D. Dodd Award. David Dockery was president of Union at that time. We had served together at the Sunday School Board before he joined the leadership staff at Southern Seminary.

The Great Commission Council was comprised of all of the presidents of Southern Baptist Convention entities. It met just before the semi-annual meetings of the SBC Executive Committees in February and October. I hosted the meetings on Friday evenings at our LifeWay facility and after the Saturday morning session we always shared lunch at a restaurant in Nashville. We also had a retreat with our wives many of the years. These times were good opportunities to find out what was going on in all our different entities and to building relationships with each other. It was a unique and very satisfying experience each time we met. I served as chairman of that group for two years while I was at LifeWay.

When Jim Carter retired, it was the natural thing and the right choice to ask Jerry Rhyne to become CFO. Jerry Rhyne had come to LifeWay as a young man and given over 30 years in ministry there. His financial experience and wisdom were known by all, and the confidence everyone had in him was deeply rooted. Jerry did an outstanding job as CFO until his retirement in recent years. We were blessed to have sound and efficient leadership in that area.

LifeWay had one of the most diverse and remarkable group of employees I have ever met, but all were great individuals with a heart for ministry. They ranged in age from young to older; they were men and women; they were from many different ethnicities.

Here are just a few:

The Sunday School Board, and later LifeWay, always looked like a very accomplished interior decorator had been working very hard every day. Things looked beautiful but were effective, too. Charles

Businaro was in charge of this area. Whatever we needed—be it seasonal changes or special promotions—Charles was always on top of it.

In our ministry with African-American churches, Jay Wells led our team. He was one of the most recognizable names in African-American leadership across the country. Jay was responsible for planning a special week at Ridgecrest designed especially for African-American leaders.

Our International Department that we began in 1998 was headed up by Luis Aranguren, who came to the United States from Cuba some years before. He did a superb job in building relationships with internationals all over the world.

Our facility team was always outstanding. Russell Vance was one of the key leaders in that effort. He was hired as an industrial engineer for logistics when he first came to LifeWay. After five years, he was promoted to be Director of Corporate Services. We could not have had a better person for that job! Although he was a Roman Catholic, he was a vibrant believer and even went on a mission trip with other employees and became one of the best street evangelists on the trip.

Steve Lawrence was the special leader of our Human Resources Division. He had a very gentle spirit, but handled delicate issues that arose with firmness, yet kindness. He led through all the changes we saw during my time as president. Whenever someone was to be replaced or terminated, Steve was the one who guided us through those moments.

Bruce Munns worked effectively in our Book Store Division and helped lead the strong surge in growth and numbers of stores during my 15 years at LifeWay. After 38 years at LifeWay, Bruce became the Divisional Vice President of Retail in charge of all retail operations.

Byron Hill came out of the hotel management field to head up our conference center ministries. His expertise and vision paved the way for us to greatly improve the facilities and services in the conference centers.

Bill Taylor followed Harry Piland in leading the Sunday School Department for LifeWay. We were thrilled to get Bill away from North Phoenix Baptist Church, although his pastor may not have felt the same way. Like Harry Piland, Bill was known everywhere for his passion for Sunday School, and did a masterful job in moving us forward in that strategic area.

T.W. Hunt was a remarkable gifted co-minister at the Sunday School Board. He was a Music and Missions professor at Southwestern Baptist Theological Seminary from 1963 – 1987. Throughout his ministry he had focused on the prayer life of the believer. From his fertile heart and mind he produced materials like "Disciples Prayer Life" and "The Doctrine of Prayer." In 1987 he joined the Church Resource team at the Sunday School Board. In 1994 we released his most popular book, "The Mind of Christ." It would be hard to imagine a more gracious and genuine believer than T.W. He and Laverne were cherished friends and partners in ministry until his retirement in 1994. I am so privileged and grateful to have served with him for 13 years before his death.

There were many key women who served in top leadership roles. Linda Lawson became the leader in our Communications Department. At that time, she was the highest-level woman in LifeWay's leadership team. Linda was an incredible journalist and helped me prepare for every major speech I made. If I ever sounded really good, it was Linda's doing!

Billie Pate was the executive assistant for Harry Piland. Harry was one of the key leaders in LifeWay, and Billie was tasked to try to keep up with Harry and to make sure he had what he needed as he traveled around the nation. Harry was 'Mr. Sunday School' and was one of the keys to the strong ministry Southern Baptists had with Sunday School. I loved serving with Harry, and Billie was excellent as his Administrative Assistant. Billie was also the chairperson for the Organizational Task Force in 1992.

Selma Wilson was the person I always went to during my 15 years there when I needed information about LifeWay. She was unequaled in her knowledge of LifeWay and its operations. Under Thom Rainer, she actually became one of the vice-presidents for LifeWay. I still call her today occasionally if I really need help, even though she is now retired!

Janice Bell came to us from US Airways. She had been one of the key leaders a U.S. Air when one of their planes crashed into the Potomac River near Reagan Airport in D.C. She saw the job posting online and soon became the head of our Customer Service area. She said if she could survive a plane crash at the airlines, she could handle Customer Service! Janice's team was our first line of contact with customers. Their ability to handle the most sensitive and detailed of inquiry was extraordinary.

Melissa Mitchell came to work as our Loss Prevention expert. A company the size of LifeWay, with 175 stores and millions of pieces shipped every year, was always dealing with thefts and inappropriate actions by various customers and even those within the organization itself. She had served in the Air Force, as a Detroit policewoman, and with the FBI before coming to LifeWay. She resolved many mysteries in the area of loss prevention and was tremendously gifted at getting guilty individuals to confess!

Melissa became as close as family to us as did her daughter, Katie. Katie suffered from cancer and went through several years of severe treatments. Carol Ann and Melissa developed a strong friendship through this trial. We both became very involved with Katie's treatments and her progress. Katie overcame hundreds of special treatments, from chemo to radiation, over several years, and won her battle. Through all those long months of treatments, we developed a great love for Melissa and her husband, James, and especially for Katie!

Buddy Dotson was one of the most vibrant employees we had. He was African-American and had a smile that was contagious. I loved to hear him pray in chapel or anywhere else we needed someone to pray. His prayers were passionate and uplifting. He was a great encouragement for all of us. He became afflicted with a muscular disease that ultimately caused him to have to move around in a motorized scooter. But that challenge never diminished his attitude and spirit. As I was finishing this manuscript today, word came that Buddy Dotson died a few days ago. Praise the Lord, he is not struggling to live any longer! Absent from the body, present with the Lord! (2 Cor. 5:8)

Roy Edgemon and his wife, Ann Marie, had been missionaries with our Foreign Mission Board before coming to LifeWay. He was 'Mr. Discipleship' and did a fantastic job building what became the best source for discipleship materials to be found anywhere. Roy was a close friend and encourager for me throughout my 15 years there and over the 14 years since we retired.

Mark Blankenship led the Church Music Department of LifeWay most of the time I was there. He is one of the premier songwriters, not just in our convention, but in the evangelical world. He and Terry York, another of our LifeWay employees, wrote 'Worthy of Worship,' one of the truly great hymns written in the late 20th century.

Each year our LifeWay Christmas Special featured our employees singing and presenting the message of Christmas. Mark came up with the idea of taking our program to the Ryman Theater in downtown Nashville and offering it as our Christmas gift to the downtown community. We did this the last few years I was president, and it soon became a favorite event for downtown workers and for senior adult groups from all over the middle Tennessee area. Steve Green joined our employees to kick off the program at the Ryman that first year.

Brooks Faulkner became one of my dearest friends at LifeWay. Our backgrounds were different, and our theological training was different, but that didn't stand in the way. He went to Southern Seminary, and I went to Southwestern. Most of our friends were not friends to both of us. However, our spirits connected quickly, and we shared the same passion for encouraging and ministering to hurting pastors. We shared many conferences together across the years to hurting ministers.

I watched Brooks care for his wife, Shirley, during many years of her struggle with bi-polar disorder. Such a condition is very fragile, and each day is a struggle. In spite of the demands of his job with us at LifeWay, he did a magnificent job in caring for her. When she was placed in a special facility toward the end of her life, he would go every day to be with her and have meals with her even after she no longer recognized him. What an incredible encourager he was to me and all who knew him with his perseverance and patience as he gave tender care for Shirley.

During one Southern Baptist Convention, Brooks became very ill. He had to be flown back to Nashville before the convention ended. He was so ill that he could not get out of his seat on the airplane and was found by the airline attendants unconscious when they landed in Nashville. He was rushed to the hospital and spent a number of days in ICU. At one point, I called him on his phone, and his wife held it to his ear. I told him, "Brooks, don't you die on me!" He meekly replied, "Yes, sir!" He later told me, "I would take a bullet for you." I believe he would, and our friendship remains strong to this day!

We have kept in close touch since retirement began. In fact, I received a lengthy email from him yesterday! In an email in November, Brooks wrote to me, he said, "In the 40 years I worked at LifeWay, no one I loved more. There is no one I wanted to emulate and learn from more than Jimmy Draper. No one I considered to be in step with the love and compassion of Jesus than Jimmy Draper." I will always cherish my friendship with Brooks Faulkner!

If I needed anything done while in Nashville, I would call Jay Johnston. He was one of the hardest working ministers I have ever known. I'm afraid I took advantage of his inability to say "No" to any invitation and must have really overloaded him through the years. I told him he had never learned to delegate, but I was the one to benefit as he became an incredible partner in ministry for me.

MUSIC CITY USA

One of our favorite people from our LifeWay days was Pam Adcock. She was in the Human Resources department when we arrived in Nashville, but I soon brought her into the President's office. To this day, she sends me the names of LifeWay personnel when they observe each fifth year of their employment. (Every employee was recognized in a special way at each fifth-year anniversary) I email all those who were there when I was president. She also has a beautiful voice and often sang for us at LifeWay.

One of the very best decisions we made at LifeWay was to bring Mike Harland from First Baptist Church of Carrollton, Texas, to succeed Mark Blankenship when he retired. Mike has done a remarkable job and has taken the music department to new achievements over the years.

There are many others I could mention, but these give you an idea of the scope of our employees. From support staff to Ph.D.'s to multiple generations and ethnicities, LifeWay is not a building, but a people of unusual and devoted service and ministry for the Lord to all who follow our Lord Jesus Christ.

After much prayer, I announced in the February 2005, trustee meeting that I would retire on February 1, 2006. I asked the trustees to begin the process of finding the next president by appointing a search committee at that meeting. I specifically asked they make every effort to bring the new president in by fall of that year to allow us several months to work together before I retired. And beginning on February 1, 2006, he would become the ninth president of LifeWay.

The committee was appointed, and by fall, Thom Rainer was elected president of LifeWay. Thom had come from a distinguished career at Southern Seminary, most recently serving as the Dean of the Billy Graham School of Evangelism and Missions. He served at LifeWay for 13 years before retiring earlier in 2019.

Thom was always gracious to me and gave me updates on major decisions, such as selling the 14 acres in Nashville and selling Glorieta. My job was to give him a sound organization and then get out of his way. During his tenure, I always let him know when I would be in Nashville and tried to stop by to see him if he was in the office. Looking back, I did not realize how much pressure was involved in being president of LifeWay, until I no longer was president when I realized the heavy load was gone. Still, I remain very grateful to have been given the privilege of serving as president.

When I retired, the trustees named the last building to be built, known as the Centennial Tower, the James T. Draper, Jr. Tower. When the property was sold, plans were made to tear down all of the buildings on that 14 acres, with the exception of the Frost building. As time came to implode the Draper Tower, Baptist Press asked me to write an article to be released the day after the building was imploded. Here is the article I wrote:

THEY IMPLODED MY BUILDING!

"It is rare for any of us to have buildings named after us. It is even rarer for us to observe the destruction of those buildings. But it happens…in fact, it just did in Nashville, where the Draper Centennial Tower was reduced to rubble in a few seconds. I've thought long about that event ever since I received the call that the building was being imploded.

"God reminded me that Jesus is the great cornerstone of our faith and of LifeWay. Biblically, the cornerstone was selected with care, laid with great ceremony, and the stone itself determined the lines of the architecture of the building. All the building took shape from the cornerstone.

"Peter reminds us that believers have come to Christ, who is 'a living stone' and that we have become 'living stones' in a great spiritual sanctuary, (1 Pet. 2:4-10) Paul reminds us that 'In him the whole building, being put together, grows into a holy temple in the Lord.' (Eph. 2:19-22) 'Living stone' is a magnificent figure of speech (1 Pet. 2:4). That appears to be a violent contradiction of language, as if we said, 'cool fire, hot ice, bright darkness, dry water.' We normally speak of someone as 'stone dead'.

"Yet the Bible calls Christ both our Stone or Rock and our Life. He has the nature of a Great Stone: fixed foundation, fortress, solid, steadfast, strong, massive, immovable. But He is the living stone. In Him is vitality, life, energy, growth, movement.

"It has never been God's intention just to have a temple for His people, but to have a people for His Temple. Every believer is a temple, but every Christian temple becomes a living stone in that vast, eternal temple that God is building.

"The living stones in the walls of the temple become the believer priests offering sacrifices within the temple. We are not only the stones in the wall, we are the priests in the temple. (1 Peter 2:5)

"This concept dignifies every life and every aspect of each life. There is no job so low or position so prestigious that it is not dignified by this high calling. All can declare, 'I am a living stone in the everlasting sanctuary that the Lord Jesus Christ is building'.

"Now, what does all this mean for those who have served in Draper Tower? That building is not LifeWay. It was simply where LifeWay served and ministered. I have walked those halls when they were empty, and in the loneliness of those moments, I often thought deeply about what LifeWay is. When these buildings were empty, LifeWay was not here. The employees are LifeWay. Their passion, devotion, abilities, heart, expertise, service, and love for Him expressed through their service and love for others – that is LifeWay!

"Have I been diminished by the removal of this building? Absolutely not! That building is not my legacy. The exceptional ministers employed by LifeWay are my legacy. Without them, I have no legacy!

"Some wonderful things occurred within those walls. However, that building never helped a church in its ministry, nor any person in their devotion to the Lord. It never designed a budget or a building for a church, nor provided a single piece of bible study curriculum or a single piece of discipleship material. It never provided retreats or conferences to strengthen church leaders, nor provided guidance for any young person in their walk with Christ. It never printed any books to promote maturity among believers, nor provided materials scrutinized for the inventory for LifeWay Christian Stores. It never wrote a song or provided choir arrangements for our churches, nor addressed any of the significant challenges facing the church in this godless world. It never won a single soul to faith in Christ.

"But the people who have served in these buildings have done all that and infinitely more. Individuals come and go, but all who serve or have served here comprise the essence and the strength of

LifeWay. The stones, steel, and mortar of that building were lifeless materials. The only thing that made that building sacred and distinct from other buildings is the extraordinary people who ministered there and still do in another place.

"When I moved to Texas, I did not cease to be who I am. I simply relocated to another place. LifeWay is the same. LifeWay still lives and ministers because those phenomenal people are LifeWay. Those of us who have been privileged to serve as the face of LifeWay for a season could not have done it without them. They will always be LifeWay Christian Resources wherever they are!"

Following 13 years as president of LifeWay, Thom Rainer, resigned in the fall of 2019. The new president of LifeWay is Ben Mandrell, an exciting young, 41-year-old pastor from Denver, CO. He is one of the bright young stars in the Southern Baptist Convention, and I am so grateful for him being there at LifeWay. He brings a fresh new "pastoral" style of leadership that is greatly needed at this time. His previous ministry position was the Storyline Fellowship in Arvada, Colorado, where he led a church plant that began in 2015 with 200 members and was running over 2000 in attendance when he resigned to come to LifeWay.

I could say a great deal about him but will say that he possesses a pastor's heart in connecting with the employees and is creating a return to a great spiritual morale at LifeWay. He and his wife, Lynley have already established their strategic leadership at LifeWay and in Nashville. The best thing I can say about him is that he values people and is focusing on building relationships with employees and all Southern Baptists as LifeWay navigates some challenging obstacles to its ministry in our technological culture. I believe he will do well and be successful in leading LifeWay to new heights of ministry to Southern Baptists and the larger Evangelical population in our land and around the world.

New LifeWay Entrance

Plaza Dedication

Jimmy speaking

MUSIC CITY USA

Jimmy & Carol Ann
40th anniversary
Glorieta, NM

Draper home

Carol Ann &
Paula Arrington

Drapers, Arringtons, Swindolls,
Charles Oglesby & Dan Taylor

WHO BUT GOD! RIDING THE WHIRLWIND
JIMMY AND CAROL ANN DRAPER

Jimmy, Bailey Smith & Morris Chapman Montevideio Uruguay

Jimmy, Ed Young & James Dobson

Mike Arrington & Jimmy

Jon & James in our elevator at home

MUSIC CITY USA

Orient Express from Bankok to Singapore

Frank & Shirley Favazza

Jimmy & Carol Ann with Billy Graham

WHO BUT GOD! RIDING THE WHIRLWIND
JIMMY AND CAROL ANN DRAPER

Our six grandchildren

17

STILL RIDING THE WHIRLWIND

RETIREMENT

We have now been retired for over 14 years and it has been a hectic but delightful time. It has been filled with many different open doors. I have preached more than 1,200 times, including 81 funerals and 24 Senior Adult Revivals. Our ministry has taken Carol Ann and me to four countries—Kenya, Uganda, Germany and Austria. Our travels in the United States have included 33 states where I have led 72 conferences and been in 25 Baptist Associations around the nation. I have also preached in nine colleges and three Southern Baptist Seminaries, plus the Bibel Seminar Bonn in Germany. Retirement has turned out to be the continuation of the whirlwind!

We are living in the home that our son, Bailey, built for us and it is a wonderful place to live. He built it during our last year at LifeWay. We only saw it five times during construction. We were able to fully occupy the home on February 1, 2006. We actually got to move the furniture in over the Christmas and New Year holidays at the end of 2005.

WHO BUT GOD! RIDING THE WHIRLWIND
JIMMY AND CAROL ANN DRAPER

One of the real blessings is to be near our children again. We did not get to watch the grandchildren grow up for the 15 years we were in Nashville as we only saw them a couple of times briefly each year. Now, Randy lives a little over a mile from us, Bailey lives six miles away, and Terri lives 30 miles away. It is great to be close to them again.

It is exciting to be near our children again and most of our grandchildren. God blessed us with three fantastic children. Here's an update on each of them:

James Randall Draper was born September 8, 1957. He has lived his life for the Lord and conducted himself and his career with integrity. He is an ordained deacon and a lay preacher. He is one of the best communicators around today anywhere. As an example, one year as he was speaking at a men's luncheon of several hundred business leaders at Cross Church in Springdale, Arkansas, pastor Ronnie Floyd texted me in the middle of Randy's talk to say, "If I could do to an audience what Randy is doing, I'd have a really big church!" Randy is good at what he does.

Randy has always been active in sports, especially basketball. Because he had been in kindergarten before beginning the first grade, he was ready to begin when he was still five years old. Because Texas had a rule that said children must be six years old before Labor Day to enter first grade, Randy fell a week late and could not begin.

We had him tested and he was cleared to begin school. That first year we paid for him to start first grade just prior to his sixth birthday. He always did well in school, so being the youngest in his class did not bother him, except when it came to playing basketball. He told us when we were in Del City and he was in the ninth grade,

STILL RIDING THE WHIRLWIND

"I am a good ninth grade basketball player, but I would be a great eighth grade player!"

He married Elizabeth Crossley on August 13, 1977. She had been raised as a Methodist and was saved at a Billy Graham Crusade in Dallas. After that, she attended First Baptist Church Dallas because of the very active youth group. She made her profession of faith and I baptized her on live television one Sunday morning so her dad could slip out of his assignment at First Methodist Church in Fort Worth and watch the baptism from his office. We love Elizabeth dearly and are so grateful that God brought the two of them together. They celebrated their 42nd anniversary recently.

Randy and Elizabeth have two terrific sons. Kyle Randall Draper was born on November 22, 1982 in Bedford, Texas. Kyle was born at 9:30 a.m., just hours before I flew to Israel that afternoon to lead a group of Baptist pastors and Jewish rabbis at the invitation of the Israeli government. Every time I showed my passport, my first grandson's picture was also in view!

Kyle was married to Lana Trout on November 14, 2009. Her parents were ranchers in western Oklahoma. She is a graduate of Oklahoma State University and was working at a bank in Oklahoma City before they married. Like his dad, Kyle is also a gifted communicator and has often preached in churches in Texas and Oklahoma. He is creative, credible, and connects well with any audience! He is doing an outstanding job in training agents in the real estate business in the use of social media to establish their careers and build their businesses. He also has developed a large following as 'Coach Kyle' mentoring individuals around the country personally and virtually.

WHO BUT GOD! RIDING THE WHIRLWIND
JIMMY AND CAROL ANN DRAPER

Kyle is outgoing and passionate about whatever he is doing at the moment. He served as Minister for Students at Fellowship Church's satellite campus in Plano, Texas, for 8 years. Kyle and Lana have blessed us with two great-grandchildren! Harrison Dane Draper was born in McKinney, Texas, on November 1, 2012. Everly Kyle Draper was born in Oklahoma City, Oklahoma, on February 3, 2015. Today they live close by and we love the opportunity to watch Harrison and Everly grow up.

Kevin Harrison Draper was born on March 30, 1985 in Bedford, Texas. He is one of the finest young men you could ever find. Kevin is creative and energetic as an entrepreneur and businessman. He has interests in lots of different projects. He is the ultimate 'people person.' If you give him a few weeks, he will know the owner and employees of every restaurant he frequents or any place he consistently visits.

He is passionate about the Lord and is involved in many Christian issues and ministries. He is presently taking the lead in the roofing jobs that Draper Construction & Commercial Roofing is repairing across Texas and Oklahoma. He is precise, efficient, and diligent at whatever he tackles.

Kevin has been very active in working with a team of real 'dreamers' to produce Christian movies. The most recent one is 'Run the Race,' which was written by his friend, Jake McIntyre. It had a strong run in theaters across the country. Kevin and the 'dreamers' are actively looking for their next movie, which might possibly be one that Kevin has written himself! He walks in every area of his life with confidence and integrity. We are so proud of him and his love for the Lord.

STILL RIDING THE WHIRLWIND

Both Kyle and Kevin are deeply committed to the Lord and are serving Him through all of their various opportunities that the Lord continues to open to them.

Randy and Elizabeth have been in Premier Designs, a direct sales jewelry company, from its founding by Andy Horner in April 1986. They continue to be active in Premier and are widely sought after for training and encouragement. They are both regular featured speakers at Premier's annual summer rallies.

On March 15, 2014, Randy formed Draper Construction & Commercial Roofing, Inc. Their main focus is commercial roofing (and some residential), but their team is widely known for always going above and beyond to make all the necessary repairs from hailstorms. The company continues to grow by word of mouth each year.

Bailey Ray Draper was born on February 11, 1960, in Hico, Texas, just before I graduated from Southwestern Seminary. We lived in Iredell, Texas, at the time and Hico was the nearest hospital just nine miles from Iredell. Like me, he loves to play all sports. He played football, basketball, and baseball throughout his middle and high school years and was always a good athlete.

When he was 16 years old, he asked me to go deer hunting with him. I had not read the 'Five Love Languages' at that time, but his love language is definitely 'quality time.' I had never been hunting but realized what a great opportunity it was for me to spend time with him. I had never fired a rifle other than the few times I fired a .22 rifle when I was a teenager, but we learned together.

There are so many hunting stories we could tell. Each trip is an incredible time to be out in the countryside and away from the chaos in our cities. We have laughed and enjoyed so much time over these years. One trip to an area near Rock Springs, Texas stands out in particular. Bailey's father-in-law, Jon Moore and his son, Mike, had joined us for that trip. One night we went into Rock Springs, about five miles away, to eat dinner.

The restaurant was an old three-story house right off the town square. After we had ordered, we noticed that there quite a bit activity going on in the kitchen and around the downstairs of the house. We noticed a little smoke in the air but didn't think anything about it. We all ate, visited together and paid the bill. As we left, we were greeted by a crowd of town people, law enforcement, and fire fighters as yellow tape had been placed around the exit like a crime scene tape. The house was on fire! We had eaten our meal and visited together while the fire was spreading, and no one had suggested we leave the restaurant!

Another time we were sitting in an elevated blind on the edge of a field up near Henrietta, Texas. We anticipated the deer coming into the fields from the woods about 150 yards away to the right. The blind faced the field and to shoot down to the right, it looked like I needed to be sitting in the right chair. I was sitting on the right but had a difficult time getting where I could fire my rifle comfortably. Then we swapped seats so I could be on the left. Then Bailey got up and motioned for me to switch back again. I whispered, "Sorry, but I didn't hear the music stop!" We both started laughing so hard we scared every deer within a mile away from us!

Bailey turned 60 in 2020 and we have rarely missed a year going deer hunting. We enjoy being out in the woods even if we don't bring anything home. In fact, we will often go years without firing our rifles even once! He says that he enjoys getting ready for deer season as much as hunting during the season.

Bailey married Kim Moore on October 4, 1980. She is the daughter of Jon and Phyllis Moore. I would describe Jon as 'a revivalist.' He is cut out of the mold of Manley Beasley and has been greatly used of God to bring renewal and revival wherever he has preached. Phyllis is an accomplished mentor and speaker for women's groups across the country. They have been cherished friends for over 40 years. Kim is a wonderful wife and mother and we love her dearly!

Bailey and Kim's first son, Jon Thomas, was born on August 30, 1991, in Fort Worth, Texas. Their second son, James Michael, was born on December 23, 1993, in Fort Worth, Texas. Both the boys are named after their grandfathers, Jon Michael Moore and James Thomas Draper, Jr. They are both remarkable young men who love the Lord and are serving Him.

Jon is one of the key leaders in the Music Ministry at Milestone Church in Keller, Texas. He is responsible for assigning those who will serve each week in the praise team and for rehearsing the group each week. He is an excellent guitar and drum player. He is a multi-talented young man who also handles the audio and video productions at the church and the graphic designs.

He married Emma Christine Lindgren on November 13, 2015, at a wonderful setting in a restored barn southeast of Rockwall, Texas. They are a wonderful pair to observe. She is a passionate believer and was on staff at Milestone Church as a special assistant to the pastor and family. Both of them now continue to serve the Lord on staff at Milestone. They recently announced we will become great-grandparents again in July 2020!

James went on to Dallas Baptist University after high school. This amazed us all as he has dyslexia and has difficulty getting what he hears into writing. He became increasingly better at doing this at DBU and made good grades, graduating in four years. In 2017, he began pursuing his Master of Apologetics degree at Southwestern Seminary. He loves his classes and continues to make good grades. He is passionate about his faith and loves the studies in the field of Apologetics. His grasp of biblical truth and its application for our lives is remarkable. We are so proud of how he is passionately following the Lord's call on his life.

We never cease to be amazed at the giftedness of both Jon and James and continue to be so proud of all they are doing and how they are serving the Lord!

From 1987-1990, Bailey built homes for D.R. Horton, the nation's top home builder. He left that company in December 1990 and began his own company, Draper Custom Homes, in January 1991. He is an excellent home builder with a positive reputation for honesty and excellence.

Just recently a high-end housing developer came to him and asked him to be one of only six builders to be allowed to build in his development. The developer told Bailey he had one of the best reputations in the Metroplex and they had to have him as one of the approved builders. That is the kind of reputation for excellence and integrity that he has developed.

Terri Jean married Michael Don Wilkinson on March 10, 1984. All three of our children were married at First Baptist Church Euless and I had the privilege to officiate in all three weddings. Mike was raised in Euless in the Methodist Church. He was saved as a teenager and mentored by Keith Moore, our youth minister at the time. Since his conversion, Mike has always been passionate about his faith. He has also consistently been strong in academics, having a double major in German and Mathematics from the University of Texas at Arlington. He was able to have a good income during his seminary years as a tutor for youth who were struggling with Mathematics.

Mike graduated from Southwestern Seminary on May 11, 1990. Terri and Mike lived with us for nearly a year while Mike was in seminary. They lived in Euless before God led them to serve on staff at Geyer Springs Baptist Church in Little Rock, Arkansas on January 1, 1991.

They served just over two years in Geyer Springs and were called to Central Baptist Church in Bryan, Texas, where Mike was Minister of Single Adults and Missions. They began in Bryan in June 1993 and served in that great church for 15 years. While there, Mike began his studies for his Ph.D. at Southwestern Seminary in August 2005 and received his Ph.D. in May 2011.

They were called to First Baptist Church of Rockwall, Texas, in 2007, where Mike served as Minister of Education for just under five years. The church has been led by pastor, Steve Swofford for decades. It was a great place for them to serve while he completed his Ph.D.

Mike was asked to come on the faculty of Southwestern Seminary and began his ministry there in May 2011. In May 2013, Mike was asked to be the Dean of the College at Southwestern, the undergraduate college for the seminary. He has served effectively there ever since. We are so proud of Mike and love him dearly. He and

Terri have an enormous opportunity to influence the students who attend the college. The name of the college was officially changed in 2018 to Scarborough College.

He and Terri have had a phenomenal impact on many students in their seminary roles. Both of them have a great heart to encourage and minister to the students.

Their first born was Wes Michael Wilkinson born on December 23, 1988, in Fort Worth, Texas. He is such an impressive young man! He has always been eager to learn. Terri homeschooled him from K-12. He went on to Dallas Baptist University and made straight "A's," before graduating in May 2011. From there, he went on to Southwestern Seminary where he graduated in May 2016.

Wes served five years as the Minister of Youth at First Baptist Church Carrollton, Texas, and then became Minister to College Students at Central Baptist Church in College Station, Texas. Central Baptist was his home church for fifteen years growing up and has a strong college ministry since it is located just a couple of miles from Texas A&M University. Some years ago Central Baptist moved out of Bryan and into College Station.

A&M has always had a great spiritual culture on campus. Some years ago, a large Bible study began on campus and is regularly attended by thousands of students. The Baptist Student ministry has been strong on campus for over 60 years. As a result, more students have come to Southwestern Seminary from A&M than from any of our Baptist Universities in the state!

Wes married Bethany Hartsfield on March 28, 2015, at First Baptist Church in Euless, Texas. They make a great team in ministering together to the Collegiate students at A&M. It is an excellent place to minister and impact students who will emerge as industry and political leaders in the future. They just announced that Bethany is pregnant with their first child. We are excited about another great-grandchild!

We heard Wes' first sermon at a small country church near Cleburne. We heard him this morning as he preached in streaming video from the church due to the restrictions on public gatherings now because of the coronavirus. He has become a remarkable preacher of the Gospel and his message today was a powerful display of God's gifts in his life.

Mike and Terri's daughter, Leigh Ann, was born April 30, 1994 in College Station. She is a terrific young lady who is a delight to us all. She loves children and has worked for a number of years in various churches caring for the younger children. Most recently she is working at the public library in Benbrook, Texas, as a valued employee. Although she has had several learning challenges, Leigh Ann is very smart, witty, cares well for others, loves the Lord, and is a positive witness for Him! We are all so proud of Leigh Ann. She is such a blessing to us and often visits us here at our home. We always are thrilled when she can come.

We believe that she will be greatly used by the Lord throughout her life because of her loving heart and her passion for the Lord. She is a welcome addition to our grandsons. She was the last grandchild and the only girl, so she stands out from all boys in that generation!

We feel that we are living out the truth of the Scripture about children and grandchildren. "Sons (Children) are indeed a heritage from the Lord, offspring, a reward, like arrows in the hand of a warrior are the (sons) children born in one's youth. Happy is the man who has filled his quiver with them." (Ps. 127:3-5)

We had a unique experience the year we retired. We got to vote on the new pastor at First Baptist Euless. We had always been the ones being voted on throughout our ministry, but we got to be part of calling our current pastor, John Meador, to be our pastor. We are thrilled to have him as our pastor. He and his wife, Kim, are special friends and we love them greatly. He is a thorough and excellent expositor of God's Word. We are blessed every time we listen to him open God's Word.

When we retired we rejoined First Baptist Euless, where we had served for 16 years before going to the Sunday School Board. The church was without a pastor at that time and Bill Anderson was the interim pastor. When the pulpit committee settled on John Meador to recommend for pastor, he flew here to DFW Airport and spent most of one day with Bill and me. Since both of us had been pastor here, he wanted to spend time with us before deciding to come in view of a call. We both could understand his apprehension of having two former pastors as members of the church.

We met at our home in the morning and Carol Ann joined us for lunch. We have loved him ever since that time. He is one of the most remarkable men I have ever met. He lost 95% of his hearing at the age of five when he had spinal meningitis. His parents did not want him to grow up without a strong connection to the hearing community, so they refused to have him learn sign language and chose to train him to read lips. He is an expert at that and functions without giving indication that he has virtually no hearing.

STILL RIDING THE WHIRLWIND

After John became our pastor, I asked him if he heard his own voice when he preached. He said he did not. It is really a miracle that he preaches from memory and does not hear his own voice. If he can see your face, he can communicate with you as any of us would do. He is also one of the best expositors of the Word of God that I have ever heard. We are tremendously blessed to have him as our pastor. His wife, Kim, is a precious lady and cherished friend. Bill and I assured him that we would be his biggest cheerleaders and help him in every needed way. We have kept that promise and support him completely.

Carol Ann and I began saving our airline boarding passes back in 1991 when we moved to Nashville. We were travelling so much that we thought it would be interesting to keep them, so we put them in a large decorative glass jar. In 2010, while moving a table in my office, my shoe bumped into the jar and one side of it broke and fell on the floor. I had always been curious how many of those boarding passes we had collected over those years. I counted them and discovered that we had over 4,100 boarding passes over those 19 years!

In February 2007, we flew to Georgia and drove up to Brewton-Parker College in Mt. Vernon, Georgia. It is a great small college that proudly declares on signs entering the campus that it is a conservative, Bible-believing school. Carol Ann met with the ladies' group on campus, while I preached in chapel and met with the ministerial students. We loved being there and were blessed. One thing I remember was meeting for lunch with about 30 ministerial students. One of the students told us that he had just learned that a teenage girl had committed suicide and he would be leaving after lunch to meet with the family and try to help them through the tragedy.

He asked me what he should tell them and what he should do. I told him to just be there, weep with them and support them, because they would not remember what he said. Just being there was the most important thing and God would lead him in what he should say. The most important thing for any family in a moment of crisis is to have their pastor there!

In 2008, we flew to Bonn, Germany, and were met by Mark Wagner, son of Billy and Sally Wagner. He was serving as an International Mission Board missionary in Germany. While there I taught several classes at the Bibelseminar Bonn which was founded in 1993 by Russian and German Baptists.

During the second World War, many German Baptists fled to Russia. As the 20th century drew to a close, many of them returned to Germany. Unhappy with the liberal theology they found in Germany, they founded the Bonn seminary to train and equip leaders for German Baptists. The president of the seminary, Heinrich Derksen, has been a dear friend for many years. We see him at nearly every Southern Baptist Convention here in the United States and regularly communicate by email.

While in Bonn we drove up to Cologne to preach in one of the German Baptist churches on Sunday. It was a special time for us as I had to once again, preach through a translator. There were a number of adults making professions of faith in that service.

The next day we drove from Bonn to a castle in Austria to spend several days encouraging and speaking to our missionaries in Germany, Austria, and Switzerland. They were facing a real crisis in their ministry in all three countries. The United States government had a policy that no U.S. citizen could remain in a country for over a certain number of years without leaving the country for six months before returning. The policy had never been previously enforced by our government.

However, it had been announced that the policy would begin to be enforced at a certain point in the next year. That meant that long-term missionaries had to leave their fields for that specified time which created a musical chairs type challenge. What would they do? Where would they go? Who would take their places? How would their ministries continue in their absence? These and other questions occupied their attention during the retreat we attended with them.

We were able to encourage them and give helpful counsel as they worked through those questions. Mark Wagner led the retreat and I spoke to the group several times during those days. Carol Ann and I shared fellowship and discussions with the missionaries gathered there as they made hard decisions about their future.

It was about this time that the Southwestern Seminary, with the support of many of our friends, named a portion of the Riley Conference Center, 'The Jimmy and Carol Ann Draper Guest Housing Center.' We are privileged to be such an integral part of the seminary that still holds my earliest memories as a two year old boy.

On March 29, 2009, I preached at First Baptist Church of Maryville, Illinois, on the third Sunday after the pastor, Fred Winters, had been shot and killed by a man who came up in the middle of his sermon and shot him on the platform. The church was obviously in a critical stage of grief and was very unsettled trying to deal with that event. I returned one week later to preach again. The services were emotional, and the mood of the congregation varied greatly from one day to the next. It was a privilege to preach three times on those two Sunday mornings following that tragedy. God blessed us and I pray we were a blessing to the church.

While at the Sunday School Board/LifeWay I had become good friends with Jerry Davis, the president of the College of the Ozarks in Point Lookout, Missouri. He had served on a group I had brought together to discuss the future of Ridgecrest Conference Center, which we operated in North Carolina. He had spent many summers there growing up and was invaluable for the discussion.

He invited me to preach the baccalaureate message at graduation on May 10, 2009. I was especially excited about the invitation when I learned that my good friend, Mike Huckabee, was the commencement speaker that day. I preached in the morning and Mike brought the commencement address after lunch. To my surprise, Jerry had led the faculty to vote to bestow the Doctor of Law degree on me on that day. I had no idea it was going to happen until it did!

The College of the Ozarks is one of the most remarkable and unique colleges in the United States. Students cannot come if they have any government assistance. They are not allowed to borrow money for tuitions and other expenses while there. They pay no tuition but work for their tuition during their college years. The academic and practical training there is excellent. They are held to strict behavioral guidelines and graduate not only with excellent degrees in a wide variety of fields, but also with strong patriotism and no debt. Five United States military generals have graduated from College of the Ozarks over the more than 100 years of its existence.

In September 2009, we had one of the most unusual opportunities we have ever had. Our good friend, Gary Dyer, had been pastor of First Baptist Church in Midland for over 15 years. He invited us to come for a Senior Adult Revival in the fall of that year. The interesting thing was that First Baptist Midland had been one of the strongest opponents of the Conservative Resurgence in our convention.

Their former pastor, Dan Vestal, had openly opposed the resurgence and had run for president of the convention against conservative candidates several times. Gary told me that there were only 30-40 people who would not come to hear me preach, but 15 years earlier it would have been 300-400!

Carol Ann's cousins, Jimmy & Ginger Floyd, were active members of that church. I was surprised to be asked to come there in light of the controversy we had come through as a convention. However, we had one of the best weeks we have ever had in any church. I preached Sunday through Wednesday and the response was remarkable. The building was filled on the lower level of the sanctuary every service and many decisions were made for Christ.

One of the real blessings for me was that Mark Blankenship, who had been Minister of Music there years before, came to lead the music. That was very special as we had served together at the Sunday School Board/LifeWay for many years before we both retired. Mark is one of the most gifted songwriters we have today. It was great to be with him again.

One of the big blessings for us that year was to be the interim pastor at Dauphin Way Baptist Church in Mobile, Alabama. We were there for nearly a year and returned home for good in October 2010. During our time there, we flew to Mobile every Saturday and returned home on Monday afternoon. It was a meaningful time for us as we already had friends in the church and Dan and Priscilla Taylor were on staff. That made the year extra special for us!

In March 2011, we began as interim pastor of Lake Arlington Baptist Church in Arlington. I had preached in that church several times over the years and was interim there until February 2012. We loved our time there. The executive pastor of the church was Eric Herrstrom whose parents were members of First Baptist Euless when he was born. He showed me the baby letter I sent to him when he was born and also the Bible I presented to him when he started to school six years later.

It was great to work with Eric over that year. The Search Committee did its due diligence and when they had carefully looked at candidates for pastor, they ended up coming back to Eric and presented him as their recommendation for pastor. The church gave him a strong secret ballot vote with overwhelming support.

At the time, Eric and his wife, Laura, had one daughter, Emma Grace. Since then, they have adopted a beautiful daughter from overseas. Eric's mother had been on staff at First Baptist Dallas when we were there. She met and married her husband there and they joined First Baptist Euless after we began our ministry there. Eric has done a remarkable job as pastor of that church now for eight years as the church continues to grow.

In April 2012, I had a great privilege of preaching at First Baptist Church of Mixon, Texas where I preached my first sermon on Sept. 3, 1950. It was such a blessing to be back in that church that had been so gracious to allow a 14-year-old preacher boy to preach in their pulpit so many years earlier!

It was about that time that through the generosity of many friends, Southwestern Seminary names one wing of the Conference Center at the seminary "The Jimmy And Carol Ann Draper Guest

Housing Center." We are thrilled to have our name associated with Southwestern Seminary.

In 2014, I was asked by Paige Patterson, president of Southwestern Baptist Theological Seminary, to be chairman of a group he called the 'Board of Visitors' at Southwestern. Paige and I had been friends most of our adult lives. I was the one who brought him to Criswell College to be the president of that fledgling school back in 1974. Our fathers had been good friends over the years. My dad was on the Executive Board of the state convention when Paige's dad was elected as Executive Secretary for the convention.

The Board of Visitors has no authority or power to do anything specific in the seminary. It meets to get a closer look at the activities of the seminary and to encourage the faculty, administration, and students. It gives all our group the opportunity to see more of what goes on in a great seminary and to make suggestions to the president for potential changes and improvements. It has been a special opportunity for all of us who are involved. The name was changed to the Southwestern Advisory Council in 2019 and we continue under that name.

We had several other important events in 2014. I served from November 1, 2013 to August 1, 2014, as the interim president of Criswell College in Dallas. I had been a trustee of the college since 2013 and ended my time as a trustee in the fall of 2019. I presided over the commencement ceremony in May 2014, and the faculty had secretly voted to present a Doctor of Divinity degree to me. Again, I didn't know until the graduation ceremony they were giving me the degree!

In November 2014, the Southern Baptists of Texas Convention

presented me with the H. Paul Pressler Distinguished Service Award. I have known Paul since he was in his twenties and I was in my late teens. My brother, George, and I helped him in his first political campaign when he ran for congress in Texas. He and Nancy have been special friends for Carol Ann and me and we were greatly blessed to receive this award.

In February 2015, I began an interim pastorate at Cana Baptist Church outside Burleson, Texas, and served in that capacity until the end of October 2016. We loved our time at Cana. It is an open country church about four miles east of Burleson. It was a sweet fellowship of believers who had become known as a haven for seminary students and their families. The previous pastor, Charles Stewart, had asked seminary students to regularly preach on Sunday evenings, so we had a large group of student families from Southwestern Seminary there.

The latest building to be built at Southwestern Seminary is a state-of-the-art building that includes the Scarborough College students, faculty, and administration. It is a remarkable building with up-to-date technologies that allow students from around the world to join internet classes. Some of our dearest friends donated several million dollars to name the 200-seat auditorium the Jimmy and Carol Ann Draper Auditorium. We were honored at that recognition and were completely surprised when it happened.

We have had some physical challenges since we retired. The only surgery either of us had in Nashville was for my orthoscopic knee surgery in August 2003. However, as we have moved into retirement, we have begun to have many other physical challenges. The first challenge was a bout I had with meningitis in June 2009. I was in ICU for six days before I was placed in a regular room and then sent home. I had been preparing for back surgery and needed a myelogram test. Apparently, the needle or injection fluid itself was tainted as I lapsed into semi-consciousness the next morning with extreme nausea.

I was unable to get into the car, so Carol Ann asked if I wanted for her to call 911. In my semi-conscious condition, I said not to do that, but to call our grandson, Kevin, to help get me in the car. They managed to get me into the car and took me back to the treatment center where I had the myelogram. In retrospect, we should have called 911! We were told at the treatment center that they did not have the facilities to treat me. Next thing I knew, I was on my way to Baylor Hospital in Grapevine in an ambulance.

Upon arrival, I was mistakenly put on a floor that had no nurses serving the floor and was basically empty. My nausea became worse and I lapsed into unconsciousness. We had called our family doctor, Dr. Randall Perkins, and thank God he came to the hospital. As soon as he saw me, he had me admitted to ICU, no doubt saving my life. He later told me that if I had not gotten to ICU as soon as I did, I would not have lived through the night.

God was gracious, and after a month of injections by nurses who came to my home twice a day, I did recover completely. Dr. Perkins said it was one miracle that I survived and a second miracle that I had no lingering side effects from that bout with meningitis. Normally patients would suffer from headaches or other symptoms after such a bout with meningitis, but I had none. This illness caused us to miss our first Southern Baptist Convention since we began attending over 50 years ago.

I did have back surgery on November 3, 2009, to remove the cyst that was pressing on my sciatic nerve and causing severe pain. The relief from pain that the surgery provided was wonderful. On November 25, 2014, I had shoulder replacement. My shoulder had gotten so painful that something had to be done. When the doctor did a sonogram on my shoulder, he said that he could not even find my rotator cuff – that it had just disappeared from where it would normally be. Shoulder replacement was the best solution to that problem.

Carol Ann had had rotator cuff surgery in June 2012, and it was a brutal surgery. She slept in a recliner for nearly three months and the recovery was intense and very painful. Her rotator cuff surgery was much more painful and more difficult to heal than my shoulder replacement.

In the spring of 2017 my brother, Charlie, underwent extensive back surgery that took nine hours. Carol Ann and I flew to Louisville to be there for the surgery. He responded strongly and was moving around easily very soon following surgery. We thought he was doing well, but in late June became very ill. I had flown to Springfield, Missouri, to conduct the funeral service for my friend Jim Wells, Registration Secretary for the Southern Baptist Convention, whom I had known since he was a college student over 50 years earlier. During that night my sister-in-law, Retta, called to tell me that Charlie had taken a turn for the worst and had died. It was June 25, 2017.

Charlie was 70 years old when he died and had a remarkable career as a pastor and then for 20 years on the founding faculty of Boyce College at Southern Baptist Theological Seminary in

STILL RIDING THE WHIRLWIND

Louisville, Kentucky. He returned from serving the Pearl Harbor Baptist Church in Honolulu, Hawaii, for five years, and began to sell church bonds as the vehicle for erecting buildings. After several years of doing that, he enrolled in New Orleans Baptist Theological Seminary to get his Ph.D. degree. After his classwork was complete, he went to North Greenville University in Tigerville, South Carolina, while he continued to work on his dissertation. Upon completion of that degree, he accepted the position at Boyce College at Southern Baptist Theological Seminary in Louisville, Kentucky, in June 1997.

Charlie's wife was Retta Wymer; they had married on June 7, 1969. Retta was a pastor's daughter and is a remarkable lady. She has worked their entire marriage and always became the office manager or executive assistant of every job she had.

Charlie is buried in the cemetery by the Pine Grove Baptist Church in Livingston, Louisiana, about halfway between Baton Rouge and New Orleans. He had served for four years as pastor while he was working on his Ph.D. It was the very best pastorate he and Retta had during their ministry together and it is fitting that he is buried by that dear church. Retta has retired and is living there in Livingston near her son, David, and his wife, Jennifer, and their children. Shelly, Charlie and Retta's daughter, married a preacher, Kyle Hardin, and they are serving in South Carolina today. We are so proud of both Shelly and David and their families.

I fell in the shower on May 26, 2019 and fractured the shoulder bone that anchors my artificial shoulder. As I write these pages, I have good use of the arm, but it is still sore each day.

Carol Ann had knee replacement surgery on June 25, 2018, and it took seven months for her to be able to walk without severe pain.

She still has lingering pain that goes from her lower back and down her leg and into her foot.

On August 26, 2019, Carol Ann stumbled and fell coming out of Ace Hardware in Colleyville and fell headlong into the pavement. Her right forehead, eye and cheekbone under the eye were bruised, her right elbow was scraped and bleeding from a large area and the right knee that had been replaced last year had a knot on it with pain and swelling. She has been in pain 24/7 ever since the fall. We are going to grow older, but it seems it will not be gracefully!

Still, we rejoice that we are vertical and mobile at this time. We are getting older but working hard not to get old in the process! Getting older is inevitable but getting old is a choice! We continue to stay busy and have not had to cancel anything from our very busy schedule of engagements.

In December 2017, we were broadsided by a car that ran a red light and totaled our car. The good news is that neither of us were injured seriously, but we did have to replace the car. We were doubly disappointed because we truly loved our car at the time and had planned to never buy another car. We had 177,000 miles on that 2005 Toyota Avalon but had to buy another one after the crash. Sadly, our newer car hasn't been nearly as good nor as comfortable.

In March 2018, Frank Page retired as president of the Southern Baptist Convention Executive Committee. His Executive Vice President, Augie Boto, was named Interim President. I have known Augie since he was a student in Baylor University. His dad was a deacon at First Baptist Dallas while we served there. Augie attended Baylor Law School and had a very successful legal career here in

STILL RIDING THE WHIRLWIND

Texas. The Executive Committee hired him as their inside legal counsel over 20 years ago.

When he was named to be Interim President by the Executive Committee, he asked me to become his Presidential Ambassador to assist him in the interim. I accepted and served with him for 15 months. We stayed in regular contact and I stood in for him when needed at meetings and conventions across the country. It was a great time for me to reconnect with many friends across the convention.

I attended five annual state conventions in the fall of 2018 on behalf of Augie and the Executive Committee. Regular contacts with state executive directors and members of the Executive Committee and staff kept me busy during those months. Augie did an outstanding job as the Interim President. It was a privilege for me to serve those 15 months with him and the Executive Committee.

One of my good friends for more than three decades was Homer Lindsay, Jr., pastor of First Baptist Church in Jacksonville, Florida. When he died, the church initiated a special award in his name, The Homer G. Lindsay, Jr. Lifetime of Ministry Award. It was an honor for me to receive that award in January 2019, at their Annual Pastor's Conference.

It was a great privilege for us was to return to The Billy Graham Conference Center, The Cove, in May of 2019. It was a great week we shared with a full-capacity group. Our dear friends, Mike and Paula Arrington and Don and Elizabeth O'Neal, attended and shared the week with us. The Christian singer Steve Green and his accompanist, Dick Tunney, sang and played for every service.

I have known Steve for over 20 years and met him when he was featured soloist for the first Christmas program that LifeWay presented at the Ryman Auditorium in Nashville. What an incredible and gifted minister he is…and an absolutely fantastic singer and song writer. Dick Tunney married Melody Ware and I did their pre-marital counselling as Melody and her family were members of First Baptist Euless at the time. Dick is one of the top pianists, composers, and arrangers of Christian music in America today.

After the conference at the Cove, they asked for us to come back in 2020 and do another conference. I never had peace about that for some reason. I knew we were facing some increasing challenges with mobility and the usual issues that come as we get older. The invitation was to come back to the Cove in September 2020, 16 months from the time I was invited and three weeks before my eighty-fifth birthday. I declined the invitation, although we both really wanted to do it!

The 2019 Southern Baptist Convention in Birmingham was the most challenging convention ever for us. With 9,000 messengers at the convention, we were the second largest convention that Birmingham ever had. The city simply does not have the facilities or infrastructure to host large conventions.

The meeting itself was in the downtown arena that seats 10,000 people. The street level was the mid-level of the arena and required going down 50 steps to get to the main floor. There were no rails to hold on to on the way down nor were there any elevators accessible to attendees.

Our hotel room was over a quarter of a mile from the arena, so it was quite a walk just to get to the convention. Both Carol Ann and I had severe limitations at that convention. Carol Ann was still having difficulty with standing and walking. I had my arm in a sling and had the same difficulty with standing and walking. Getting down to the platform where we needed to be was a very difficult challenge for us. We were absolutely worn out by the end of the convention. It was the most difficult of all the conventions we had attended. We have only missed one convention in 53 years, and this was by far the hardest for us.

Following the convention, we were home one day and then drove to Lubbock, Texas, to preach for my friend, David Wilson, at Southcrest Baptist Church. I had preached there in July 2018, and they wanted us back the following summer. I preached back-to-back for three services. We drove home on Monday and were scheduled to fly into St. Louis, Missouri, on Friday, and then drive over an hour to Farmington, Missouri, for a Saturday Associational Conference, and preach on Sunday at First Baptist Church of DeLassus, Missouri. Our original plans were to arrive in St. Louis on Friday so I could speak on Saturday at the associational meeting. We made the flight and took off for St. Louis. Less than 30 minutes outside of St. Louis, the pilot announced he had been instructed to turn around and come back to DFW because of severe weather in St. Louis.

The plane returned to DFW and we had to be up before 4:00 a.m. the next morning to catch a 7:00 a.m. flight to St. Louis. If all went well, we could still make the associational conference in time for me to speak. The flight went well, but as we landed in the midst of more storms, I noticed that lightning strikes were all around the airport. These strikes shut the airport down temporarily as we were made to wait on the plane for more than an hour before we could deplane.

The pastor and a deacon were waiting for us and we headed straight to our meeting. The rain was coming down in such torrents it took 1-1/2 hours to get to the church. When we finally did arrive,

WHO BUT GOD! RIDING THE WHIRLWIND
JIMMY AND CAROL ANN DRAPER

I preached just before lunch and then again afterward. We had a few hours to catch our breath before dinner with the pastor's family.

I preached at the church the next morning to about 100 people. It's always a surprise just how many people will attend when I go to a church. I never know until I get there. We had a sweet service and the pastor drove us back to the airport for our 5:30 p.m. flight. When we checked in, we noticed the flight before and after our flight had been cancelled due to severe weather in Dallas.

For several hours our flight showed on time, but it was delayed many times. We finally loaded the plane at 7:00 p.m. We were just getting settled when a flight attendant told us we had been upgraded to First Class. We then moved up to First Class. After waiting quite a while for take-off, we were told to deplane, take our luggage, and stay close to the gate.

We got word around 9:00 p.m. that the flight was formally cancelled, and we began making alternative plans. I called Randy and asked for his help booking a room at the Hampton Inn I'd seen across from the airport. He got us one of the last three rooms there that night.

The American Airlines flight options were complicated, lengthy and physically too hard for us to accept, so we asked Randy to find us tickets on Southwest Airlines and fly into Dallas Love Field. The earliest flight he could find the next day didn't depart until 8:00 p.m. on Monday. We stayed at the Hampton Inn but had to be out by 11:00 a.m. Southwest Airlines would not let us check in for our flights until two hours before departure. That meant we couldn't check our luggage for many hours after that. It was a long nine hours at the airport without any regular restaurants anywhere near our terminal.

STILL RIDING THE WHIRLWIND

We put together a sparse lunch from a modest food provider with a limited menu, but that was our only option for all those hours.

When we finally left that evening on the 8:00 p.m. flight, we arrived home 26 hours later than we had originally planned. When we went over our travel for the weekend, we discovered we had been travelling to an airport, in an airport, or in an airplane for over 30 hours of that long weekend. Those two weeks of nonstop travel were all enjoyable trips, but also some of the most exhausting ones we've ever had.

After the brutal and demanding summer in 2019, we realized that our age and resilience had reached a point where we just could not keep up a pace like we had that month. I had already declined the invitation from The Cove because of our physical concerns and we had decided to be very cautious about booking flights in the future. I have logged over 3-1/2 million miles on American and Delta alone, not counting the numerous other airlines I have flown. Now, it seems the miles are catching up with us as we are finally feeling our age!

God has blessed us in myriad of ways since we started on this whirlwind. I have written 31 books. This volume will be number 32 and is the first one Carol Ann and I have done together. We have traveled in 36 countries around the world doing partnership crusades, ministering to missionaries, and participating in special events. We have been privileged to meet Christian leaders, heads of state, and other leaders beyond the United States. We have met believers and Christian leaders across America, along with Presidents, Congressmen and Congresswomen, governors, and mayors.

We have had more opportunities opened to us than we could ever have imagined and certainly never expected. When I was elected president of the Southern Baptist Convention, Carol Ann said, "I think the Lord has played a trick on the whole Southern Baptist Convention!" We both felt so unworthy and undeserving of such responsibility. That has been true of our whole life's journey. God has always surprised us with his Amazing Grace. We were saved by grace and we have certainly served by grace!

Gary Inrig wrote a wonderful book entitled 'Hearts of Iron, Feet of Clay' (Moody Press, 1979) which was a detailed study of the book of Judges. One of the issues he quickly raised in the book was what he called 'The Second-Generation Syndrome.' In that early chapter of his book he discussed the difficulty of passing on our vision and convictions to our children and grandchildren.

Chapter two of Judges describes how the nation faithfully served the Lord during the lifetime of Joshua and the elders who outlived him. They had seen the miraculous things God had done. Then another generation was born who did not know the wonders God had given to Israel (2:7-13).

Inrig writes, "The second generation has a natural tendency to accept the status quo and to lose the vision of the first generation. Too often the second-generation experience is a second-hand experience. Church history is filled with examples of it, and sadly, so are many churches. The parent's fervor for the Lord Jesus Christ becomes the children's formalism and the grandchildren's apathy."

What caused the children and grandchildren to lose the vision of the parents? Inrig continues: "They knew about his deeds. But they did not know Him or acknowledge Him. They had lost touch with God. Here we come to the heart of the second-generation syndrome. It is a lukewarmness, a complacency, an apathy about amazing biblical truths that we have heard from our childhood, or from our teachers."

This underscores to us the great difficulty in seeing succeeding generations follow in the spiritual footsteps of their first-generation Christian parents. To see godly children of godly parents is something that happens frequently, but to see generation after generation follow in that heritage of faith is difficult to find.

We are a couple most blessed of God. Our strong godly heritage goes back at least to our grandparents. My grandfather was a Baptist preacher for 54 years. He and my grandmother were married for over 50 years. My father was a Baptist preacher for 36 years until his death at the age of 52. He and my mother were married 33 years. My parents had three sons. All three of us became Baptist preachers. Our marriages have been centered in the Lord and our children all have followed in the pattern of faith first revealed in my grandparents.

At least back to Carol Ann's grandparents there is an unbroken succession of strong believers who honored the Lord with their lives, trusted in Him for their salvation, and demonstrated that faith through their commitment to the local church.

Our children married committed believers. Our oldest son, Randy, is a committed deacon and lay preacher. Our youngest son, Bailey, is a devoted deacon, Sunday school teacher, and faithful member of his church. Our daughter, Terri, married a minister and they have served in local churches for 20 plus years and he is now the Dean of Scarborough College at Southwestern Seminary.

Carol Ann and I have six grandchildren. All of them have a personal relationship with Jesus and all love and serve the Lord. Two of them are ministers on staff at their churches. All of them are active in their relationship with the Lord and share that readily with others. We have two great-grandchildren and they already speak of their love for Jesus even though they are too young to understand all that being a Christian means. What an incredible blessing it is to have five successive generations walking in the grace and presence of our Lord Jesus Christ!

How did it happen? What has been the secret? I can only venture some observations about our family.

1. The Bible was honored and revered in each generation of our parents and grandparents as being the completely reliable and inerrant Word of God.
2. Never have any of us ever heard our parents fighting, shouting at each other, or in any way mistreating one another. Love, kindness, and grace were lived out before us and are present in each of these generations.
3. Regular involvement at all church services, and usually all activities, was a given in our lives. We never knew we had a choice, yet we never felt we were made to attend church! It is just how we lived our lives.
4. We were taught compassion, hospitality, and generosity. Each of our homes have been havens for friends and others to whom we ministered. We learned that it is really more blessed to give than to receive!
5. Integrity, consistency, and obedience to God have been the characteristic of each family. We all learned early on to stand for what was right and to oppose what was wrong. And we learned to do it in a strong and firm, yet kind, way. Convictions don't have to brutalize others.

6. Christian morality and honesty were practiced and lived out in our homes. Consistency, faith, and character have always been strong qualities in our families. We simply live by the clear teachings of God's Word to treat others with respect, to be individuals of integrity and honesty, to practice what we believe, and to be grateful for everything God allows into our lives.
7. Daily fellowship with the Lord and drawing strength from His Word continues to be a strong pattern in our lives.
8. Forgiveness and grace has always been present. All of us understand that we are frail and sinful and in need of forgiveness and grace, so we learned to forgive others as we ourselves need forgiveness. We have avoided family squabbles, disputes, and divisions. Our family really enjoys being together.
9. All of these things are wrapped up in our unswerving conviction that the Lord Jesus Christ has a plan for our lives, and we have found our fulfillment in Him.

In her personal journey with the Lord, Carol Ann was led by the Holy Spirit to write out her prayer/confession to God to declare what His Word says about her. It applies to all of us equally well.

WHO BUT GOD! RIDING THE WHIRLWIND
JIMMY AND CAROL ANN DRAPER

WHO I AM IN CHRIST
I CONFESS……

I am an **AWESOME** spirit being,
made in His Image and saved by His Grace;

TOTALLY LOVED by God,
in spite of my performance;

COMPLETELY FORGIVEN through
the Blood of Jesus Christ, who died for me;

DAILY EMPOWERED by the Holy Spirit
who lives in me, and
desires to live through me.

ABSOLUTELY NOTHING can touch my life
apart from Gods permission!

I am a **CHILD** of the **ETERNAL KING**,
WELCOMED into His presence at any time and
for any reason.

I am Heaven Bound and Joy Filled.
I am His **'SPECIAL TREASURE'** and He knows 'me' by **NAME!**

Carol Ann Draper

STILL RIDING THE WHIRLWIND

My dad once told me, "The debt we owe to the past is to leave the future indebted to us." We are deeply indebted for the godly heritage we received. We pray that our legacy will be passed on, not just to two succeeding generations, but many more to come. God's greatest gift to any of us is our family. Let each of us make sure we have begun and continue a legacy of faithfulness for our children and grandchildren.

We have always tried to live by God's Word. God's word through Moses in the Book of Deuteronomy has been our guide throughout our marriage. "The Lord our God, the Lord is one. Love the Lord your God with all your heart, with all your soul, and with all your strength. These words that I am giving you today are to be in your heart. Repeat them to your children. Talk about them when you sit in your house and when you walk along the road, when you lie down and when you get up. Bring them as a sign on your hand and let them be a symbol on your forehead. Write them on the doorposts of your house and on your city gates." (Deut. 6:4-9)

We have children and grandchildren who love the Lord and are faithfully serving Him. Our love for each other is stronger today than ever before and we rejoice in God's grace and providence that has shepherded us throughout our lives. The best part of these last 14 years of retirement is that we (Carol Ann and Jimmy) get to be together all the time! For much of our soon to be 64 years of marriage we have been riding the whirlwind of God's sovereignty. We would not change anything in our lives, except we would like to have done better in everything we did. We have found that obedience to God is really the key to genuine happiness, satisfaction, and fulfillment in life! God is good all the time! All the time God is good!

WHO BUT GOD! RIDING THE WHIRLWIND
JIMMY AND CAROL ANN DRAPER

As we have completed these pages, we have been carefully abiding by the quarantine orders currently in force in America as we combat COVID-19 that attacked our nation in March 2020. All church services have been cancelled and creative ways to worship the Lord have been introduced all across the nation. This has opened up many new opportunities for us. The last four Sundays we have gotten to listen to our grandson, Wes, as he preached the streaming video service at Central Baptist Church in College Station. The church is in the final stages of calling a new pastor. We are so grateful that due to the COVID-19 quarantines we had this wonderful chance to hear him preach.

Businesses have shut down and restaurants have closed except for carry-out orders. Life is different than any of us have ever seen before. The uncertainty of when life will return to an open society for all of us is weighing heavy on everyone. As believers, how can we face the uncertainties that now threaten our health and economies? Should we panic or live in fear, or is it possible for us to remain strong in the midst of these perilous days? God's Word has an answer for us today.

In 701 B.C. the dreaded Assyrian army came marching out of the north, pushing southward through Syria into Israel and on south toward Jerusalem. Fields ripe for the harvest were abundant before them. Behind them they were bare, swept clean by hungry troops or simply burned to the ground. Hezekiah first sought appeasement by paying enormous tribute to Sennacherib, the Assyria King.

Then Sennacherib had second thoughts - how could he afford to march on to face other enemies with such a formidable fortress as

STILL RIDING THE WHIRLWIND

Jerusalem, ungarrisoned by loyal Assyrian troops and governed by Hezekiah whose loyalty was to be doubted?

He decided he could not, so he demanded that Hezekiah open the gates of Jerusalem and submit to the Assyrian army. Following God's message delivered by Isaiah the prophet, Hezekiah refused to comply with the demand. Sennacherib had Hezekiah mocked and taunted, and the Assyrian army surrounded Jerusalem. Then God sent down an angel to deal with the besieging army. One angel! One night! The mighty army was no more! 185,000 invaders perished in their camp, and Jerusalem was saved. The jubilant city rang with hymns of thanksgiving and praise.

Ps. 46 is the first in a trilogy of praise psalms (46,47,48) celebrating God's deliverance of Jerusalem from the Assyrians. This psalm was penned to commemorate the victory, immortalizing the triumph of the angel of the living God over the mighty army of Assyria.

So great and glorious was the victory and so marvelous the deliverance that Jew and Christian alike have turned instinctively to Ps. 46 whenever disaster strikes, and it seems that all hope is lost. This psalm assures us that God can handle, in His will, in His own good time and way, things which seem like total disasters to us.

This remarkable Psalm tells us three eternal truths we can hold on to today in the midst of the global threat of COVID-19. Where is our help in time of trouble? That answer lies in the power of God!

First GOD IS STILL SOVEREIGN IN OUR WORLD TODAY. (Ps. 46:6) Make no mistake about it. This is our Father's world. Though marred by the sin of man, God is still in control. He is still the God who makes everything work together for good to those who love Him and are called according to His purpose (Rom. 8:28). Cataclysmic events (Ps. 46:2-3) are simply reminders that man is not sovereign. Although man knew about and predicted it's eruption, man was powerless to stop the eruption of Mt. St. Helen's. Never fear. Our Refuge is safe no matter what upheavals may come.

Three times in this psalm we meet the word "Selah" – "There, what do you think about that!" or "How about that!" Whatever is tearing us apart now, take courage. God has not changed. "There, what do you think about that!"

Second, GOD ALONE IS OUR SECURITY – (Ps. 46:1) The very first word in the Psalm is "God." We are secure in Him because of His PRESENCE. "A helper who is always found in times of trouble." This could be more literally translated, "Abundantly available for help." The word "trouble" literally means "in tight places." We are certainly in "tight places" in our country today! God is an available tower where any helpless creature can quickly find safety and security. "Refuge and strength" are words of salvation.

REFUGE gives the external aspect of salvation: God is unchanging, and we find shelter in Him! STRENGTH implies the dynamic aspect: God is within to empower the weak for action. Both are summarized in the words "a very present help in trouble." He is ready to be "found" and He is "enough" for any situation.

He says, "There is a river – its stream delights the city of God." He supplies refreshing streams that bring new life and freshness so that strength, life, health and joys are possible. The stream provides grace, healing, life, and happy triumphant praise. God is in the midst of His beloved city. He is the river of gladness.

STILL RIDING THE WHIRLWIND

History tells us to which river the psalmist is referring. Hezekiah had taken the wise and practical steps to ensure that Jerusalem had an unfailing water supply, no matter how long the siege. The spring of Gihon located below the steep eastern hill of Ophel in the deep Kidron Valley was Jerusalem's most ancient water supply. It was exposed to enemy attack, so Hezekiah diverted the spring through a conduit, 1,777 feet long and hewn out of solid rock, into a reservoir inside the city's walls. He then completely covered the ancient spring so that the enemy would not know it was there. Throughout the fearful siege there was "a river, the streams whereof make glad the city of God."

Without that hidden river, Jerusalem would have fallen, not from the strength of the foe without, but from weakness and failure within. Instead, the city had a secret river that kept it strong. And vs. 5 tells us that "God is in her midst." He is in the midst of our lives today, just as He was in the midst of Jerusalem when the ruthless Assyrians threatened the city from without.

He is always "in the midst." Through every experience – He is there! He is within us – the Holy Spirit dwells in us. He is "Emmanuel," God with us! Our nation is not likely to ever fall from external enemies as we are a strong military nation with a vibrant economy. But our nation is vulnerable to destruction from within. When we become so arrogant and believe we are adequate for any enemy, the end of our great nation is near. Our hope cannot be in our military or economic strength. Our only hope is to turn to God! He is the "river" and is always in our midst if we will trust in Him and obey His instructions. Join us in praying that God will once again prove Himself strong and mighty within our nation. He has done it in the past. "Lord, do it again!"

WHO BUT GOD! RIDING THE WHIRLWIND
JIMMY AND CAROL ANN DRAPER

We have prayed over the years that as our family enlarges, our children will want their own personal relationship with the Lord Jesus as they mature into adults passed on to their own families. We pray they will love the Lord Jesus personally and have a strong and vital relationship with Him! "I have no greater joy than this, to hear that my children are walking in truth." (3 John 4) To our great joy, that is happening in all our family today. For that we give our Lord Jesus Christ the praise!

"Therefore I tell you: Don't worry about your life, what you will eat or what you will drink; or about your body, what you will wear. Isn't life more than clothing? Consider the birds of the sky: They don't sow or reap or gather into barns, yet your heavenly Father feeds them. Aren't you worth more than they? Can any of you add one moment to his life span by worrying? And why do you worry about clothes? Observe how the wildflowers of the field grow: They don't labor or spin thread. Yet I tell you that not even Solomon in all his splendor was adorned like one of these. If that's how God clothes the grass of the field, which is here today and thrown into the furnace tomorrow, won't he do much more for you – you of little faith? So don't worry, saying, what will we eat? Or What will we drink? Or What will we wear? For the Gentiles eagerly seek all these things, and our heavenly Father knows that you need them. But seek first the kingdom of God and His righteousness, and all these things will be provided for you. Therefore don't worry about tomorrow, because tomorrow will worry about itself. Each day has enough trouble of its own" (Matt. 6:25-33)

STILL RIDING THE WHIRLWIND

Jim & Wanda Jean Hickey

10th Anniversary at Euless

15th Anniversary at Euless

WHO BUT GOD! RIDING THE WHIRLWIND
JIMMY AND CAROL ANN DRAPER

Us with Randy's family

Bailey's family

STILL RIDING THE WHIRLWIND

Terri's famnily

All the grandkids

WHO BUT GOD! RIDING THE WHIRLWIND
JIMMY AND CAROL ANN DRAPER

Our kids all grown up

Draper Auditorium at Southwestern Seminary – Don & Elizabeth O'Neal

Kyle's family

Our great grandchildren Everly & Harrison

WHO BUT GOD! RIDING THE WHIRLWIND
JIMMY AND CAROL ANN DRAPER

Barry Creamer presents Jimmy with Criswell doctorate

Jimmy at SW Seminary

STILL RIDING THE WHIRLWIND

Huge Feral Hog

Nice buck!

Hunting with Bailey

JimmyDraper.com

www.ingramcontent.com/pod-product-compliance
Lightning Source LLC
Chambersburg PA
CBHW070123080526
44586CB00015B/1537